THE BOOKS OF

FIRST & SECOND THESSALONIANS

LOOKING FOR CHRIST'S RETURN

AMG PUBLISHERS

TWENTY-FIRST CENTURY
BIBLICAL COMMENTARY SERIES®

THE BOOKS OF

FIRST & SECOND THESSALONIANS

LOOKING FOR CHRIST'S RETURN

MIKE
STALLARD

GENERAL EDITORS
MAL COUCH &
ED HINDSON

The Books of First and Second Thessalonians:
Looking for Christ's Return

Twenty-First Century Biblical Commentary Series®

Published by AMG Publishers
6615 Standifer Gap Road
Chattanooga, TN 37421

ISBN–13: 978–0–89957–827–9

First Published: September 2009

Cover Design by ImageWright, Inc.
Editing and Text Design by Warren Baker
Editorial assistance provided by Weller Editorial Services, Chippewa Lake, MI

Printed in United States of America
POD

To my brother Jimmy
who assisted me in this project and
who joins me in eagerly awaiting the return of the Lord

Twenty-First Century Biblical Commentary Series®

Mal Couch, Th.D., and Ed Hindson, D.Phil.

The New Testament has guided the Christian church for over two thousand years. This one testament is made up of twenty-seven books, penned by godly men through the inspiration of the Holy Spirit. It tells us of the life of Jesus Christ, His atoning death for our sins, His miraculous resurrection, His ascension back to heaven, and the promise of His second coming. It also tells the story of the birth and growth of the church and the people and principles that shaped it in its earliest days. The New Testament concludes with the book of Revelation pointing ahead to the glorious return of Jesus Christ.

Without the New Testament, the message of the Bible would be incomplete. The Old Testament emphasizes the promise of a coming Messiah. It constantly points us ahead to the One who is coming to be the King of Israel and the Savior of the world. But the Old Testament ends with this event still unfulfilled. All of its ceremonies, pictures, types, and prophecies are left awaiting the arrival of the "Lamb of God who takes away the sin of the world" (John 1:29).

The message of the New Testament represents the timeless truth of God. As each generation seeks to apply that truth to its specific context, an up-to-date commentary needs to be created just for them. The editors and authors of the Twenty-First Century Biblical Commentary Series have endeavored to do just that. This team of scholars represents conservative, evangelical, and dispensational scholarship at its best. The individual authors may differ on minor points of interpretation, but all are convinced that the Old and New

Testaments teach a dispensational framework for biblical history. They also hold to a pretribulational and premillennial understanding of biblical prophecy.

The French scholar René Pache reminded each succeeding generation, "If the power of the Holy Spirit is to be made manifest anew among us, it is of primary importance that His message should regain its due place. Then we shall be able to put the enemy to flight by the sword of the Spirit which is the Word of God."

The Thessalonian epistles were probably the first letters written to the churches by the apostle Paul. F. F. Bruce said: "They were written not more than twenty years after the death and resurrection of Jesus, at a time when the gospel was already making headway in the Gentile world. . . . The letters reflect basic Christian teaching of the period—teaching maintained both in the church of Jerusalem and in the Gentile mission."

Richard Mayhue observes: "Resulting from his several months' stay in Thessalonica, Paul formed a lifetime relationship with the church as her first pastor. He left the priceless legacy of his two correspondences for churches throughout the ages to study as a superlative example of evangelism and church planting, biblical shepherding, and doctrinal commitment."

John Stott says: "These letters set the church in a theological, indeed an eschatological context. . . . Paul emphatically returns to the central verities of the Christian faith, that Christ died for our sins, that he was raised from the dead and that he is coming back again. One can hear the threefold acclamation: 'Christ has died! Christ is risen! Christ will come again!'"

Contents

I. The Book of 1 Thessalonians

Introduction: Background of 1 Thessalonians 1

1. *Opening Remarks* 7
1 Thessalonians 1:1

2. *A Testimony of Thanksgiving* 13
1 Thessalonians 1:2–10

3. *The Testimony of Paul's Ministry* 25
1 Thessalonians 2:1–20

4. *The Testimony of Timothy's Ministry* 45
1 Thessalonians 3:1–8

5. *Praying for the Church* 55
1 Thessalonians 3:9–13

6. *Morality and Genuine Love* 61
1 Thessalonians 4:1–12

7. *The Comfort of the Rapture* 73
1 Thessalonians 4:13–18

8. The Day of the Lord 1 Thessalonians 5:1–11 85

9. A Church in Harmony 1 Thessalonians 5:12–22 99

10. The Faithfulness of God 1 Thessalonians 5:23–28 113

II. The Book of 2 Thessalonians

Background of 2 Thessalonians 125

11. Encouraging the Church 2 Thessalonians 1:1–5 133

12. The Judgment of God 2 Thessalonians 1:6–10 143

13. The Focus of Paul's Prayer 2 Thessalonians 1:11–12 157

14. Prophetic Issues about the Day of the Lord 2 Thessalonians 2:1–12 165

15. The Call of God 2 Thessalonians 2:13–17 185

16. Dealing with Unruly Believers 2 Thessalonians 3:1–18 193

Appendix A. The Day of the Lord 203

Appendix B. The Identification of the Restrainer 213

Bibliography 217

Notes 219

SECTION 1

The Book of 1 Thessalonians

Introduction

Background of 1 Thessalonians

Author

Three general views have been advanced for the authorship of 1 Thessalonians. First, following the liberalism of the nineteenth century, some denied that Paul had anything to do with the book. It is, according to this viewpoint, a later second-century work using first-century names. The alleged lack of agreement in style between 1 Thessalonians and other known works of Paul, such as Romans, 1 Corinthians, and Galatians is invoked to support this claim.[1] In response, one must recall that arguments based on stylistic differences sometimes stand on shallow ground since they can assume an unwarranted lack of breadth in the expressions of any one author. Paul, as an extremely educated man, could certainly have written in varying styles, depending upon the circumstances and themes of the moment.

A second view is that Paul did not write the letter alone, but that all three of the men listed were involved. Perhaps one of the men (even other than Paul) was the main author, but input was gained from the others on the missionary team. For example, on this view, if Silas was the main author with input from Paul and Timothy, any stylistic differences with other epistles by Paul could be explained without rejecting Paul's influence in 1 Thessalonians.[2] Strong arguments can be made that all three of the men were involved, not the least of which is that all three are named. Both epistles to the Thessalonians begin with "Paul and Silvanus and Timothy to the church of the Thessalonians." Aside from the opening verse in 1 Thessalonians, any authorship is only mentioned once after that—Paul in the singular ("For we wanted to come to you—I, Paul, more than once"; 2:18). Yet 1 Thessalonians is written in a plural style (e.g., "*We* give thanks," not "*I* give thanks") for the most part of the letter.

A third view is the traditional view that Paul wrote 1 Thessalonians. To be sure, he may have had assistance or input from Silas and Timothy, but he must be declared to be the writer. The fact that the plural style is used is not significant. There are many "we" sections in the book of Acts, but it is not generally understood that there are multiple authors because of it. Moreover, the three exceptions to the plural style in 1 Thessalonians are highly instructive: 2:18 (cited above), 3:5 ("When I could endure it no longer, I also sent to find out about your faith"), and 5:27 ("I adjure you by the Lord to have this letter read to all the brethren"). These examples are important in that they surface the real relationship of significance. Paul is the apostle who was the father of the church at Thessalonica. In that light, it is most likely that Paul included Silvanus (Silas) and Timothy in the greeting to the church as a courtesy, since they served with Paul on his missionary journey. Furthermore, the style of the letters is chiefly Pauline, and Paul was stated as the author by early church authorities Polycarp, Ignatius, and Justin. Pauline authorship is also mentioned in *The Shepherd of Hermas* and in the Marcion and Muratorian canons.

Finally, the closing of 2 Thessalonians is helpful in coming to a conclusion about Paul's authorship of 1 Thessalonians. He mentions that he signs with his own hand: "this is a distinguishing mark in every letter; this is the way I write" (2 Thess. 3:17). This is in light of possible fraud on the part of others about a letter from Paul (2 Thess. 2:2). Yet the opening of 2 Thessalonians mentions Silvanus and Timothy just as in 1 Thessalonians. The inclusion of the other two men cannot be used to diminish the Pauline source for 2 Thessalonians. The same is most likely true for the earlier letter. Therefore, there is no reason to doubt the authenticity and genuineness of 1 Thessalonians and Paul's authorship.

Date

As with most books of the Bible there has been some debate about the actual time of the writing of 1 Thessalonians. Some have argued for a date of composition in the early 40s. This is based largely on the assumption that the edict by Emperor Claudius that expelled the Jews from Rome (Acts 18:1–2) can be dated as AD 41. Then the meeting of Paul with Aquila and Priscilla after they fled Rome took place in Corinth. Apparently, after a few months Paul started a long-term ministry in Corinth for a year and a half (18:11), and Silas and Timothy were present for most of that time (18:5). From there the first letter was written to the Thessalonians bearing the names of Paul, Timothy, and Silas. On this basis, Karl Paul Donfried dates the book as being written around AD 43.[3] If that is correct, the book could be the first book penned by the apostle Paul.

However, the date of the edict by Claudius cited in Acts 18:2 is far from certain. F. F. Bruce points out that there was more than one occasion when Rome expelled the Jews.[4] Moreover, the mention of Gallio as proconsul of Achaia in Acts 18:12 places the account almost a decade later according to inscription evidence. Therefore, those who hold this view must accept that Luke is combining two of Paul's visits to Corinth into the story of one visit.[5] This nonhistorical approach to Luke's writing of the book of Acts must be rejected.

Various interpreters opt for a second view in which the composition of 1 Thessalonians is placed in the decade before AD 70. The reasons given for this later date are many and depend largely on some discovered correlation in Acts or elsewhere to the content of the letter.[6] One particular version of this approach sees the various problems of the epistle as reflecting the theological problems Paul faced, such as Gnosticism—issues supposedly taken up in such other letters as Colossians. According to this view, since Colossians was written around AD 64, then a similar date must be declared for 1 Thessalonians. In response, one must protest that assertions about Gnosticism are overabundant in our day. Furthermore, even if it is granted that Colossians is partially a response to some form of early Gnosticism, we must agree with Bruce that there is nothing "in either of the Thessalonian letters which requires a gnosticizing tendency at Thessalonica for its explanation."[7]

The best option is a third one, which places the composition of 1 Thessalonians in the early 50s. This makes the epistle one of the earliest of the New Testament books, perhaps the earliest except for Galatians. Most scholars date 1 Thessalonians in AD 50 or 51, based on the contents of the epistle and the extrabiblical evidence for the date of Paul's confrontation with the Jews before Gallio in Corinth (see Acts 18:12), from which Paul authored the letter.[8] The extrabiblical evidence is actually the Delphic inscription, which gives a letter from Claudius to Thessalonica acknowledging Gallio as proconsul of Achaia.[9] The date of Claudius's writing is certain, thus confirming the date of 1 Thessalonians within a few months.

City of Thessalonica

The most probable historical account of the founding of Thessalonica was that Cassander founded it in 315 BC and named it for his wife, the half sister of Alexander the Great. As an ancient city it had been named Therma for many hot springs nearby. When the Romans conquered Macedonia in 168 BC, they divided it into four districts or provinces, making Thessalonica the capital city of one of them.

Thessalonica was the crucial seaport of Macedonia in the first century. With its safe harbor, it served as a strategic place for commercial, social, and military activity. The famous Roman road *Via Egnatia*, or Egnation Way, traversed the city and connected Rome with the whole region north of the Aegean Sea. The city's location greatly added to its importance for the spread of the gospel message that Paul preached.

It was in this major cosmopolitan city of 200,000 people that Paul and Silas, on Paul's second missionary journey, established a church (1 Thess. 1:9). Its population consisted of Greeks, Romans, Asians, and a good contingent of Jews. During World War I this city served as a military base for the allied armies, and during World War II the city was taken by the German army. The Jewish population of 60,000 was exterminated under Adolf Hitler's reign of terror. Thessalonica is one of the few of the New Testament cities that have continued through history to exist today.

Establishment of the Church

The starting of the church at Thessalonica (around AD 49 or 50, during the second missionary journey) did not come easy. Luke gives the record of the tumultuous events that took place there in Acts 17:1–10. After being beaten and jailed in Philippi, Paul and Silas had traveled through Amphipolis and Apollonia to come to Thessalonica.

There was a synagogue of the Jews in Thessalonica, and Paul "reasoned with them from the Scriptures" (Acts 17:2) and preached "This Jesus whom I am proclaiming to you is the Christ" (Acts 17:3). It had been his custom to begin at the synagogue with the preaching of the gospel. The converts to Paul's message included a great multitude of Greeks and leading women of the city (Acts 17:4) as well as some of the Jews out of the synagogue.

Jealousy on the part of the Jews produced a strong reaction to Paul's successful ministry, and a riot ensued as the city went into an uproar. When they did not find Paul and Silas at Jason's house, they dragged Jason and other Christians before the city authorities (Acts 17:6–8). The net result of the riot was that Paul and Silas had to leave the city by night to go to Berea (Acts 17:10).

Occasion

Why Paul wrote to the church seems clear when we note that he was ripped away from the church by persecution (Acts 17:10, 1 Thess. 2:17). This left the church and its new converts in a state of anxiety, and the apostle wanted to comfort them and guide them with his letters.

In the first epistle Paul encourages them in their suffering (2:2, 9; 3:3–5) and the gentleness with which he had treated them (2:7–9). Further, he uses the background of their situation to highlight the teaching of the coming of the Lord to bring comfort (4:18) and to examine the teaching of the future Day of the Lord (5:2) with all its horrors and persecution. It is also possible that Paul is responding to the false idea that those who had died as believers had missed the coming of Christ for the church.

Structure

While a detailed outline of 1 Thessalonians will be obvious throughout the following chapters, comment will be made at appropriate places concerning the high-level outline of the body of the epistle that Paul himself gives in 1:9–10.

Paul's Outline in 1 Thessalonians 1:9–10	
How you turned to God from idols (1:9)	*1 Thess. 2:1–3:13*
To serve a living and true God (1:9)	*1 Thess. 4:1–12*
To wait for His Son from heaven (1:10)	*1 Thess. 4:13–18*
Who delivers us from the wrath to come (1:10)	*1 Thess. 5:1–11*

Significantly, Paul generally follows the chronological outline of events described in 1:9–10 when he addresses those topics in 2:1–5:11.[10]

Another interesting observation is the mention of the coming of the Lord near the end of each chapter of the book. With the exception of the first chapter, the word *parousia* ("coming") is used. However, it can still be said that each chapter ends with a focus on His coming.

Such an observation does not necessarily assist in understanding the outline or structure of the book. In the outline used above, the second section (1 Thess. 4:1–12) contains no mention of the coming of the Lord. Furthermore, chapter divisions are not always useful for seeing how a Bible book is organized. Therefore, it is best to see these references to the coming of the Lord as simply a reinforcement of the theme that is building all the way from chapter 1. In short, Paul's main interest in writing to the Thessalonians is the doctrine of last things as a matter of comfort to the church.

The Focus on Christ's Coming	
Chapter 1	*1:10—to wait for His Son from heaven*
Chapter 2	*2:19—For who is our hope or joy or crown of exultation? Is it not even you, in the presence of the Lord Jesus at His coming (parousia)?*
Chapter 3	*3:13—so that He may establish your hearts unblamable in holiness before our God and Father at the coming (parousia) of our Lord Jesus Christ with all His saints*
Chapter 4	*4:15—that we who are alive, and remain until the coming (parousia) of the Lord, shall not precede those who have fallen asleep*
Chapter 5	*5:23—may your spirit and soul and body be preserved complete, without blame at the coming (parousia) of our Lord Jesus Christ*

Basic Themes

Several ideas dominate Paul's first letter to the Thessalonians in addition to the aforementioned highlighting of the second coming of Christ. The persecution and suffering of the saints, including Paul himself, receives major attention (1:6; 2:1–2; 2:14–17; 3:1–10). Its presence in the experience of the Thessalonians requires two things—that they look to the future when God would begin to make all things right and that they not fall away from the truth under pressure.

That last point is why the epistle stresses to a great degree the need for believers in Christ to walk a blameless, holy, and worthy walk before God in spite of such a predicament. Paul reminded them of how blameless he had walked before them (2:10). Negatively, he tells them he had feared that Satan had drawn them away (3:5). He wants them to be established in holiness (3:13). He informs them it is God's will for them to be sanctified and to avoid immorality (4:3–7). In light of Christ's coming, the saints are to be alert and sober (5:6). Paul warns them to "abstain from every form of evil" (5:22). The apostle's final wish was for God to sanctify them entirely and make them without blame at the coming of Jesus (5:23).

CHAPTER 1

Opening Remarks
1 Thessalonians 1:1

Preview:

Paul, along with Silvanus (Silas) and Timothy, sends greetings to the entire assembly of believers at Thessalonica. In doing so, Paul invokes the position of the Thessalonians in God and Christ and wishes for them both grace and peace, common terms of greeting in his letters. The close association of Christ with God shows that He is on equal footing with the Father.

This chapter ("Opening Remarks") and the next ("A Testimony of Thanksgiving") combine to form Paul's introduction to his epistle. The apostle wrote to the church saints of Thessalonica out of a deep concern for their welfare. After being suddenly removed from their midst due to persecution, he was concerned for their continuance in the faith. For this reason he had sent Timothy (3:2) to follow up on the progress and development of their Christian faith. Were they holding fast to the truth Paul had taught them? Or were they caving in to the extreme pressures of persecution? Paul's tone reflects tenderness throughout the epistle (2:7, 11; 3:12).

Paul's opening remarks in 1 Thessalonians are almost identical to those in 2 Thessalonians. The latter adds the words "from God the Father and the Lord Jesus Christ" to the entire opening expression (2 Thess. 1:1–2). This should not be thought a significant difference since 1 Thessalonians 1:3 mentions "our Lord Jesus Christ in the presence of our God and Father."

Salutation (1:1)

The greeting Paul gives is also similar to what he would go on to write in other letters. He identifies himself and then his associates who were with him, Silvanus, or Silas, and Timothy. Silas and Timothy had been companions of Paul on his second missionary journey. Silas had followed Paul when the apostle split with Barnabas over the issue of taking John Mark along on the journey. John Mark had turned back earlier (Acts 15:38), and Paul refused to let him go along. So Barnabas took John Mark and Paul took Silas. The young man Timothy was a convert picked up by Paul at Derbe and Lystra (Acts 16:1).

The Jewish name of Paul was Saul (*Saulos*, or "asked for"), which was the Greek form of the Hebrew *Shaoul*. The name Paul meant "little." D. Edmond Hiebert points out the significance of the shift:

> He is always called Saul in Acts until his clash with Bar-Jesus at Paphos, when Luke suddenly writes, "Saul, the one also Paul." . . . Thereafter he is always called Paul in the Acts as well as in the epistles. This change to the use of his Roman name is peculiarly appropriate at the time he was entering upon his position of leadership in the evangelization of the Gentiles. As a Jew who was born a Roman citizen (Acts 22:28), he doubtless carried both names from birth. Apparently the two names were chosen by his parents because of their resemblance in sound. It was a common practice for Jews of the dispersion to have a Jewish as well as a Roman name.[1]

The name Silvanus is a Roman name that meant "wood" or "woodland." Luke always, in the Acts, calls him Silas, while Paul in his epistles always calls him Silvanus (cf. Acts 18:5; 2 Cor. 1:19). Silas initially appears in Scripture in Acts 15:22 where he accompanies Paul and Barnabas to Antioch after the Jerusalem Council. He is called one of the "leading men among the brethren" in the Jerusalem church. Paul chose Silas to be his traveling companion on his second missionary journey after an argument erupted with Barnabas over John Mark (Acts 15:36–41). The closeness of Paul and Silas as colleagues in the ministry can be surmised in light of the nature of their work together, especially the endurance of persecution in the Philippian jail where they sang hymns together (Acts 16:25) followed by the oppression that arose in Thessalonica (Acts 17:5–10). After the second missionary journey, Silas is no longer mentioned in the accounts with Paul. One later biblical reference shows that he became a messenger for the apostle Peter, delivering 1 Peter to believers throughout Pontus, Galatia, Cappadocia, Asia, and Bithynia (1 Pet. 1:1; 5:12). Thus Silas had the privilege of working for and with the two greatest apostles.

The name Timothy means "honoring God." This young man who ministered on occasion with Paul is mentioned more than twenty times in the New Testament. Only Barnabas among Paul's traveling companions is mentioned more. Timothy had a Greek father but a Jewish mother (Acts 16:1). Paul would come to look on Timothy as the closest reflection of his own ministry. "For I have no one else of kindred spirit who will genuinely be concerned for your welfare," Paul told the Philippian church about Timothy (Phil. 2:20). Timothy was considered more than a brother in Christ. He was a spiritual "son" to the apostle (1 Tim. 1:2; 2 Tim. 1:2) and greatly loved. Paul trusted Timothy's maturity to the point that he sent him to Thessalonia to encourage the believers in light of their affliction and persecution (2 Thess. 3:2). That Paul had a lasting and close friendship with Timothy is clear from the fact that the connection, which began with the second missionary journey where he met Timothy (Acts 16:1), ended with Paul's last known letter to Timothy (2 Timothy). According to Christian tradition, Timothy died as a martyr in Ephesus.

The Recipients (1:1)

The recipients of the letter are identified as "the church of the Thessalonians." The word "church" (*ekklēsia*) was the normal word for an assembly. It referred to a "group or company" assembled together for some purpose (e.g., Acts 19:32, 39, 41). The word was taken over by the early Christians to refer to the church as a group of believers fulfilling the functions that Christ had intended (Matt. 16:18; 18:15–17; Acts 2:41–47). Sometimes the reference in the New Testament is to the church as a whole, or the universal body of Christ (Eph. 1:22). But most of the time the word references a local assembly at a given location, for instance, the church of the Thessalonians located in the town of Thessalonica.

The exact makeup of the church in Thessalonica is debated. It was probably a small congregation of mostly Gentiles. The largely Gentile background of the assembly can be seen in Paul's statement that they had turned from idols to serve a living God (1:9). Presumably Jews would not have been involved in idol worship. However, in their history the Jews had on occasion dipped into idolatry in syncretistic ways (recall the reason for the Babylonian captivity). So their presence in the congregation should not be ruled out on that basis alone. Acts 17:1–4 indicates that Paul and Silas had some success in preaching the gospel in the synagogue of the Jews at Thessalonica.[2]

The church is described as "in God the Father and the Lord Jesus Christ." The placement of both the Father and Christ on equal footing is clearly intended as Paul viewed Christ as God in the flesh (Rom. 9:5; Phil. 2:5–11;

1 Tim. 3:16). G. K. Beale notes, "The point of Paul's close connection of *God* and *Jesus Christ* is to point to the deity of the latter, which is further suggested by calling Jesus *Lord* (*kurios*). The clear implication is that the Father and Son are two divine persons. . . . This particular connection is also apparent throughout the two epistles, where the names are similarly linked in order to indicate that the position or function of God is also the position or function of Christ."[3] The language used in 1 Thessalonians 1:1 would have been understood by both Jews and pagans to mean that Jesus is somehow divine.[4]

The full designation of Jesus as the *Lord Jesus Christ* signifies the full weight of heaven behind the fledgling church. He is Lord (*kurios*) who rules and reigns. He is Jesus (Savior) who has delivered the Thessalonians from their sins. He is Christ (Anointed One) who was prophesied in the Old Testament. They had received this One whom the Jews had rejected and were being persecuted for their relationship with Him.

The church's position in relation to God is no doubt mentioned at the outset to fortify believers in the midst of the persecution. To be *in God and in Christ* was to be in a position of protection and security. Paul would go on to remind them of God's work on their behalf (1:4–5) and His watch care over their lives (5:9–11).

Greetings (1:1)

The special greeting of "Grace to you and peace" in verse 1 is peculiar to Paul. *Grace* was a common greeting among Greeks. The greeting of peace (shalom) was the common greeting among the Hebrews. While it is possible that these words are the modern equivalent of "Hello" or "Greetings" in modern use, it is likely that Paul's intention is stronger. By his usage the apostle gave to these words a richer and deeper meaning to convey the message of the gospel, which comes by way of grace (Rom. 4:4–5; Eph. 2:8–9) and brings peace with God (Rom. 5:1). Martin eloquently notes that, by wording the greeting this way, Paul "turns a perfunctory 'hello' into a theologically meaningful salutation."[5] The fact that this grace and peace were "to you" implies that the Thessalonians had this as a reality in their lives and were to have a deeper experience of both grace and peace in the midst of their situation.

Study Questions

1. What lessons can we draw from Paul having associates with him on his missionary journeys? What input do you think they had on Paul's letters to the Thessalonians?

2. Does God look upon the churches in your city as one church or many churches?
3. Does He look at the church in a different way today than in New Testament days?
4. Can you demonstrate from the first verse the deity of Jesus Christ? How would this have brought comfort to the Thessalonians? How could it bring comfort to you today?
5. Did Paul's greetings of grace and peace have any deeper meaning than was customary in that day?

CHAPTER 2

A Testimony of Thanksgiving
1 Thessalonians 1:2–10

Preview:

Paul highlights his great gratitude to God for the Thessalonians for several reasons. The saints at Thessalonica had turned to God from idols beginning when Paul had first preached in the city. After that, they maintained their faith in the midst of severe suffering and persecution. Finally, they longed for the second coming of Christ.

Paul's letters, except for the epistle to the Galatians (Gal. 1:1–3), begin with thanksgiving. While the Galatian believers had failed Paul by listening to the Judaizers, no such disappointment can be found in the church at Thessalonica. No doubt the "we" would include Silas and Timothy, but the spirit of constant gratefulness is a major quality seen in Paul's life (Rom. 1:8; 1 Cor. 1:4; Eph. 1:15–16; Phil. 1:3; Col. 1:3; 2 Thess. 1:3; 1 Tim. 1:12; 2 Tim. 1:3). The editorial "we" is also part of Paul's writing style (1 Thess. 2:18; 3:1). But no doubt Paul prayed with Silas and Timothy for the believers and expressed thanksgiving in those prayers.

Paul's concern for the believers at Thessalonica gives way to joyful thanksgiving as he begins to rehearse all that God had done in them and among them. The entire epistle is filled with this recitation of joy and thanks. The following items are a few of those mentioned by the apostle:

Giving Thanks and Prayer (v. 2)

"Give thanks" (v. 2) is in the present tense, and along with the "always," it indicates in this context that Paul's gratefulness was constant and ongoing. Paul does not thank the Thessalonians. He thanks God who was at work in the lives of the Thessalonians. This outline follows the pattern Paul uses in several other epistles.[1] The giving of thanks in verse 2 includes "all of you" and is done with specificity, "making mention of you." The first chapter especially forms the basis for Paul's attitude of thanksgiving toward the Thessalonians. The tenderness of the verse is clear when one remembers that "Paul is a spiritual parent to the Thessalonians (2:7–8, 11), and just as little children are never far from the thoughts of their parents, so Paul is continually mindful of his children, the Thessalonians."[2]

Paul's Joy and Thanks
Gives thanks for the believers (1:1–10)
Praises the church for their suffering (2:14)
Views them as his joy or crown of exultation (2:19)
Calls them his glory and joy (2:20)
Rejoices in Timothy's good report of them (3:6)
Desires greatly to see them again (3:10)
Reminds them of God's faithfulness (5:24)

Remembering the Church's Testimony of Service (1:3)

"Constantly bearing in mind" actually comes from the terms for "remembering" (*mnemoneuontes*), a common word in Paul's letters, and "constantly" (*adialeiptōs*).[3] Most likely the Thessalonian believers were coming to mind for Paul's prayers and thanksgiving because he had heard reports of their spiritual development. These reports came from Timothy who noted specifically for Paul their ongoing faith and love (1 Thess. 3:6). Thus the apostle was always remembering three things about the Thessalonians. First was their *work of faith*, second their *labor of love*, and third their *steadfastness of hope* (see also 1 Thess. 5:8; 1 Cor. 13:13; Gal. 5:5–6; Col. 1:4–5). D. Edmond Hiebert points out, "Here for the first time, chronologically, in Paul's writings we have this famous triad: *faith, love, hope*. But Paul's stress is not on these virtues alone, but rather on what they produce. They are active ingredients of the Christian life, finding expression in active work, patient toil, and enduring constancy. Thus Paul does not link these basic virtues with that which is beautiful, poetic, and ethereal, but rather with that which is toilsome and difficult. They are seen to their best advantage amid the rugged demands of daily life."[4] Paul's words reveal the essence of the Christian life and how the believers at Thessalonica had satisfied the demands of that life.

The first expression of the triad, *work of faith,* is an interesting one since most of the time in Paul's writings the terms *works* and *faith* are at odds. Usually Paul is speaking of justification by faith and faith alone apart from any work or works of the Law (Rom. 3:27–28; 4:5; 9:32; Gal. 2:16; 3:2, 5). However, there are some other Pauline uses that bring the two terms together in a positive way. In Galatians 5:6 the apostle mentions that "faith working through love" is important for the person who has already come to Christ. In that passage, faith works itself out in the life of the believer through acts of love. Perhaps another way of describing *work of faith* is that activity which is inspired *by* faith. Faith can encourage and lead to work (cf. Eph. 2:8–10).

First Thessalonians 1:3 is the only verse in Paul's letters in which the terms *labor* and *love* are brought together. Love is not the object of the labor. The expression "labor of love" is that wearisome toil that is prompted by an all-consuming love. The labor (*kopos*) designated that toil or exertion that continued until fatigue set in. Thus the Thessalonian believers are being described by Paul as laboring until they dropped from weariness. But what is the object of the love described in the expression "labor of love"? It certainly includes love for those being ministered to, in this case, those under the influence of the Thessalonians. This understanding is assured by Paul's later wondering if his labor was in vain (1 Thess. 3:5–8). In the context, the concern occupies his mind partly due to the reciprocal relationship of kindly longing between the church and its missionary founder. Although the word *love* does not occur in this section, its imprint is everywhere and helps to inform the meaning of 1 Thessalonians 1:3. However, one more factor can be seen in this connection. The labor of love, as with the other two phrases in the triad, is "in our Lord Jesus Christ." The framework for love worked out toward others is the position of the believer in Christ. Just as faith is in God and hope is in God, love is directed toward God. Consequently, it is not stretching the point to suggest that love for others stems from love for God who has already blessed the believer immensely. Harold Ockenga adroitly observes, "It is love which moves the Christian religion, beginning with God in the redemptive plan, continuing in Christ, who laid down His life for us, and ending in the believer with a manifestation of a selfless life of service."[5]

In the third expression of the triad, "steadfastness of hope," the word *steadfastness* (*hypomonēs*) speaks of a patient endurance the church maintained under the heavy weight of persecution. This fortitude came by way of a fixed *hope* (*elpidos*) directed toward the Lord. In light of the overall end-times focus of both 1 and 2 Thessalonians, it may be that Paul places this expression last to highlight it as the anchor needed by the believers at Thessalonica as they wrestle with teaching about the coming of the Lord.[6] To be sure, the ultimate solution is the second coming of Christ when He will begin to make all things right, including the rightful judgment of those who oppose the Thessalonians (2 Thess. 1:5–12). Leon Morris comments on the progression of the expressions in the following way: "This verse brings before us that conjunction of faith, hope, and love which we find in a number of places in the New Testament. . . . First Corinthians 13:13 is especially important, for that chapter is about love, not faith or hope, yet at the climax the other two appear quite naturally. It was apparently an accepted Christian practice to join the three. While the linkage is found in several places, the order varies. In this verse hope comes last as a climax, which is very fitting in a letter in which hope is given so much emphasis."[7]

Thus, at the outset of his first epistle to the Thessalonians, the apostle Paul attempts to push the saints forward in hopeful expectation based on Christ. He does this by reminding them that their present success in spite of circumstances proved the work of God in their lives. Similarly, early in 2 Thessalonians, Paul says that the very presence of persecution and difficulty was proof of their worthiness for God's coming kingdom (2 Thess. 1:5).

Remembering the Church's Election by God (1:4)

Paul has confidence. Paul could maintain confidence in the church because of "knowing" (*eidotes*) What did Paul know? He knew that the brethren of Thessalonica were beloved and chosen by God. His knowledge was not based on the performance of the believers, though he had seen the result of God's work in them. It was based on God's grace and activity directed toward the Thessalonians and their public embrace of the gospel message.

They are loved. Paul uses the term *brethren* (*adelphoi*) more than seventy times in his New Testament letters, fourteen times in 1 Thessalonians alone. This usage sets the tone for the highly personal nature of the exhortation Paul is sharing with the Thessalonians. This personal nature is further reinforced when he calls the believers at Thessalonica "beloved" (*ēgapēmenoi*), which is a perfect passive participle. Its implication is that the brethren have a love focused on them from the past that has continued into the present without stopping (see 2 Thess. 2:13). God loves them Himself and will continue to do so. This would be an endearing and comforting thought to them at the time of their present circumstances.

They are chosen. The King James Version has "your election of God," while the NASB has "His choice of you." This is a reference to the Bible doctrine of election spoken by Paul elsewhere (1 Cor. 1:27, 28; Eph. 1:4; Col. 3:12) and in other portions of the New Testament (John 13:18; 15:16; Acts 9:15; James 2:5; 2 Pet. 1:10). The Bible doctrine of election and its corollary doctrines of predestination and foreordination have been controversial throughout church history. Seemingly opposed to the doctrine of the sovereignty of God is the concept of human responsibility. William MacDonald explains both sides of the argument this way:

> The doctrine of **election** teaches that God chose certain people in Christ before the foundation of the world (Eph. 1:4). It does *not* teach that He chose some to be damned. If men are finally lost, it is because of their own sin and unbelief.
>
> The same Bible that teaches election also teaches human responsibility or man's free choice. God makes a *bona fide* offer of salvation to all people everywhere. Whoever comes to Christ will find a warm welcome.
>
> These two doctrines, election and freedom of choice, create an irreconcilable conflict in the human mind. But the Bible teaches both and so we should believe both even if we can't harmonize them.[8]

No unbeliever should use the doctrine of election as an excuse not to believe on the Lord Jesus Christ. No believer should use the doctrine of election as an excuse not to witness and share Christ with unbelieving family, friends, or neighbors. Yet the truth of the teaching provides great comfort for those who have trusted in Christ and know that God has a plan for their lives from before the foundation of the world. F. F. Bruce comments, concerning the Thessalonians, "While the election took place in God's eternal counsel, its effects are seen in the lives of the elect, as they were seen now in the lives of the Thessalonian Christians."[9] It is this observation that gives Paul confidence toward the recipients of his letter.

Remembering the Gospel's Power of Transformation (1:5–10)

The gospel message preached by Paul and his helpers on that second missionary journey is described as "our gospel." It was not peculiar to them and was the same gospel that other apostles had preached—the death, burial, and resurrection of Christ from the dead (1 Cor. 15:1–4). But it was a personal matter between Paul and the church. As the main messenger, he could identify the gospel as belonging to him (and the missionary team) as he personally delivered it to the Thessalonians (cf. "my gospel" in Rom. 2:16).

Presentation of the gospel (1:5). Paul also notes how this gospel message came to them. It was more than just words spoken—"for our gospel did not come to you in word only." The phrase "in word only" in context is usually taken along the lines of "speech unaccompanied by the convincing power of the Holy Spirit."[10] In harmony with this notion is the fact that Paul mentions a fourfold claim for his presentation of the gospel. It came (1) in power, (2) in the Holy Spirit, (3) with full conviction, and (4) with a lifestyle that proved the truthfulness of what was preached. Thus it is possible to see a combination God uses to the highest effectiveness: The inerrant Word of God proclaimed with "full conviction" as absolute truth (Matt. 24:35; Isa. 55:11) is proclaimed in the power of the Holy Spirit by a godly messenger (see Acts 8:29–40). This kind of presentation produces amazing results.

While the above outline gives the general gist of Paul's statement, some of the specifics need further comment. It is in the realm of possibility that the mention of power and the Spirit together is speaking of the apostolic use of signs and wonders, a work of the Spirit to authenticate the apostle's message (see 2 Cor. 12:12). However, against this view are several lines of evidence. First of all, Paul's later discussion of the Thessalonian acceptance of his gospel message focuses on the work of the Word of God in the believers who had received the message (1 Thess. 2:13). Moreover, in the same section there is a downplaying of apostolic authority on the part of Paul (1 Thess. 2:5–6), something that would be hard to do if apostolic signs and wonders were the power by the Spirit that is meant in 1 Thessalonians 1:5. Finally, the later remembrance of the Thessalonian embrace of Paul's gospel emphasizes the godly character that the missionary team had shown in its behavior toward the saints (1 Thess. 2:9–10). This is in harmony with the last part of verse 5—"what kind of men we proved to be among you." Such a focus might get diminished within the powerful declaration of a message associated with signs and wonders. Therefore it is best not to see any reference to signs and wonders in 1 Thessalonians 1:5, but to see God's Spirit powerfully making the Word of God effective in those who hear.

However, for the above conclusion to hold entirely, the expression "with full conviction" needs to be explored. The word *conviction* means "certainty" or "full assurance." The understanding implies that the Holy Spirit powerfully uses the Word of God to convince hearers of its truth or grant full assurance to them. Contrary to this approach, some interpreters have taken the term instead to speak of Paul's own deep conviction, which is spoken of on almost every page of all his letters and no doubt characterized his preaching ministry (see 1 Thess. 2:11).[11] So the question is whether the conviction mentioned in the passage is something the Holy Spirit performs and produces in the Thessalonians or is something found in the hearts and minds of the givers of the gospel. The focus appears to be on the link between this full conviction and the Holy Spirit that has just been mentioned. Therefore, the best solution is to take the expression as referring to the ministry of the Holy Spirit in convincing the Thessalonians of the truth of Paul's message.[12] In the end the Thessalonians could take heart because all of these things were for their sake.

Reception of the gospel (1:6–9). Those believers at Thessalonica received the gospel message and had their lives transformed. This is what the gospel message is supposed to accomplish in all who will receive it. Note the following eight ways the Thessalonians received the truth of the Word of God and were transformed in that reception:

Transformation of the Thessalonian Believers
1. They became imitators of Paul and the Lord (v. 6).
2. They received the word of the gospel in spite of the threat of persecution (v. 6).
3. They received the word of the gospel with great joy in the Holy Spirit (v. 6).
4. They became an example of what believers should be to other churches and to other believers elsewhere (v. 7).
5. They became faithful in the proclamation of the Word of God (v. 8).
6. They had a testimony of great faith throughout the region (v. 8).
7. They left their idols to serve the true and living God (v. 9).
8. They were intensely interested in prophetic truth and were awaiting the return of the Lord Jesus Christ and the resurrection (v. 10).

They became "imitators" (v. 6) of Paul and his associates because they had seen how they responded to the persecution they faced when they were with them. Of course, this was also true of the Lord Jesus, whose suffering on the cross was from the human perspective a persecution. Because of these divine and apostolic examples, the Thessalonian believers were prompted to receive the Word of God "in much tribulation" (v. 6) as persecution swirled around them (cf. 1 Cor. 11:1).

Beyond merely imitating Christ and the apostles by suffering, Paul praises the Thessalonians doing so with the "joy of the Holy Spirit" (v. 6). To do seems odd when one contemplates the pain associated with the trials of persecution. The answer of course is the supernatural work whereby the Holy Spirit produces joy in their hearts. This connection of joy with the Spirit is not surprising since Paul had elsewhere taught that joy was part of the fruit of the Spirit (Gal. 5:22). In addition, later God would inspire Paul to write, "We exult in our tribulations" (Rom. 5:3). In the apostle's mind, this is because of the presence of the Holy Spirit in the hearts of believers, a presence associated with the production of love (Rom. 5:5).

The result of the Thessalonian believers' joyful endurance of trials is that they became an example for other believers in their region who would hear about them (v. 7). In this way they model the character of Christ to believers in various places who may be in similar circumstances. The particular regions Paul mentions are Macedonia and Achaia. Paul himself had quickly endured persecution in Macedonia, a region north of Greece proper, when he ended up in jail at Philippi along with Silas (Acts 16:16–40). In addition, the apostle knew trials and persecution in Corinth, which was in Achaia (central and southern Greece) and was the location from which Paul wrote the Thessalonian letters. The believers had probably heard about the Thessalonians' joyful endurance from the missionary team. The saints at Thessalonica could take heart precisely because their own behavior under severe pressure was being used in the lives of others.

Part of the reason that people could know the glorious example of the Thessalonians was because the Word of God had "sounded forth" (v. 8) (*exēchētai*) from their church. Even beyond the near regions of Macedonia and Achaia, the faith of the Thessalonians had instructed others. Specifically, Paul may be referring to Aquila and Priscilla who had come from Rome and may have heard about the Thessalonians and recounted the public reputation with the apostle Paul (Acts 18:1–2).[13] The imagery of the phrase "sounded forth" is of a trumpet blowing or ringing out with strong force or reverberation. Some expositors down through church history have suggested the imagery may be better pictured as thunder rather than a trumpet.[14] Regardless, the imagery speaks of the great impact the church had on its surrounding area and the level of testimony that resonated around them. As a result of this public testimony, the missionary team's praise was not needed for others to know about the Thessalonians' great ministry (v. 8). Paul in the next verse voices that this is to the extent that the public testimony of the Thessalonians includes how they had received the missionary team (v. 9).

The powerful testimony of transformation is brought to full force by Paul's next statement in verse 9: "and how you turned to God from idols to serve a living and true God." This implies that most of the believers at Thessalonica had been saved out of a pagan background.[15] But now, in finding Christ and turning to God, they had left their idols to serve the Lord. This is the essence of biblical *conversion*. The impact of this kind of conversion at Thessalonica would indeed have produced the response of the pagans who resided there (Acts 17:6). William MacDonald amplifies what this means: "Notice that they **turned to God from idols**, not from idols to God. It wasn't that they had become fed up with their idols and then decided to give God a chance. No, they turned to God and found Him so satisfying that they dropped their idols."[16]

The description "a living and true God" needs some explanation (v. 9). On the face of things the comparison is obvious. Those who were pagans were worshipping false gods presented in the form of idols (statues or items with physical form) that were dead. The idols could not talk, interact, or intervene in the affairs of humans. In contrast, the God of heaven is a living (*zōnti*) God. The word "true" (*alēthivō*) is a rare word in Paul's letters. In this context it carries the idea of "real," a twin idea to living. The false idols were more than simply dead. Such a notion might imply that they were once alive. However, Paul's statement is stronger. These false idols simply were not real; they did not exist. On the other hand, the living God of Christians and Jews did exist. So, in the end the Thessalonians turned to the God who is there and away from that which is not there.[17] It is possible that the idolatry at Thessalonica was not as oppressive as that which Paul found later at Athens where he was grieved severely over its pervasiveness in the Athenian culture (Acts 17:16). However, there is evidence of a wide range of cultic worship in Thessalonica that would have offended the Christian sensibilities of the missionary team.[18]

A connection can be seen between verses 3 and 9. The *work of faith* relates to "turned to God from idols." The *labor of love* can be seen reflected by the words *to serve the living and true God.* The *steadfastness of hope* finds its complement in "to wait for His Son from heaven." The interpreter of 1 Thessalonians must also at the point of verses 9–10 notice the summary that Paul uses to introduce the body of his entire letter. Chapters 2 and 3 will deal with their *turn to God from idols*. First Thessalonians 4:1–12 covers the idea of what it means *to serve a living and true God*. First Thessalonians 4:13–18 teaches how *to wait for His Son from heaven*. 1 Thessalonians 5:1–11 registers the hope that Christ will *deliver us from the wrath to come.*

Waiting on the coming of the Lord (1:10). Verse 10 begins to chart a course on prophetic matters concerning the return of the Lord that becomes prominent throughout 1 and 2 Thessalonians. The Thessalonians were an eager group of believers who had the characteristic posture "to wait for [God's] Son from heaven." This theme is prominent throughout the New Testament as believers are exhorted to look for the return of Christ (John 14:1–3; Titus 2:13). The Greek word for "wait" (*anamenein*) occurs only here in the New Testament, but Paul does teach the same concept with different Greek words in several other places (1 Cor. 1:7; Phil. 3:20; Rom. 8:23; Gal. 5:5).[19] This idea does not mean that believers should just sit around passively before the coming of the Lord. It means that every believer should live expectantly in the light of His coming as he goes about his daily life. One implication of this characteristic of the Thessalonians is that it is not wrong for believers today to get excited about the possibility of the Lord's return. Too often a false dichotomy is set up that says if you look to the future, you will be no good for the present.

The Thessalonians were waiting for God's *Son*. The sonship of Christ is arguably a major doctrine in the Bible. But the precise rendering of the term is not always clear due largely to the fact that Jesus is called the Son of God in more than one way. In Christ's high-priestly prayer in John 17, Jesus seems to push back the Father-Son relationship into eternity past. This would then be a reference involving the Trinitarian relationship of Christ to the Father in the Godhead. In other words, the term *Son of God* would imply the deity of Christ. In Luke 1:35 the teaching is that Jesus is called Son of God precisely because of the virgin birth and incarnation. In Romans 1:4 he is declared to be the Son of God by virtue of his resurrection from the dead. However, none of these are probably what is meant here in 1 Thessalonians 1:10. Instead, it is better to see the term "Son" here as referring to the idea that Jesus will one day rule as king of Israel (see Ps. 2:7; 2 Sam. 7:14; John 1:49; Heb. 1:5). Jesus is the Christ, the Anointed One, the Messiah who will one day come to rule and reign in kingdom glory (2 Thess. 1:5–12).

Jesus will come from "heaven" (*ouranōn*). The word is in the plural. It could conceivably carry the idea of Jesus returning out of the heavens. That is, he appears in the sky to deliver his people. However, the Jewish character of the term is most likely in view. Hebrew had no singular form for heaven.[20] The context emphasizes the true and living God. Therefore, the point being made is that Jesus is coming from heaven, the abode of God. Lest there be any doubt about who Paul meant, this Son of God is clearly identified as Jesus, the one who was raised from the dead. This identification highlights the fact that the coming of Christ that is envisioned is a personal one. The second coming of Christ is not the coming of the Spirit on the Day of Pentecost or when a person dies. He was the one who died for their sins as the gospel message makes clear. But he did not stay in the grave. He rose from the dead and ascended to the Father as Lord and Christ who would one day return personally. This entire panorama of Jesus' work would be in the background of Paul's understanding as He stressed the Thessalonians' forward look.

The result of that personal coming of Jesus is that He "delivers us from the wrath to come." The word *delivers* (*puomenōn*) means "to rescue" or "to save." The word is used several times by Paul in his letters but only one other time in the Thessalonian correspondence. In 2 Thessalonians 3:2 Paul asks the Thessalonians to pray that the missionary team would be "delivered from perverse and evil men." Hence, the word is simply a common expression for "rescue."

The term "wrath to come" raises the question as to the particular wrath that is in view. The Bible says that those who have not believed in Jesus have the wrath of God abiding on them (John 3:36). This current wrath on the lost is not in view here in 1 Thessalonians 1:10, since what is being described is a wrath *to come*. Another possibility is that the wrath refers to the judgment of God in hell for unbelievers. Certainly the Thessalonians, since they have received the gospel, are not destined for eternal fire. However, this interpretation also seems to fail due to the context of the entire book of 1 Thessalonians. The outline point in 1:10 that speaks of deliverance from wrath is taken up in 1 Thessalonians 5:1–11. The fact that the Thessalonians are exempt from wrath is taught in 5:9. Moreover, the context of that section speaks of it as the "Day of the Lord" (5:2). Thus what the Thessalonian believers will be exempt from is the Day of the Lord's wrath.

Two main views exist concerning the nature and time of the Day of the Lord's wrath. Those interpreters who generally hold to the doctrine of a posttribulational rapture (Christ raptures the church at the end of the tribulation) often equate the day of the Lord's wrath with the wrathful event of the second coming of Christ as portrayed in Revelation 19. Those interpreters who hold the doctrine of a pretribulational rapture (Christ raptures the church before the beginning of the tribulation) often see the Day of the Lord as equivalent to the seven years of the Seventieth Week of Daniel (Dan. 9:24–27). In other words, the Day of the Lord is not an event, but a time period or duration of seven years in which God pours out His wrath on the whole earth as described in Revelation 4–19. The pretribulational view of the rapture of the church sees a two-phase second coming and is no doubt the correct interpretation, as our later discussions will show throughout 1 and 2 Thessalonians. The definition of the Day of the Lord is so crucial in this matter that an appendix discussing it has been provided (see appendix A).

Study Questions

1. Do you work in your church's ministry until you are weary? Why do you serve the Lord in your church?
2. How does the Bible doctrine of election affect the church? Why is it so difficult to understand?
3. Has your life been transformed by the gospel? How does your life compare to that of the believers at Thessalonica? How would you describe your life now compared to before the time you were saved?
4. What is your attitude toward the coming of Christ? Are you eagerly anticipating the return of the Lord? Is your life any different today because you look ahead with hope?

CHAPTER 3

The Testimony of Paul's Ministry 1 Thessalonians 2:1–20

Preview:

Paul reminds the Thessalonians that when he first arrived in the city, he had preached the Word of God with boldness under suffering, pure motives, the gentleness of a mother, and hard work. The church's response was positive so that the apostle longs to minister to them again.

This section begins the part of Paul's outline from 1 Thessalonians 1:9 where he discusses how the Thessalonians turned to God from idols. Paul's discussion of this point goes from 2:1 to 3:13 and consists of the testimony of Paul's ministry, the testimony of Timothy's ministry, and a special prayer of Paul. The comments in this chapter will cover the testimony of Paul's ministry as it impacted the Thessalonians.

The Lord Jesus Christ sent the disciple Ananias to go to Saul of Tarsus to lay hands on him so he could receive his sight (Acts 9:12). Ananias complained because he knew of Saul's reputation for putting believers in prison. But Jesus gave His reason for sending Ananias: "Go, for he is a chosen instrument of Mine, to bear My name before the Gentiles and kings and the sons of Israel; for I will show him how much He must suffer for My name's sake" (Acts 9:15–16).

Saul of Tarsus became known as Paul the apostle and did indeed suffer for the sake of the Lord. As noted previously, this was part of his testimony at Thessalonica (Acts 17:1–10) and was a major reason for his writing to the church. He wanted to vindicate his character and teaching in the midst of the evil reports associated with the persecution at Thessalonica.

The Character of Paul (2:1–12)

Paul's entrance to Thessalonica. Paul appeals to something that the Thessalonians already "know" (*oidate*), namely, "that our coming to you was not in vain" (v. 1). The reference could include the previous mention in 1:5 of the believers' knowledge of the character of the missionary team.[1] However, it is best to take it as referring to the immediate and previous context of 1:9. One reason is the closer proximity of the verse to 2:1. In addition 1:9 mentions the kind of reception the Thessalonians gave to Paul and his traveling companions. This description fits appropriately with the "coming" of the team to Thessalonica that is portrayed in 2:1. Finally, if, as suggested, 1:9–10 gives the outline of the book and 2:1 begins the first section of the Pauline outline, the verse must hark back to 1:9. Thus what is being emphasized is not so much the character of the men (Paul, Timothy, and Silas) who came to Thessalonica, but the coming of the team in ministry success.[2]

Therefore, Paul could speak of his reception as not "in vain" (*kenē*). Paul's coming had met with great success and could not in any way be construed a failure. It could also be said that His words were not hollow or empty words void of any precise content. The two ideas of the character of the preaching and the result of the proclamation by Paul and his associates should both be included in the understanding. As F. F. Bruce notes, "The Thessalonians' positive response to the gospel and subsequent energy in spreading it abroad bore sufficient testimony both to the quality of the preaching and to the power that accompanied it."[3] However, even if both ideas are included, the focus on the production of results may be emphasized in light of the good end summarized in 1:9.[4] Such a thought is supported by the fact that in 1 Thessalonians Paul's other use of the phrase "in vain" refers to his fear that his work had not produced the desired effect (1 Thess. 3:5).

Paul's boldness under suffering. While Paul's suffering had been well known, he reminds the Thessalonians about what happened to him and Silas before they arrived at Thessalonica. At Philippi they had "already suffered and been mistreated" (v. 2; cf. Acts 16:23–24). The Philippian experience had preceded the efforts to spread the gospel at Thessalonica by only a short time (Acts 16:31–17:9). Paul's testimony no doubt included his welcome in that city. The opposition to Paul they had clearly witnessed themselves. Beyond that, the stopover in Berea (Acts 17:10–15) became an occasion for some Jewish opponents from Thessalonica to follow Paul and stir up others against him. Thus the Thessalonians would have known not only of the mistreatment of Paul but of the entire history of what had transpired. However, Paul's focus in this verse is on the Philippian experience that was in the immediate background as he came to Thessalonica. Mal Couch identifies the impact of Paul's words about his suffering: "*Suffered* (*propaschō*, aorist active participle) and *mistreated* (*hubrizō*, aorist passive participle) are strong words that show the intensity of the hatred against Paul preaching the gospel. *Hubrizō* means to treat insolently. . . . The truth is not popular, and satanic opposition against it is always bitter."[5]

Paul declares, "We had the boldness in our God to speak to you the gospel of God amid much opposition" (v. 2). Though the missionary team suffered for the faith, they continued to preach the gospel with boldness. This particular expression for boldness (*eparrēsiasametha*) occurs only here in Paul's letters and in the Prison Epistle of Ephesians where he asks for prayer that he might declare the truth fearlessly (Eph. 6:20). The term on its own can carry the idea of speaking boldly. The use of it with the verb to speak (*lalēsai*) intensifies the notion. This boldness to share the gospel comes from God himself (*in our God*) and is not something that Paul summoned on his own strength.

The word *gospel* is "good news" and should be understood here in the conventional sense as the death, burial, and resurrection of Jesus Christ (1 Cor. 15:1–4). Paul uses the term *gospel* seventy times in his New Testament writings. In 1 Thessalonians it occurs six times (1:5; 2:2, 4, 8, 9; 3:2) and in 2 Thessalonians twice (1:8; 2:14). In this section of 1 Thessalonians, the gospel that came to them in power by the Spirit (1:5), was committed to Paul by God (2:4), was imparted by Paul (2:8), and was the essence of his proclamation (2:9) was the good news that Paul boldly proclaimed when he was with the saints at Thessalonica. This gospel was "of God" probably in the sense that God was the originator or source of the gospel. Thus one cannot accuse the missionary team of preaching their own story.

Paul adds an enigmatic expression when he notes that his bold preaching was displayed "amid much opposition." Is Paul suggesting that his preaching to the Thessalonians was in the midst of opposition while he was at Thessalonica? If so, does that cause a problem with his earlier statement that they received him "not in vain" (2:1) and appeared to believe God's message gladly (2:13)? Others have suggested that the reference is to the boldness the missionary team exhibited *after* having been persecuted. That is, after the Philippian experience mentioned earlier in the verse, Paul and his friends came to Thessalonica and preached the Word of God boldly in spite of past experiences.[6] They were not deterred. However, the preferred and simplest reading of the verse leads to the interpretation that Paul continued to preach in the midst of opposition while he was at Thessalonica. This fact is certainly born out in the Acts account of his ministry in that city (17:5ff.). There is no contradiction to the statement that the Thessalonians received him gladly. In every place Paul went, there were those who accepted Christ and those who rejected Him on the strongest terms.

Paul's pure motives. Paul's exhortation or appeal (*paraklēsis*) was done with the purest of motives. Three false motives are addressed by the apostle in 2:3—error, impurity, and deceit. He categorically denies that he or any of his associates had engaged in any preaching ministry based on these motives. His denials are strong. The need for the denials is made clear by Bruce: "So many wandering charlatans . . . made their way about the Greek world, peddling their religious or philosophical nostrums, and living at the expense of their devotees . . . that it was necessary for Paul and his friends to emphasize the purity of their motives and actions by contrast with these."[7]

To base his ministry on "error" (*planēs*) would involve Paul in deception or leading people astray. Paul denies his preaching is error or that it has any intention of directing people off course. To be involved in *impurity* (*akatharsias*) is a reference to the Gentile religions and their unclean, impure sexual religious ceremonies. This term is chiefly unique to Paul, although Matthew records Jesus using it on one occasion to compare the Pharisees to whitewashed tombs full of *uncleanness* (Matt. 23:27). The apostle uses the term another time in 1 Thessalonians to contrast impurity with the sanctification that God wants for all believers (1 Thess. 4:7). To use *deceit* (*dolō*) or trickery to gain or fool an audience was part of the accusation against Paul. He denies all three charges and reminds the Thessalonians of his character when he was with them.

In contrast to the negative traits of error, impurity, and deceit, Paul notes that the missionary team was approved by God to be entrusted with the gospel (2:4). To be "approved" (*dokimazō*) means to be accepted by testing. So the gospel has been "entrusted" (*pisteuō*) to his faithful preachers: "But how can the Thessalonians know that Paul and his helpers have been tested by God and were thus entrusted with the gospel of God? May not any errorist or fake religionist set up the same claim? He may, but he will be exposed at once. If he does not bring the gospel, and that the pure gospel, that already exposes him as *not* being attested by God, as *not* being entrusted with the gospel by God."[8] The word "examines" in 2:4 is the same Greek word that is translated earlier in the verse as "approved." Paul is willing to bare his heart and ministry and to allow God to judge it, examine it, test it, or put it on trial. This would stand in stark contrast to those who were charlatans and used the ministry for gain. The team did not try to "please" (*areskontes*) men, but God (2:4). He would later in the letter contrast this behavior with those who killed Jesus, killed the prophets, and drove out Paul (2:15). Additionally, he would later argue for the Thessalonians to follow his teaching on how to please God (4:1).

Paul further reminds the Thessalonian believers in 2:5 that he did not come to them with "flattering speech" (literally, "a word of flattery"). "*Flattering*" (*kolakeias*) is a rare word, occurring only here in the New Testament. The general idea of the expression is exaggerated praise. Such an approach would certainly be man-pleasing and self-serving. Paul distances himself along with his missionary team from such nonsense. That Paul did not come to them with such speech the Thessalonians knew quite well ("as you know"). However, he adds another point that God knows ("God is witness"). Paul and his team did not come to the Thessalonians with any pretext for greed. "Pretext" here refers to a falsely alleged motive or excuse. The ministry of Paul was not an excuse to make money. Greed might easily offend the sensibilities of a Jewish man who understood the implications of idolatry. Paul would later write the books of Ephesians and Colossians, in which he would name greed and covetousness as types of idolatry (Eph. 5:3–5; Col. 3:5). This may be why Paul invokes the witness of God on this last point and not just the testimony of the Thessalonians.

Continuing a similar line of discussion, Paul notes that he did not "seek glory from men" (2:6). The word translated "seek" (*zētountes*) is a frequently used word meaning to desire or covet. Here "glory" (*doxan*) probably means *praise*—Paul did not desire the praise of people. The universal nature of Paul's attitude is clear when he says, "either from you or from others." At no time did he have an agenda of producing a personal following that especially esteemed him as an apostle. Thus he adds the qualification: "even though as apostles of Christ we might have asserted our authority."[9] The plural word "apostles" initially raises a problem. Does Paul in using the term label both Silas and Timothy as apostles? The rest of the New Testament does not designate them so. It could be that the word is being used in a general sense as missionaries, that is, "ones sent out." However, Paul's mentioning of authority appears to imply more. The best approach is to see Paul using his own personal authority as an apostle to represent the authority that the team as a whole, led by an apostle, possessed.[10] These men, especially the apostle Paul, deserved to be esteemed by people because of how God was using them. They could have brought that to the forefront by insisting on their rightful status, but they refrained. In the end, God's approval of Paul was all that mattered. What people said about him was meaningless. God Himself called Paul into the ministry and gave him the gospel to carry to the mission field.

Paul's gentleness. Paul describes his ministry as one of gentleness (2:7). Here "gentle" (*ēpioi*) simply implies being kindhearted to another person.[11] The overriding image in the passage is the analogy of Paul's relationship with the Thessalonians to that of a nursing mother who cares for her children. A mother "tenderly cares for" her children. This expression (*thalpē*) literally carries the idea of keeping warm but is generally used to signify the idea of comforting or cherishing. This is especially sharpened by the reference to "her own children" as opposed to someone else's children. It is an appropriate metaphor since Paul and his missionary team had spiritually birthed the believers in Thessalonica. They were indeed his children in that sense. The metaphor occurs elsewhere in Paul's writings when he emotionally and personally tells the Galatians, "My children, with whom I am again in labor until Christ is formed in you" (Gal. 4:19). The idea of cherishing within the family unit is also mentioned in a different direction by Paul when he notes that husbands should cherish their wives (Eph. 5:28–30).

The idea of gentleness on the part of Paul and the missionary team is also highlighted by other expressions in the passage. First, the apostle refers to "having thus a fond affection" (*omeiromenoi*) for the saints at Thessalonica (2:8). The term carries the tone of longing for someone else and as such is quite a personal expression. It is also an ongoing act or state, not a single event in Paul's experience. It characterizes his heart and mind.

Second, the man of God reminds the Thessalonians that he was pleased to preach the gospel to them, but even beyond that, to impart "also our own lives" (2:8). Leon Morris notes that even when Paul is emphasizing other points, the gospel is not far from his mind.[12] However, the main thrust here is that Paul and the team had imparted their very lives to the Thessalonian converts. This means more than their willingness to lay down their lives for them in death, although the thought would contain such a notion. The meaning is something akin to "to put ourselves at your disposal, without reservation."[13] Think of it this way: the missionaries had decided to use some of their God-given time on earth in behalf of others, in this case the Thessalonians. Such commitment is at the heart of the missionary enterprise and Christian ministry. Bruce comments that the example became a lesson learned by the Thessalonian believers, because later Paul bragged that the Macedonian Christians ministered in generosity for others when they "first gave themselves to the Lord and to us by the will of God" (2 Cor. 8:5).[14]

Another way that Paul highlights the idea of personal gentleness and kindness in the passage is his statement that the saints had "become very dear to us" (2:8). Here "dear" (*agapētoi*) is used as a statement of direct address in many of Paul's letters and could be translated "beloved" (e.g., Rom. 12:19;

1 Cor. 10:14). This continues the focus in the entire passage on how special all believers are to Paul (cf. 1 Tim. 6:2). They are loved, not just by God, but by the missionary team.

Paul's testimony of labor. Paul further reminds the church of how he worked and labored among saints, calling his toil "our labor and hardship" (2:9). "Labor" (*kopon*) is the same word found in 1 Thessalonians 1:3. "Hardship" (*mochthon*) is used only by Paul in the New Testament—here and in 2 Corinthians 11:27 and 2 Thessalonians 3:8. It connotes hard labor and exertion. The two terms appear to be synonymous in this passage. No doubt this text would compare to the words near the beginning of the epistle in which he praises the Thessalonians for their work of faith and labor of love (1:3). Theirs had been a toil that had brought fatigue. Paul reminds them that he, too, had the same kind of work and toil when he was with them.

What was the nature of Paul's labor among them when he was "working night and day" (2:9)? In this verse he is not stressing his preaching and teaching, but his trade of being a tentmaker (Acts 18:3; 20:34). He made tents during the whole time he stayed with them. The purpose of this practice was "so as not to be a burden to any of you" (2:9). Here "burden" (*epibarēsai*) naturally carries the thought of a load weighing someone down. Paul practically gives the identical presentation in 2 Thessalonians 3:8. Apparently the apostle did not want to be a financial drain on the new converts who certainly could have taken Paul on for support. Paul had a right to expect this (1 Cor. 9:1–14; 1 Tim. 5:17–18). But he also knew that the brand-new church had other concerns, and he did not want to be accused falsely by others over money issues.

The reference to both God and the Thessalonians as witnesses of Paul's behavior in financial matters (2:10) echoes the statements "you know" and "God is witness" in 2:5. Paul apparently has a clear conscience relative to both God and his brothers in Thessalonica. In verse 10, the apostle describes his actions with three terms. "Devoutly" (*hosiōs*) labels his conduct as being in a holy manner pleasing to God. The term is used only here in the New Testament. The next descriptor is "uprightly" (*dikaiōs*). It carries the idea that Paul's deeds in the midst of the Thessalonian believers were right and just before God. Finally, Paul uses the word "blamelessly" (*amemptōs*). No person in Thessalonica could place a charge against Paul for his work ethic in their midst. This particular expression is used only here and in 1 Thessalonians 5:23 where Paul envisions the Thessalonians themselves presented blamelessly and entirely sanctified when they one day stand before Christ at his coming.

The encouragement of a father. Paul gave the example of a nursing mother in 2:7. Now he gives the metaphor of a father encouraging his children in 2:11, while once again noting that the Thessalonians already know that what he is saying is true ("just as you know"). Paul once again uses three descriptive verbs to portray the way he dealt with them as a father.[15] The apostle begins by noting his "exhorting" (*parakalountes*) of them. This term is a common one in Paul's writings, occurring in various forms more than fifty times. It can mean to urge, entreat, request, summon, or encourage. To exhort someone is sometimes to urge them on in something or to warn and command them. Other times it carries more the idea of giving comfort. Paul's use of the word in 1 and 2 Thessalonians covers both ideas. Of the other nine times it is used in these two books, four times it means to urge to do something. Five times it means "to comfort." Which does it mean here? The parallel to the second descriptive verb supports the view that Paul speaks of comforting. "Encouraging" (*paramuthoumenoi*) can only mean to comfort or cheer the heart. This would be extremely appropriate in light of the persecution common at Thessalonica. The other time it occurs in Paul's letters is when the apostle tells the Thessalonians to encourage or comfort the fainthearted (1 Thess. 5:14). Therefore, in 2:11 the first two descriptive verbs are probably synonyms that mean "to comfort." Paul had comforted the Thessalonian converts as a father comforts his children. The third descriptive verb is "imploring" (*marturomenoi*).[16] This word, different from the first two terms, usually means "to testify or witness" but can signify the notion of insisting on something. Here Paul is reminding the Thessalonian believers that he insisted, virtually begged, them to accept the truth when he came to them.[17]

Worthy of God. The goal of all of the encouraging, comforting, and urging is that the believers would walk in a manner worthy of God and the destiny He has for them (2:12). "To walk" (*peripatein*) is a frequent expression in the New Testament that denotes the course of one's life. To urge people to walk a certain way is to advocate that they live by following the prescribed path. The way they are to live is in a manner "worthy" (*axiōs*) of God. Living in a worthy manner means living in a manner that is suitable or fitting for what is desired. In this case, to live worthy is in view of God who determines what is acceptable and what is not.

Paul speaks elsewhere of receiving a believer in the Lord in a manner worthy of the saints (Rom. 16:2) and of Christian conduct being worthy of the gospel of Christ (Phil. 1:27). Moreover, he gives the same exhortation as that found in 1 Thessalonians 2:12 in Colossians 1:10 where he commands the saints to "walk in a manner worthy of the Lord to please Him in all respects, bearing fruit in every good work and increasing in the knowledge of God." A similar thought is found in Ephesians 4:1 where the apostle entreats the saints to "walk in a manner worthy of the calling with which you have been called." The calling had been explained in the earlier sections of Ephesians. The believers were saved. They were called as part of God's family. Now, they were to live like it.

These references in Colossians and Ephesians come close to the heart of what Paul is saying to the Thessalonians in 2:12. The depth of meaning comes from how God is described in the verse: "who calls you into His own kingdom and glory." Thus the meaning of the entire verse is that the Thessalonian believers are to live their lives well in light of what God is doing for them. The phrase "who calls" (*kalountos*) points to the summons of God in the work of salvation. One might expect a reference here to a past, accomplished work of salvation similar to that mentioned in Ephesians 4:1. However, as D. Michael Martin notes, "The present participle 'who calls' looks not to the conversion of the Thessalonians in the past but focuses on the ongoing calling that anticipates the future dawning of the age to come."[18] While some interpreters see the reference to God's own kingdom and glory as some present rule of God, usually through the church, the overall context of such a notion does not fit the Thessalonian correspondence, which is futuristic in focus.[19] Hence, to understand this section of Paul's thoughts, one must understand him to be telling the Thessalonian believers to live in light of God's coming kingdom of which they are already citizens.

The Response of the Church (2:13–16)

The reception of the Word of God. Paul's defense of his ministry now gives way to a reminder of how the church responded to him when he came to Thessalonica to minister. He mentions again (2:13) his gratitude to God in light of the Thessalonians as he did at the beginning of the epistle (1:2). His reason is their reception of the Word of God. Paul describes this reception in several ways.

First, they received "the word of God's message," or literally, "a word of hearing" (*logon akoēs*). Here "received" (*paralabontes*) for all practical intent means that the people had outwardly received the message. "Accepted" (*edexasthe*) means that they inwardly embraced the preaching of Paul[20]—that is, they believed that his preaching was true and they appropriated the message for themselves. The content of this proclaimed word primarily includes the gospel, that is, the death, burial, and resurrection of Christ and the need to accept him by faith to have forgiveness with God. It is this gospel that he shared with them upon his arrival in their city (Acts 17:1–3). Paul also mentions the gospel earlier in the second chapter of 1 Thessalonians four times. Altogether in the epistles to the Thessalonians he uses the term eight times. Throughout this section Paul seems concerned about people being saved, or justified, as a result of accepting the gospel (see especially 2:16).

Second, they rejected the notion that Paul's preaching was just the word of men (2:13). They recognized the special quality of what they were hearing. Traditions passed down by people were not necessarily a bad thing in Paul's thinking. If the traditions are rooted in the truth about God and Christ or in apostolic authority, they were to be followed (2 Thess. 2:15; 3:6; 1 Cor. 11:2). However, the apostle was leery of the traditions of his fathers (his Jewish heritage) when such traditions did not lead to Jesus Christ (Gal. 1:14). He also showed concern about human thought in general when he told the Colossians, "See to it that no one takes you captive through philosophy and empty deception, according to the tradition of men, according to the elementary principles of the world, rather than according to Christ" (Col. 2:8). While this Colossians passage is an exhortation to those who already believe in Jesus, Paul in 1 Thessalonians 2:13 is grateful that the saints in Thessalonica had gotten off to a good start in their attitude about the words of the apostolic proclamation. While they recognized they were listening to humans, they had not concluded that the message was manmade.

Third, they understood that preaching as it really was—the Word of God being proclaimed (2:13). This is, of course, the flip side of the previous point. The source of the message was not humans, but God himself. Paul's proclamation was divine truth. One interesting discussion in this connection is the relationship that the phrase "word of God" has to the written Word of God in the Bible. The passage is certainly speaking about the oral message given by the apostolic missionary team. However, that oral message no doubt contained arguments from the Old Testament text concerning the Christ. We know this because of Paul's debates in the synagogue for three Sabbaths that started the Thessalonian experience and generated the first Christian converts (Acts 17:1–4). Nonetheless, we are forced to conclude that Paul's preaching also included extrabiblical testimony to the oral traditions about Christ, which had not yet been written down. It is clear that the book of Acts had not yet been written with its testimony of Paul's conversion on the road to Damascus (Acts 9:1–19). However, it is unreasonable to assume that Paul did not share this testimony with the Thessalonians, for it was a major part of his life story (Acts 22, 26). Thus the expression "word of God" refers both to the written content of the Old Testament and to oral tradition and testimony in harmony with that written word. Regardless, the source of all of the proclamation is God.

Finally, they experienced in their own lives the results of believing the gospel and God's word for their lives. "*Performs [its] work* is the present indicative of *energeō*, which expresses the idea that the Word of God causes things to happen."[21] John states those results in his gospel: "Many other signs therefore Jesus also performed in the presence of the disciples, which are not written in this book; but these have been written that you may believe that Jesus is the Christ, the Son of God; and that believing you may have life in His name" (John 20:30–31). However, the status of being saved is probably not all that is meant by the expression. "Believe" is in the present tense, signifying the present state of the faith of the Thessalonians. Therefore, the ongoing work of the power of God may be in view.

The imitation of the churches in Judea. Not only did the Thessalonians receive salvation and eternal life through faith in Jesus Christ, but they also "became imitators of the churches of God in Christ Jesus that are in Judea" (2:14). That is, they followed the pattern of other godly churches in Judea. In what way did they imitate those churches? They endured persecution from the Jews just as the Judean churches did. The apostle's discussion leads into a sensitive area to modern readers offended by negative statements about Jews. However, Paul, as a Jew, offers a clear and concise presentation that neither criticizes Jews simply because they are Jews nor gives any hint of replacement theology in which the church replaces national Israel in God's overall plan. In short, Paul and the letter of 1 Thessalonians cannot be accused of anti-Semitism.

In Acts 17 Luke summarizes the Jewish opposition to Paul and the Thessalonian believers. Apparently the apostolic missionary team had some measure of success while Paul reasoned in the synagogue. Some Jews, God-fearing Greeks, and women joined themselves to the team and its message (v. 4). This caused jealousy in some of the Jews who formed a mob to find Paul and Silas in particular (v. 5). Failing to find them, they forcefully took Jason and other new Christians in Thessalonica to the city authorities angrily and falsely accusing them of violating the decrees of Caesar (vv. 6–7). The situation was so tense that the new converts sent Paul and Silas away by night to Berea (v. 10). However, the same Thessalonian Jews became incensed over Paul's ministry in Berea and sent a delegation to Berea "agitating and stirring up the crowds" (v. 13). Consequently, the experience of the Jewish Paul in Thessalonica, as well as the ongoing experience of the Thessalonians themselves relative to many Jews in the city, was an extremely hostile and negative one. It is this experience that forms the backdrop to Paul's statements in

1 Thessalonians 2:14–16. It must be understood that when he speaks of the "Jews" (1 Thess. 2:14), he means the unbelieving and rebellious Jews and not all Jews everywhere since many had come to the truth both in Judea and in Thessalonica.

Paul gives several statements portraying the actions of the rebellious Jews that the Thessalonians faced and that the Judean Christians faced. The two experiences were the same. First, both had endured suffering at the "hands of [their] own countrymen" (2:14). It would be obvious that the Jews in Judea persecuted the mostly Christian Jews in that region as Paul mentions. Jews would be persecuting Jews as far as nationality goes. However, things are not so obvious for the Thessalonians. It is clear that the congregation was made up of mostly Gentiles, although as said earlier, there were several Jews who came to Christ and helped make up the initial members of the assembly. Does this fact mean that the term "own countrymen" should include both Jews and Gentiles? If both are included, the statement makes sense. However, it is also true that if only Jews are in Paul's mind, the statement makes sense. The thrust of it would still be true since Macedonians had persecuted Macedonians. Therefore, one should not try to soften Paul's statements about these particular Jews by suggesting that Gentiles are also included, since he is clearly focusing on the Jewish opposition that was in the past and ongoing experience of the Thessalonians.[22] Jewish opposition led to Gentile opposition, the Jews also went to Berea, and Paul highlights the Jews throughout the remainder of this passage. These details cannot be glossed over. The Thessalonians had "endured" (*epathete*) the same plight as the Judean churches. This particular term is rarely used of any positive experiences. Its association with enduring negative things is so strong that it could be translated "suffered."

Second, in history the Jews had been largely responsible for killing the Lord Jesus and the prophets of Israel (2:15). Such a statement is quite consistent with the tenor of the entire New Testament, including Jesus' teaching. Jesus tells the scribes and Pharisees of his day, who represented "this generation" of those who rejected Christ, that they were guilty of "all the righteous blood shed on earth, from the blood of righteous Abel to the blood of Zechariah" (Matt. 23:34–35)—the entire history of the Old Testament.[23] He says this in the context of the nation's rejection of many prophets sent by God. In the parable of the vine-growers, Jesus also asserts that the nation would reject and kill the Son of God when he came after a long line of prophets who had been rejected (Luke 20:9–18). Peter's sermon on the Day of Pentecost contains clear words: "this Man [Jesus], delivered up by the predetermined plan and foreknowledge of God, you nailed to a cross by the hands of godless men and put Him to death" (Acts 2:23). The "you" in this statement is the "men of Israel" of verse 22. Peter says this as a Jew speaking to Jews.

At this point, it must be said that one must be careful with such a truth so as not to read more into it than the statement bears. For example, it is not really right to give the moniker of "Christ killers" to the Jews as a race because of such a passage. Acts 2:24 also notes that God Himself had something to do with the death of Christ as part of His design, plan, and working in the world. The Gospels clearly tell us that the Roman soldiers were the immediate murderers of Christ. Although his death was instigated by the Jews, it was Roman authority that actually killed him. It can also be said that there is a higher sense in which no one killed Jesus, since he gave his life freely for others (John 10:18). Theologically, we can also remember that all sinners bear some responsibility for the death of Christ, since it is our sin that made his death a necessary substitution (2 Cor. 5:21). Consequently, statements in the New Testament, including those here in 1 Thessalonians, should not be viewed as an open door to practice anti-Semitism, for we all bear some blame for the death of Christ.

Third, Paul describes the Jews as those who drove him and his missionary team from Thessalonica and Berea (2:15). He uses the simple expression "drove us out" to make the point. The expression "drove out" (*ekdiōxantōn*) means to persecute severely or harshly even to the point of forcing someone out or somewhere else. This was exactly the experience of Paul and Silas when the Jews of Thessalonica stirred up trouble to the point that Paul had to leave both Thessalonica and Berea (Acts 17:10, 14). The Thessalonians were well aware of this history lesson.

Fourth, Paul describes the Jews as "not pleasing to God" (2:15). This expression forces an immediate contrast to the earlier verses in chapter 2 where Paul voices a great desire to please God (2:4). The Jews who rejected the message of God in Christ were not eager to please God and were therefore not like the Thessalonian believers. Correspondingly, Paul does not use terms of endearment when discussing them.

Fifth, Paul notes that the Jews were "hostile to all men" (2:15). The word translated "hostile" (*enantiōn*) means "contrary" or "opposite." When applied to people, it would naturally signify hostility toward someone. The difficulty of the phrase is in discerning in what way or ways the Jews were hostile to *all* men. Morris reminds us of the statement by Tacitus that the Jews were "haters of the human race."[24] This should be viewed skeptically while being aware of some Roman bias. The apostle goes on to explain his meaning: "hindering us from speaking to the Gentiles that they might be saved" (2:16). The hostility he has in mind is the hostility the unbelieving Jews had toward the gospel itself, which identified Jesus as the Jewish Messiah who came to give eternal life to those who believe in him. The term *hindering* (*kōluontōn*) explains how the Jews were hostile to all men, not wanting any to accept Paul's gospel. The term means "to prevent, hinder, block, or keep away from." By their persecution of Paul, the unbelieving Jews were not only trying to keep his voice out of the synagogue but also out of the entire city. They did not want the Gentiles to accept Paul's notion of the Jewish Messiah. That means that they hindered the Gentiles from being saved whenever their persecution accomplished its goal. The word saved (*sōthōsin*) is the usual word for the deliverance that comes when a person trusts Christ as Savior.

The response on the part of the unbelieving Jews brought a twofold judgment in Paul's estimation (2:16). First, their actions bring "the result that they always fill up the measure of their sins" (2:16). This refers to the fact that they are filling up their cup for judgment in the future. Hiebert points out why the Jews were so hostile:

> The Jews' opposition to the work of the missionaries among the Gentiles was not due to the fact that they were seeking to win Gentiles. The Jews themselves were vigorously engaged in this period of their history in actively proselyting Gentiles. Their fierce opposition was due to the fact that Christian missionaries offered salvation to Gentiles without demanding that they first become Jews. Everywhere the Jews showed themselves wildly jealous at Paul's success in winning Gentiles to the Christian faith directly.[25]

Second, this state of sinfulness has evoked the wrath of God upon the unbelieving Jews. The wrath is said to have come upon them "to the utmost" (2:16). It is a picture of a hammer ready to fall at any moment upon national Israel. Those who believe the message of Paul would be received by God and His Christ. However, those who reject that message will ultimately receive judgment. But which judgment is meant and what is its character? If the apostle meant the judgment of hell, that would be true enough but something that is true of all who reject Christ.

Another option is to see the wrath as a temporal destruction that is awaiting the Jews as a whole. God's patience will be ended and His wrath will be poured out on the nation. Though Israel had faced many past judgments of God, now they had rejected their Messiah. In the not-too-distant future, within twenty years of the Thessalonian experience, God would judge Israel. In AD 70 this took place when Roman legions under Titus sacked the city of

Jerusalem and destroyed the temple. The Jews were scattered throughout the world, fulfilling the teaching of Scripture (Deut. 28). This is a judgment that had been predicted by Jesus himself (Matt. 23:37–38; 24:1–2).

A final option is that the wrath meant here is the Day of the Lord's wrath that is coming at the end of the church age, a topic brought out by Paul in 1 Thessalonians 1:10 and explicated in 5:1–11. This is a time predicted in the Old Testament prophets that would be the time of Jacob's trouble—a time of distress for and judgment upon the nation of Israel that serves as a cleansing of the nation before it inherits its glorious kingdom (e.g., Jer. 30:1–11; Joel 2:1–3:3). Such an end-time judgment is probably the intended meaning, although Paul is not specific. Regardless of its identification, the fate of the unbelieving Jews, like the fate of all those who reject God's Christ, is one of darkness and gloom.

Paul's Desire to Minister to Them Again (2:17–20)

Paul's desire to see the Thessalonians. The apostle reminds himself and his readers that he has been "bereft of [them] for a short while" (2:17). This calls to mind the fact that he and Silas had been abruptly sent away because of the turmoil at Thessalonica. The word *bereft* means to be made an orphan by separation. It is a rare word occurring only here in the New Testament. Paul, who had earlier applied the metaphors of a nursing mother and encouraging father to his relationship with the saints, now uses a more enigmatic picture. This portrait gives the imagery of being ripped away from family, for this is how he viewed the believers at Thessalonica.

Paul visualizes the separation as only temporary. The phrase "a short while" (*kaipon hōras*) is literally a "time hour." The expression carries the weight of "an hour of time" or "short amount of time." Paul anticipates that he will not be separated from them for a long time. He also points out that he was absent "in person, not in spirit." The first part of this wording, "in person," is literally "in face" (*prosōpō*). It is a usual Hebraic expression for the whole person that has come down to us in modern times. When we say, "We want to see your face," we really mean the whole person. It is the same word that occurs later in the verse when Paul notes his eagerness "to see your face." The phrase "not in spirit" is actually "not in heart." The word translated "heart" (*kardia*) reflects the inner person. The similar idea of being present in spirit occurs in 1 Corinthians 5:4 where Paul tells the Corinthians to deal with the man who has committed incest in the congregation. There he tells them that when they are assembled to deal with the situation, he will be present with them in spirit (*pneumatos*). In 1 Thessalonians 2:17, the idea of the heart as the inner person reflects the same sentiment so that the use of "spirit" in the translation is justified. Paul comes across as almost mystical, but we should probably stop short of saying so. Instead, it is better to suggest that there is a spiritual reality of union with Christ and all other believers that each individual follower of Christ possesses. It could also reflect Paul's heartfelt belief that he is there in Thessalonica in the spiritual teaching he has left behind. His imprint is left all over that congregation even though he is not physically present.

Paul finishes his statement about his temporary separation from the Thessalonians by noting in strong language that he is "all the more eager with great desire to see your face." The term "all the more" (*perissotepōs*) implies that the separation actually increased Paul's desire to see them, causing him to be eager to a *greater degree*. The verbal expression "were eager" (*espoudasamen*) implies being eager and zealous, making every effort or taking pains to bring about whatever one is eager for. The apostle heightens the strength of the statement even more when he adds that he is eager with "great desire." The word translated "desire" (*epithumia*) means great desire or passion as it is translated in 1 Thessalonians 4:5. It can refer to either good or bad forms of desire. Here the apostle Paul demonstrates with powerful wording that he possesses an excited anticipation and great need to see the Thessalonians once again. They no doubt appreciated this word from their spiritual father.

Satan's opposition. In 2:18 Paul explains that the proof of his eagerness to see the Thessalonian believers is in the attempts he made to go back to them. His desire is reiterated by the statement "We wanted to come." Now Paul abandons his normal use of the term *we* by adding—"I, Paul, more than once." The apostle makes it personal and intense by mentioning his name. It is his own personal desire to see them that resulted in more than one attempt to go to them. He does not say how many times he tried to come to them, only that it was more than once, using the idiomatic expression "once and twice" (*hapax kai dis*).

Paul tells the saints, however, that he could not come to them because "Satan thwarted us" (2:18). *Satan* means adversary, opponent, or accuser. There can be no doubt that the term refers to the leader of the fallen angels, the great opponent of God. Paul refers to him in 2 Thessalonians 2:9–10 as one who assists the Antichrist in the last days with powerful signs and false wonders and great deception. Here in 1 Thessalonians 2:18 the word is definite—"the" Satan—clearly identifying him as the fallen angelic creature of great power and not some human adversary. Paul believed and understood rightly that there was a cosmic, usually unseen world where angels and demons live and work. Furthermore, the biblical worldview is that such beings interact with the affairs and lives of humans. In this case, Satan had specifically hindered Paul's attempts to return to Thessalonica. The verb used by Paul, "thwart" (*enekopsen*), generally means to hinder and contains no special hints of how it is done. Whether that meant Paul was sick (2 Cor. 12:7–10), had a legal issue with authorities in Thessalonica, or faced general opposition to the gospel, he does not say. It is clear that he viewed Satan as actively involved in trying to hinder, delay, or disrupt ministries of the Lord by whatever means. Without referring to Satan, Paul said the same thing generally to the Romans when he could not come to them because he had been concentrating on places where the gospel had never been preached (Rom. 15:20–22).

Paul's crown of exultation. The apostle asks the Thessalonians a rhetorical question (2:19): "Who is our hope or joy or crown of exultation?" Since the question is personal ("who" not "what"), certain people are perhaps to be expected as the answer. There are three expressions (once again) that Paul uses in stating the query. The word *hope* often carries with it a futuristic flavor, something that surfaces in the next part of the verse (cf. 1 Thess. 1:3; 4:13; 5:8; 2 Thess. 2:16). *Joy* is the usual word for being filled with a sense of happiness, pleasure, and gladness. The last phrase is the most telling—"crown of exultation." The word *crown* (*stephanos*) refers to a wreath that serves as a crown. In the culture of Paul's day, such a crown was often a reward given at the end of an athletic contest. The apostle makes such a reference in 1 Corinthians 9:24–25: "Do you not know that those who run in a race all run, but only one receives the prize? Run in such a way that you may win. And everyone who competes in the games exercises self-control in all things. They then do it to receive a perishable *wreath*, but we an imperishable." Paul exhorts the Corinthians to follow his example in living well so that he will win a reward for his Christian holiness. That the apostle is speaking of something else to the Thessalonians will be seen below. In another epistle, Paul looks to the future when God will give him a crown of righteousness for loving the appearing of the Lord (2 Tim. 4:8), a crown available to all who do the same. However, in 1 Thessalonians 2:19, Paul describes the crown as one of *exultation*. This word (*kauchēseōs*) means pride or boasting. Paul is asking, "Who is our hope or joy or crown of boasting?" In other words, who can we brag about?

Paul gives an answer to his rhetorical question in the form of another question (2:19): "Is it not even you, in the presence of our Lord Jesus at His coming?" In this statement he identifies what he means by his hope, joy, and crown of boasting. It is the Thessalonians themselves. But he is not setting them above all other converts he has made and other believers he knows. For he also refers to the Philippians as his joy and crown (Phil. 4:1). He is not saying that he cherishes them in his heart as special, although he certainly does so. Rather, he envisions a day when everyone else will know what he knows about them—who they really are in Christ. He adds the qualification "in the presence of our Lord Jesus at His coming." When the Lord returns Paul could take great satisfaction that the Thessalonians would be part of the church triumphant. They were trophies of spiritual warfare. Paul closes with a statement and not a question: "You are our glory (*doxa*; 'boast') and joy." One is easily reminded of the boasting the apostle has done about the Thessalonians already in this letter. Such boasting will continue until the return of the Lord.

One final note needs to be mentioned. The word "coming" in 2:19 is *parousia*, a word used commonly by Paul in many ways. Assuming a pretribulational rapture of the church (something to be established later on), is the parousia here a reference to the coming of Christ for His church before the tribulation period, or is it a reference to his coming to earth at the end of the tribulation when He comes to establish His kingdom on earth? The word is not a technical term (in the sense of meaning the same thing in every text) and can be used to describe either event. The idea of mentioning the Thessalonians as a crown could lend itself to the understanding that the latter case is in view since the kingdom is when rewards are realized. However, in the pretribulational scheme, the church appears before the judgment seat of Christ following the Rapture where judgments about Christians are made and rewards established that will find fulfillment in the later kingdom age. Thus this approach leads to a draw between the two views. In the end it is probably the other passages in 1 Thessalonians that use *parousia* that mark the difference (3:13, 4:15, 5:23). If, in those passages (to be discussed later) a pretribulational rapture is in view (and it will be shown that it is), then it is likely that the parousia in 2:19 is also referring to the same event.[26]

Study Questions

1. How did Paul preach when he came to Thessalonica? Compare this to the kind of preaching you hear today.
2. Have you ever suffered true persecution for the Lord? Do you think you would continue to boldly proclaim the gospel if you were persecuted for sharing your faith?
3. How does your reception of the gospel of Christ compare to that of the Thessalonians?

4. Have you ever led anyone to Christ? What kind of relationship do you have with them? Is it like the relationship Paul had with the believers at Thessalonica?
5. Do you have a ministry for the Lord? How does Satan desire to oppose and prevent ministry?

CHAPTER 4

The Testimony of Timothy's Ministry 1 Thessalonians 3:1–8

Preview:

Paul had sent Timothy to encourage and strengthen the faith of the Thessalonians. The good news that Timothy brought back to Paul about the progress of the Thessalonians ironically strengthened the apostle.

The Lord knows the need for fellowship, and in ministry he had originally sent the Seventy out two by two (Luke 10:1). As Paul ministered in Thessalonica and in Corinth and the surrounding areas, he had Silas and Timothy with him. It fell to Timothy to get information from the Thessalonian believers on how they were doing and to pass that report on to Paul. Timothy was someone Paul trusted and hoped would keep him posted on what was happening in the lives of the saints. We get a glimpse of Paul's sincere relationship with Timothy by reading the apostle's two New Testament letters written to him. Also, the spirit of his view of Timothy is captured by his statement to the Philippians, "I have no one else of kindred spirit who will genuinely be concerned for your welfare" (Phil. 2:20).

The Work of Timothy (3:1–5)

The sending of Timothy. Paul could hardly stand to be out of touch with news of the church at Thessalonica. Therefore, he decided to be left alone at

Athens (3:1; cf. Acts 17:15–16). The desire to know their fate was so strong that the apostle commented that he could "endure it no longer" (3:1), a statement that he would repeat in 3:5. The word translated "endure" (*stegontes*) means "to bear or stand up under." In this passage it implies a mounting pressure that needed to be relieved. Paul seems to be at wit's end. The Thessalonians' situation was so important to him that he thought it best to depart from his usual mode of team ministry and stay alone in Athens. "Thought it best" (*eudokēsamen*) can signify "appear well" or "take pleasure in." Here it appeared best to Paul—that is, it seemed the best option—to stay at Athens alone.

However, the word for "thought it best" is in the plural—"we thought it best." This raises the possibility that Silas was still with Paul after the sending of Timothy to Thessalonica. In what way, then, could Paul be staying alone? The answer is found in Paul's ability to look at the entire sweep of events. F. F. Bruce nicely summarizes the probable sequence of events:

> After Paul was escorted to Athens from Beroea (Acts 17:13–15), both Silvanus and Timothy followed him there; Paul . . . with the concurrence of Silvanus . . . then sent Timothy back to Thessalonica to see how the young church was faring, and Silvanus went back on some other errand to Macedonia. It was, according to Luke, while he was waiting for Silvanus (Silas) and Timothy to rejoin him in Athens, after his first arrival there, that Paul had the encounters described in Acts 17:16–34. Shortly after Timothy, and then Silvanus, left him, he went on from Athens to Corinth, where he was rejoined by Silvanus and Timothy on their return from their respective Macedonian errands (Acts 18:5). Soon after their return this letter [1 Thessalonians] was sent.[1]

Consequently, there is no need to doubt Paul's statement that he was going to be alone. It is also just as possible, as stated earlier, that Paul is using an editorial "we," speaking only of himself, so that perhaps Silas has already left at the point he sends out Timothy.

Paul's description of Timothy, the one he sent to the Thessalonians, is appropriate for someone on the apostolic missionary team (3:2). He is called "our brother," indicating the spiritual connection of brotherhood that occurs when someone trusts Jesus Christ as Savior. Not only was Paul the apostle his spiritual "father" (1 Tim. 1:2), but Paul claims Timothy as a brother on equal footing. Again, it is hard to tell if Paul is using an editorial first person plural when he says "our brother." If not, he is reminding the Thessalonian believers that Timothy was a spiritual brother to them as well. Thus he could be trusted in the same way that Paul trusted him.

Next the apostle designates Timothy as "God's fellow worker in the gospel" (3:2). "Fellow-worker" (*sunergon*) is a word that occurs in the New Testament thirteen times, all but one by the pen of Paul. In all occurrences without exception, it refers to a Christian who is a servant of God in the church for the sake of the gospel of Christ. The term implies a sharing or community of service before God. Timothy is one of many names that Paul invoked over the years, such as Priscilla and Aquila (Rom. 16:3), Luke (Philemon 24), Urbanus (Rom. 16:9), and Titus (2 Cor. 8:23) among others.

One must not shrink from the qualification that Timothy is a fellow worker *in the gospel of Christ.* The shared labor and efforts were not vaguely knit together; they were centered with clarity on the most central truth of the Christian faith. The agenda was the same for Paul and Timothy. Such a statement has ramifications for ongoing modern debates about ecumenicalism. The drive to have a forced unity of churches in our day based on all kinds of modern or postmodern notions will ultimately fail. If it were to succeed in any form, its work could not be considered Christian since it is not based on the ancient, historical, and truthful facts of the death, burial, and resurrection of Jesus. That is the apostolic pattern. On the other side are those professing believers who also distract from the most important truth among Christians by focusing on extrabiblical traditions that lead into an oppressive legalism. On either side, Paul's message forces the cross of Christ to the center as the basis for working together as Christian believers.

The task of Timothy. Paul had already hinted at the purpose for Timothy's apostolic mission to the Thessalonians—he needed to know how they were doing. However, in 3:2 he gives another purpose directly related to the Thessalonians themselves. This mission is described as a twofold task: (1) to strengthen and (2) to encourage them (3:2). "To strengthen" (*stērixai*) means "to fix, make firm, or establish." This implied the provision of emotional, mental, and spiritual support from the missionary team, and Timothy in particular, toward the persecuted church. Paul does not flesh out any details. Whether he intends for Timothy to help the church in organizational and leadership matters, we simply do not know. However, there is the basic notion of building up the church to handle its circumstances. "To encourage" (*parakalesai*) in this context may not mean to console the Thessalonian believers as if they needed comfort as much as it means for them to be encouraged to remain in the spiritual battle they faced.[2] However, the earlier reference in 2:11 using the same term shows that the idea of giving comfort goes hand in hand with urging the troops to stay in the battle. In addition, Paul tells the Thessalonian believers that Timothy was sent to "encourage you as to your faith" or "in behalf of your faith." Such a desire on his part is not a contradiction to his earlier praise of the great faith of the Thessalonians (1:3–8). No matter what your status, the perils of persecution have the potential to diminish the light of faith. Paul wants Timothy to stave off any regression in the faith of the Thessalonians.

The above point is made clear in 3:3 where Paul gives the results he wants Timothy's work on encouragement to bring: "so that no man may be disturbed by these afflictions." Paul wants no losses at all among the believers. The current persecution was not to shake their faith in the Lord. The word *disturbed* (*sainō*) is used only here in the New Testament. It can mean to be continually wavering, upset, or shaken. It also can have the meaning of being led astray from the right way.[3] In other words, some in the community might entice the Thessalonians to give up their faith to avoid persecution. Based on the context, the "afflictions" (*thlipsesin*) spoken of refer to intense troubles that come upon a person from without due to the pressure of circumstances or the antagonism of people, although it is possible that hostile attempts to draw away the faithful believers were subtle.[4] However, based on the account in the book of Acts, the hostility was frontal and direct (Acts 17:5–9). An interesting contrast is presented in the book at this point. Later on in 5:4–9, Paul teaches the Thessalonians that they are exempt from the Day of the Lord's wrath, the time of trouble that is described as a destruction that comes suddenly like birth pangs (5:3). This is different than the tribulations they now must face with courage.

The Bible constantly reminds believers that their destiny in this life includes affliction, opposition, and persecution in a general sense even if they are exempt from the coming Day of the Lord. In 3:3 Paul states with certainty, "For you yourselves know that we have been destined for this." Here "destined" (*keimetha*) means "to be set, appointed, or laid out." The New Testament confirms that affliction and trouble were to be the lot of all believers everywhere (Phil. 1:29; 2 Tim. 3:12). In fact, the Scriptures warn us: "Beloved, do not be surprised at the fiery ordeal among you, which comes upon you for your testing, as though some strange thing were happening to you; but to the degree that you share the sufferings of Christ, keep on rejoicing; so that also at the revelation of His glory, you may rejoice with exultation" (1 Pet. 4:12–13). Later, in Paul's second letter to the Thessalonians, he would tell them that persecution, as a necessary evil in this life, serves as a positive indicator of their relationship to God and His coming kingdom (2 Thess. 1:4–5). Paul had taught these things to the Thessalonians when he was with them (3:4). They knew in advance that persecution would come, and it did. They should not be surprised. The apostle had seen it over and over again. In fact, he had once been one of the persecutors himself until God graciously changed his life (Acts 8:1–3)

Another comparison can be made with the persecutions described in 2 Thessalonians 2:2, although the false teaching might be coming from within the ranks of the church rather than without. In that second epistle, Paul warns the saints at Thessalonica not to be "quickly shaken," in language similar to this passage in 1 Thessalonians. The issue of allegiance to truth also appears, since what is at stake is the truth of whether the Day of the Lord had already come. In 2 Thessalonians 2:2, Paul cautions his readers to beware of false letters or reports alleged to be from him that are written by someone trying to deceive them (2 Thess. 2:3). Paul had earlier reminded them that his message did not come from error or deceit (1 Thess. 2:3), that they had received his words as the Word of God (1 Thess. 2:13), that people would attempt to lead them astray (1 Thess. 2:15–16), and that the great deceiver Satan wanted to prevent them from continuing in the truth (2:18). Thus, on this account alone, the afflictions of the Thessalonians as described in Paul's first letter should not be taken as general troubles, but as serious persecution partly involving deception and false teachers. The main form of persecution is through open and hostile opposition by the Jews as Paul outlines in 1 Thessalonians 2:14–16 and Luke delineates in Acts 17.

The purpose of Paul. Paul repeats the statement from 3:1 that he cannot endure being without knowledge of the Thessalonian church any longer; although here he changes from "we" to "I," making his statement extremely personal, as he had in 2:18. He could no longer hold back sending Timothy. Paul wanted "to find out about your faith," the faith of the Thessalonian believers (3:5). Were they holding up under the persecution? Were they continuing in their faith? Were they still following Christ? Paul's heart yearned to know the answers to these questions.

One of the reasons Paul sends Timothy to find out the status of the church in Thessalonica involves spiritual warfare: "for fear that the tempter might have tempted you" (3:5). The phrase "for fear that" (*mē pōs*) can be translated "lest." The import of the statement would be "lest the tempter might have tempted you." The "tempter" (*ho peirazōn*) is clearly Satan who was named directly in the earlier statement in 2:18 (cf. 2 Thess. 2:9). This description of Satan echoes the temptation account of Christ (Matt. 4:3) and the deception by the serpent in the Garden of Eden (Gen. 3:1–6). Paul uses the same language when teaching the Corinthians (1 Cor. 7:5; cf. 2 Cor. 11:3). In this context, Paul is concerned that Satan will use the persecutions and afflictions of verse 5 to move the Thessalonians away from their steadfast faith.

Earlier, in 2:1, Paul said that his coming to the Thessalonian believers was not in vain. He had much success and accomplishment in the work at Thessalonica. But now in 3:5 he shows concern that what started out victoriously might be defeated and become a wasted opportunity, work done "in vain." Paul wanted lasting results that would make a mark in eternity for God, not the flash-in-the-pan success that would only gain the approving eye of man. The apostle was always apprehensive in his ministry about his labor of service. In a parallel passage of sorts, he informs the Galatians that he was careful in how he appeared "for fear that I might be running, or had run, in vain" (Gal. 2:2). Similarly, Paul exhorted the Philippians to continue to hold to the truth so that "in the day of Christ I may have cause to glory because I did not run in vain nor toil in vain" (Phil. 2:16). One should be careful not to accuse the apostle of selfish motives in the matter—he is not just wanting his results to last for his own credit, although future reward is not a bad incentive. His great love and endurance for the Thessalonians preclude such a thought.

The Report of Timothy (3:6–8)

That the book of 1 Thessalonians was not written until Timothy returned to Paul with news of their state is proven by 3:6—"now that Timothy has come to us from you." The abrupt change to discuss the present rather than the past may mean that Timothy's arrival had just occurred, and it may be the major event prompting Paul's writing of the letter.[5] In returning, Timothy had brought back great news! The idea of bringing good news (*euangelisamenou*) is the standard word that often means to give or preach (in context) the gospel of Christ, the good news about His death and resurrection. In all other contexts in Paul's writings, he uses it to mean preaching the gospel relative to the salvation of individuals through Christ. This is the only occurrence where he uses it to refer to good news in general.[6]

The first part of Timothy's good news declaration concerns their "faith" (*pistin*) and "love" (*agapēn*). The obvious meaning (not directly stated but understood from verse 2) is that they had continued in their faith in God and love for people, which Paul had so lavishly praised them for in the first chapter (1:3). The persecutions had not knocked them off the walk of faith and their continuing service to God and others. Most commentators point out the similarity to the combination of faith and love in Galatians 5:6—"For in Christ Jesus neither circumcision nor uncircumcision means anything, but faith working through love." Faith in God does a work in the heart that works itself out in relationships by means of love. The good news for Paul was that the Thessalonians were still on track in this area.

The second part of Timothy's good news announcement is that the Thessalonians were maintaining a fondness for Paul (and the missionary team). Several expressions in the verse make this point, especially, "You always think kindly of us" (3:6), literally, "possess a good memory of us." As to the adjective "good" or "kind" here, Bruce notes that it "means not merely that they remembered them well (in the sense of not having forgotten them) but that their memory of them was happy and friendly, whereas they might have recalled them with bitterness as visitors who brought them nothing but trouble."[7] Paul notes that the Thessalonian believers thought this way "always" (*pantote*). The idea is that when Paul came to mind—and that was no doubt often—their memories were pleasant and positive: "The Thessalonians had not allowed hostile propaganda to distort their recollections of the visit of the great apostle. They still looked back on it with joy."[8]

There is another way that Paul expresses the good news that the Thessalonians had continued to embrace him in a personal and positive manner. He describes his elation over the fact that they were "longing to see us just as we also long to see you" (3:6). The terms used here ("longing" and "long") come from the word *epipotheō*, which means "to yearn for or desire greatly." Although not using the same terms, Paul had noted his own longing to see the Thessalonian saints back in 2:17. He does, however, use the same word when telling the Romans and Philippians of his great yearning to see them (Rom. 1:11; Phil. 1:8). In doing so, the great missionary is simply acknowledging the reality of a pastoral heart that every true minister bears.

Paul sums up the results of the good news about the Thessalonians by saying, "For this reason, brethren, in all our distress and affliction we were comforted about you through your faith" (3:7). In a small way the tables were turned. Paul had hoped to comfort them in spite of their suffering and had sent Timothy to do so. But ironically the great apostle is being encouraged by the testimony of the Thessalonians who have continued on even in the midst of persecution. Thus Paul now is better able to endure the troubles he faces. The nature of those troubles is not clearly stated. It could be that the apostle has in mind the ongoing struggles of the ministry to spread the gospel in pagan lands where rejection and opposition are ever before them.[9]

Paul now intensifies the depiction of the results of the good news he has received: "for now we really live, if you stand firm in the Lord" (3:8). It is somewhat enigmatic for the apostle to talk about "really living," for there is no adjective used in the verse to describe living. He asserts that he will now live if the Thessalonians stand firm. It is the entire context that suggests the weight of the idea of "really living." The idea is that Paul was now free to go about his life and ministry with one less concern on his mind. With the Thessalonians on the right path, his pastoral heart could rest easy. Nevertheless, Paul writes with a condition in mind that produces a slight twist on the interpretation. He is not actually rehearsing the past accomplishments of the Thessalonians. Instead, he is suggesting that he will have ongoing freedom to live out his ministry if the believers at Thessalonica continue to stand fast in the Lord. His intention is to let them know what their continued stand under pressure would mean for his own life and ministry.

Paul's statements are very personal and heartfelt throughout this entire section. The pathos of his soul is evident in the opening three chapters of this letter:

> Paul does not often give us a glimpse into what oppressed him in his labors. We have such a glimpse here. When one sits in a comfortable study and reads this short phrase, he may wonder at the fervor with which the apostle writes about the comfort the Thessalonian firmness and loyalty afforded him; if one could sit for a while in Aquila's shop where these lines were written, he would rather wonder how Paul could write with so much restraint and would catch something of the mighty spirit throbbing in Paul's great heart.[10]

Timothy's trip to Thessalonica and the report that came back with him to Paul provide the door by which such a large, noble, and godly heart can be seen.

Study Questions

1. What is the benefit of having a helper in the ministry? Do you minister with someone at your church?
2. How does Paul's designation of Timothy as a brother show Paul's humility?
3. What causes Paul to be concerned about the Thessalonians turning from their faith? What would cause you to turn from your faith?
4. How can persecution and affliction cause a person to turn away from God? Can a believer ever be prepared for persecution?

5. What is the importance of believers encouraging other believers? How often do you share an encouraging word with family members and fellow Christians?
6. Have you ever given anyone a reason to rejoice over the progress you are making in your Christian walk?

CHAPTER 5

Praying for the Church
1 Thessalonians 3:9–13

Preview:

Paul prays that he will be able to return to Thessalonica to help the saints grow to completion. Specifically, he prays primarily that they will grow in love and holiness. In this way the believers will be ready when God's kingdom arrives.

The Lord Jesus Christ instructed His disciples "that at all times they ought to pray and not to lose heart" (Luke 18:1). One of the most important topics in the Bible is prayer. Prayer was the habit of the Lord Jesus Christ (Matt. 26:38–45; John 11:41–42; 17:1–26). If it was necessary for Him, it ought to be evident for believers that prayer is an essential ingredient for their Christian walk.

Certainly He has instructed us in this matter of praying. We are to pray according to His pattern (Matt. 6:9–13) and are invited to ask Him for answers (Matt. 7:7–11). We are encouraged to pray according to our desires (21:21–22) and to do so in faith (Mark 11:22–24). Further, believers are to pray in Christ's name (John 14:13–14) based on being filled with His word (John 15:7) and to do so that He might be glorified (16:23–24).

Paul definitely followed the example of Jesus. Actual prayers or the content of prayers are situated in many of the epistles he wrote (Rom. 1:8–10; 1 Cor. 1:4–9; Eph. 1:16–23; 3:14–21; Phil. 1:9–11; Col. 1:9–12; 1 Thess. 3:9–13). It is the apostle's prayer for the church at Thessalonica that concerns us here.

The Basis for the Prayer (3:9–10)

Paul introduces his prayer for the Thessalonians with a lengthy rhetorical question (3:9–10). By this means Paul lays the foundation for the statement of prayer to follow in 3:11–13. The rhetorical question begins, "For what thanks can we render to God for you. . . ?" The question may be understood to mean what *kind* of thanks.[1] The apostle seems to be suggesting that the basis for thanksgiving to God for the Thessalonians is boundless and has no limits. His heart is overflowing with a sense that he owes something to God in light of the Thessalonians. Another way to say this is that it would be impossible to give God all the thanks that He is owed, the task is so great. Nonetheless, he asks what thanks we can *render* to God. Here the term "render" (*antapodounai*) signifies the paying back of an amount, that is, to repay—hence, "render . . . in return," as the text says. Paul uses the word in a negative, vengeful sense when he teaches the Thessalonians that God will repay those who are persecuting them at the second coming of Christ (2 Thess. 1:6; cf. Rom. 12:19). Here it is used in a positive way to indicate the great debt that is owed to God on behalf of what the Thessalonians have meant to Paul.

What the Thessalonians have meant to the apostle is nicely summed up in the words "for all the joy with which we rejoice before our God on your account" (3:9). Specific actions by the Thessalonians must be drawn from the earlier context, that is, their continued faith and love. Here Paul pictures the great joy that has resulted because of them (on their account). Not only is the thanksgiving directed to God, but the rejoicing is "before our God." This expression specifies that the rejoicing is done in the presence of God. Martin is correct in exclaiming that this is "an indication that the giving of thanks envisioned here is in the context of prayer . . . not simply a moment of pleasant reflection."[2]

Moreover, the apostle gives further remarks that bring the entire enterprise of thanksgiving before God into the context of direct prayer to Him—"as we night and day keep praying" (3:10). The term "night and day" should not be conceived in such a way as to "denote prayer at two set times, but rather continued prayer."[3] They prayed as a regular habit at all times of the day, sometimes formally and other times as things would come to mind. The continual nature of the praying is brought out by the present tense of the verb "keep praying" (*deomenoi*). This particular word for praying focuses on asking for something and not the praise aspect of prayer that has just been emphasized in the previous context. Paul characterizes his own prayers as made "most earnestly" (*huperekperissou*). This is a rare expression used only by Paul in the

New Testament. Outside of this passage, he tells the Ephesians that God is able to do "abundantly beyond" our wildest dreams when we petition the throne of heaven (Eph. 3:20). Paul also uses the same term later in 1 Thessalonians 5:13 when he tells his readers they should esteem church leaders "very highly." The word takes the reader to the thought of going beyond the normal boundaries.

In light of the petition focus of Paul's prayer, the apostle wants something from God as he explains in 3:10. First of all, he is asking that God would allow him to see the Thessalonians once again. He stated this desire earlier (2:17), and now that wish forms the basis of his prayer. Second, he wants to "complete what is lacking" in the faith of the Thessalonians. The word "complete" (*katartizō*) means to put in order or to put into proper condition. It contains the concept of mending, restoring, or equipping.[4] The term "what is lacking" (*husterēmata*) conveys the idea of shortcomings or deficiencies. What was lacking in their faith is not stated clearly by the apostle. Perhaps they needed more thorough teaching on Bible doctrine or how to live the Christian life. Though the report from Timothy was positive about their faith, Paul may have desired to share in the encouragement of their faith so that they would be even stronger under persecution. Thus he envisions a strong Christian faith that continues to grow in toughness under pressure.

The Prayer Offered (3:11–13)

The actual prayer of Paul is now given in the final three verses of chapter 3. It is a prayer directed to heaven. God the Father is mentioned twice (vv. 11, 13). Jesus is mentioned three times: "Jesus our Lord" (v. 11), "Lord" (v. 12), "Lord Jesus" (v. 13). There is little doubt who Paul invokes and where he believes the real answers lie. The use of the designation "our God and Father *Himself*" intensifies the expectation Paul has about both the direction of his petition and the source of the answers he expects to receive.

In addition, it must be duly noted that there is a theologically significant and close connection between the Father and the Lord Jesus as the recipients of the prayer and the ones invoked by the prayer. This mirrors the first verse of the book where Paul says the Thessalonians are a church "in God the Father and the Lord Jesus Christ." The deity of Christ was mentioned relative to that passage and must be highlighted here even more. For non-Catholic Christian theology based on the Scriptures, a believer prays only to God. For the apostle to invoke both the Father and Christ in his prayer implies the deity of Christ Jesus. Leon Morris comments, "This not a formal Trinitarian definition, but it is the kind of understanding of the nature of the Godhead that led inevitably to the formulation of the dogma of the Trinity. It is all the more impressive in that it is done incidentally. . . . In that Paul feels no necessity to produce arguments to demonstrate this we must feel that the point was accepted just as fully by the Thessalonians as by the apostle."[5] Thus it is from the vantage point of this understanding about Christ that in the prayer itself the apostle asks for two things as outlined below.

Prayer for Paul and his associates. Paul begins by crying out to our "God and Father Himself and Jesus our Lord." God and Father are associated together, indicating the kind of relationship we have as believers with God. Jesus had taught His followers to approach God as "Our Father" (Matt. 6:9). The term "Father" speaks of relationship. God is not just a vague God in the heavens, but one who actively relates to us so we can call Him our Father (Gal. 4:6). The apostle uses the term "Himself" to highlight this special, personal nature. This relationship comes to us through the person of "Jesus our Lord" (3:11). God the Father reveals the Son so the Son can be received by faith (Matt. 16:13–20). The petition is addressed to both the Father and the Son though the usual Christian approach is to pray to the Father in the name of the Son by the power of the Holy Spirit. This shows that God allows variety of form in the matter of prayer.

The request made for Paul and his associates is that the Lord would direct the missionary team back to Thessalonica to visit the believers (3:11). Here the verb "direct" (*kateuthunai*) means "to guide, make straight, or lead." The only other time it is used by Paul is when he breaks out in prayer for the Thessalonians in his second epistle to them: "may the Lord *direct* your hearts into the love of God" (2 Thess. 3:5).[6] What does Paul want God to direct in 1 Thessalonians 3:11? The apostle wants God to direct "our way to you." The term *way* is the common word for *path* that occurs over a hundred times in the New Testament. Paul is asking God to provide a way for their paths to cross once again that he might minister to them. Wanamaker suggests that this could be the real occasion for the letter as Paul wants to let them know he wants to return. Also, Wanamaker correctly notes that this longing stems at least in part from Paul's abrupt departure from the city due to the persecution.[7]

Prayer for the church. Paul now gives attention to prayer for the church at Thessalonica. He asks, "May the Lord cause you to increase and abound in love" (3:12). "Increase" (*pleonasai*) means "to become more or cause to become rich." "Abound" (*perisseusai*) means "to go beyond the barrier, to have an over supply or abundance, to be exceptionally rich." The two words together speak of God doing "exceeding abundantly" (Eph. 3:20) in their lives. Paul focuses this abundance in his prayer toward "love." One can note at this point that Paul's prayer for the Thessalonians in 3:12 is answered (and perhaps goes on being answered). In 2 Thessalonians 1:3 the apostle praises the Thessalonians for the fact that "the love of each one of you toward one another grows ever greater (*pleonazei*)."

Love is one of those words that is often described (1 Cor. 13) but is difficult to define. One practical definition is that love is giving to the needs of others without any thought of reward. In other words, if love is to be genuine, it must rise above petty selfishness or even vengeance against enemies. These things might be a temptation to the Thessalonians as they faced their persecutors. So Paul prays that God will grant them a superabundance of love "for one another, and for all men" (3:12). This would include their enemies as well as brothers and sisters in the Lord. Paul reminds them of the fact that he, too, has this superabundance of love toward the Thessalonian believers ("just as we also do for you" (3:12). He is not praying that God would grant something to them that he is not willing to have in his heart himself. The apostolic model is there to be imitated.

The final part of his petition is the words "establish your hearts unblamable in holiness" (3:13). To "establish" comes from a word from which we get the English word *steroid* and means "to make strong, fix, set up, establish, or make firm." "Unblamable" (*amemptous*) means "beyond the ability to find fault." It does not mean that they would be sinless or that they would never be accused of wrongdoing by the world. But they were to give no reason for their faith or morals to be questioned. They were to be established "in holiness before our God." To be holy is to be separated from sin and to Christ.

The Thessalonians were to be established unblamable "before our God and Father" (3:13). Paul's prayer looks into the future because this standing before God will be "at the coming of our Lord Jesus with all His saints" (3:13). The word "coming" in 3:13 is the word *parousia* discussed earlier. The passage clearly notes that in 3:13 the coming of the Lord Jesus is "with all his saints." Within a pretribulational view of the book, this is often taken to refer to the disembodied saints who are returning with Christ to unite with their resurrected bodies at the time of the pretribulational Rapture or to the presence of Christ with the saints when they are taken to heaven at the pretribulational Rapture to be in the Father's house.[8] Paul, at the end of the letter, gives another prayer in which he prays that God will sanctify the Thessalonians completely and they will be blameless at the coming (*parousia*) of Christ (1 Thess. 5:23). Apparently Paul sees a process that will culminate when Christ returns, and he wants the Thessalonians to be ready for that day.

Comparison to Paul's other prayers. The prayer statements given in Paul's New Testament writings are numerous. They thus show that the apostolic heart is one of communion with God no matter what the venue. While each of Paul's letters are occasional, that is, meant for specific occasions and circumstances, the prayers of Paul as he writes often contain some of the same elements and at times a similar overall thrust. For example, in Ephesians 3:14–20, the apostle prays that the Ephesian Christians would become "rooted and grounded in love" and that they would "know the love of Christ which surpasses knowledge." This fits Paul's desire for the Thessalonians to increase in their love (1 Thess. 3:12). In the end it is quite natural for the apostle to break out in prayer in his letters due to the big heart God had given him.

Study Questions

1. How often do you pray for others? Do you pray more for yourself or for others?
2. Does your church spend more timing praying for recovery from physical illness or the development of spiritual growth?
3. How does one believer help another believer to have greater faith?
4. Does your church abound in love? How do you know?
5. Are you ready if the Lord should come today? Would your life be characterized as blameless?

CHAPTER 6

Morality and Genuine Love 1 Thessalonians 4:1–12

Preview:

Paul calls the Thessalonian believers to continue in holy living and moral purity, including abstinence from sexual immorality. He wants them to excel even more in genuine love toward one another and to live a life with a pure testimony before the unbelieving world.

This section represents the part of Paul's earlier outline from 1:9b—"to serve a living and true God." The previous sections covered how the Thessalonians turned to God from idols in light of the work of the Paul-led missionary team. The next sections deal with eschatological, or end-time, information that Paul wants them to understand. However, for this section he discusses the need for their continued service to God until that time would arrive.

The Christian life is no ordinary life. When a person receives Jesus Christ as his Savior, trusting in His death and resurrection as the only hope of heaven, that person receives a quality of life based on the life of God Himself (1 John 5:12). He has become a partaker of the divine nature "having escaped the corruption that is in the world by lust" (2 Pet. 1:4). Sin brought down the human race, but the salvation of the cross has lifted up the saints.

While no one is saved by good works, baptism, keeping the commandments of God, or any other service rendered to God, the salvation believers have received ought to make a difference in how they live. This would be as significant to the believers at Thessalonica as it is to us today because of the immoral licentiousness that troubled that part of the world in Paul's time.

> Thessalonica was part of that debased Greco-Roman culture. The city was rife with such sinful practices as fornication, adultery, homosexuality (including pedophilia), transvestism (men dressing like women), and a wide variety of pornographic and erotic perversions, all done with a seared conscience and society's acceptance, hence with little or no accompanying shame or guilt. Unlike people in Western nations today, the Thessalonians grew up with no Christian tradition to support laws and standards that forbid the grosser manifestations of immorality. Pagan Greek society apparently did not have civil laws to prohibit immoral behavior.[1]

This debauched lifestyle emanated not from a secular society. The religion of the day with its temple prostitution was an everyday staple. No doubt many of the Thessalonians had been saved out of pagan lifestyles, and now they were going to walk a new way. Paul sought to reinforce this to the church at Thessalonica in the opening verses of chapter 4.

The Exhortation to Holiness (4:1–2)

The opening word of chapter 4 ("Finally") appears on the surface to indicate a shift in the direction of the book. The word translated "finally" (*loipon*) actually means "as for the rest" and does not mean that Paul is beginning his last discussion. In Philippians Paul uses the term twice (3:1; 4:8) to mark a transition (common in secular literature of the day) to a section of practical exhortation.[2] It would carry the same weight perhaps as our modern English transitional words "in addition." However, the word "then" ("therefore") in 4:1 ties the statements back to what has gone before. This is not surprising. Paul's prayer for the Thessalonians is that they would practice love and be blameless before God. Now the apostle gives exhortations fitting with that prayer as he speaks on the subject of purity.

Paul makes both a request and an exhortation to the Thessalonian believers "in the Lord Jesus" (4:1). The word "request" (*erōtōmen*) means "a simple question calling for a response." The apostle is not asking for a favor but is giving a request with apostolic authority behind it. The results should be that the question is met favorably by Thessalonian behavior. In this way the term "exhort" (*parakaloumen*) in the verse carries basically the same import as the word "request." Paul's urgent plea and counsel are based on the Thessalonians' relationship with Christ ("in the Lord Jesus"). It is on this basis that Paul can exhort them to a high standard of living.

The starting point for Paul's request is the *instruction* that the Thessalonians had already *received* from him when he was with them (4:1). The word "received" (*parelabete*) implies that they had heard the teaching of the apostle and his missionary team. Apparently the teaching went beyond the basic gospel of Christ for salvation and into the territory of Christian behavior or ethical living. The term "instruction" is not in the original language text but is helpfully supplied to smooth over the statement and make the meaning clear. Paul tells the Thessalonians that what they had received was "how you ought to walk and please God" (4:1). Both concepts of walking and pleasing God have already been addressed in the letter (2:4, 8, 12, 15). The phrase "ought to" (*dei*) means that it is necessary or the subject must do what is mentioned either out of a sense of compulsion or necessity. This much the Thessalonians already knew. Paul in a parenthetical way reminds them that he knows that they already practice what they know ("just as you actually do walk"). The present tense of the verb "walk" (*peripateite*) yields the notion of "actually." They are at the moment walking in a manner pleasing to God.

However, Paul wants the Thessalonian saints to "excel still more" (4:1) in this matter of pleasing God. The word "excel" (*perisseuēte*) means to overflow or have in abundance. Used in this context, it carries the idea of performing abundantly well. The qualifier "still more" (*mallon*) is repeated later in 4:10. Apparently the apostle envisions progress in the matter of holy living and not a perfect state at which a believer arrives. Yet the starting point for improving in their walk is the original teaching when Paul was at Thessalonica: "For you know what commandments we gave you" (4:2). The term "commandments" (*parangelias*) refers to orders, precepts, or instructions. It is as if the apostle says, "You remember my preaching." By this statement the apostle is buttressing the thought processes of the believers so that they somehow believe they already have enough information to live the kind of life that he asks even if he wants them to go beyond the level of success they now have. That the prior preaching of Paul when he was with them is sufficient is made clear by his statement that the commandments were given "by the authority of the Lord Jesus" (4:2)—literally, the commandments were given *through* the Lord Jesus. There is no greater authority than Christ. Thus the Thessalonians who had received the preaching of Paul as the Word of God (2:13) must continue with that attitude and posture toward the things that had been taught.

God's Will Is Moral Purity (4:3–8)

Abstinence from sexual immorality. Knowing the will of God is not always easy. Nowhere does the Bible state directly what job we should have, who we should marry, or where we should live. We must discern these matters through the principles of the Bible and the exercise of prayer. However, in some cases matters are stated directly where there is no question. In 4:3 we find such a statement: "For this is the will of God, your sanctification; that is, that you abstain from sexual immorality." The word "will" (*thelēma*) refers to the desire or wish of someone, in this case God Himself. The direction of God in this matter cannot be waved off as a cultural matter. It is God's will for Christians today to take to heart this direction.

The idea of "sanctification" (*hagiasmos*) is holiness or being set apart from sin (4:3). While abstention from sexual sin is not all there is to the will of God, it is still true that holiness is not possible without purity in this particular matter. The meaning of the word "abstain" (*apechesthai*) leaves no room for a view of moderation. Paul will use the term later, perhaps with the same general thought, when he tells the Thessalonians to "abstain from every form of evil" (1 Thess. 5:22). The general idea is that believers must keep away from sexual sin. Only *complete* withdrawal from sexual sin is envisioned in 4:3.[3]

Sexual immorality (*porneia*) often has a broad meaning and refers to illicit sexual intercourse and would include all the immoral practices of false religions in Roman and Greek culture.[4] The Thessalonian believers were to follow the will of God and separate themselves from any and all such practices:

> The strong position of the New Testament against impurity in all forms shows that Christianity did not adapt its moral standards to the practices of contemporary society. Its moral demands stand in stark contrast to the immoral practices of that day. The Christian church insisted that abstinence is an essential and ever-present need for the development of personal holiness and God-pleasing conduct. Unlike the pagan cults, it refused to tolerate, much less foster, immoral practices among its members.[5]

Control of the body. Paul stated the general principle to abstain from sexual impurity in 4:3 and will summarize it again in 4:7. In verse 4 he gets more specific and personal—every believer should "know how to possess his own vessel in sanctification and honor" (4:4). The term "know" (*eidenai*) in this context means to understand how to do something. The content of what to know has already been given the Thessalonians in Paul's visit to them. The apostle almost speaks "as though it would be impossible for any believer who knows what this sin really is to engage in it."[6]

The word "vessel" (*skeuos*) in 4:4 has been taken by some to refer to a man's wife since Peter refers to the wife as the weaker *vessel* in 1 Peter 3:7. Such use is also found in the early second-century Greek writings the *Epistle of Barnabas* and the *Shepherd of Hermas,* while the later church father Augustine held to this view.[7] In this interpretation one would see the marriage relationship as part of Paul's teaching here. In other words, a man must know how to treat his wife, namely, being faithful to her.[8] The strongest argument in favor of this view could be that the meaning of the word "possess" (*ktasthai*) is "to *acquire."* The idea would then be that the believer should know how to acquire his spouse and presumably keep her in faithfulness in order to put down his own impure desires (cf. 1 Cor. 7:2–5). However, there seems to be more than marriage involved in Paul's words here. Many of the sins of that day had nothing to do with marriage, and the likelihood is that "vessel" refers to a person's own body. Such meaning can be found in Paul's writings elsewhere (Rom. 9:22–23; 2 Cor. 4:7). This is bolstered by the fact that Paul's overall approach, especially in this passage, supports a high view of marriage, which the idea of wife as vessel may not accommodate. Thus every believer is to "possess" (a valid way to take the word), or gain control over, his own body. Two words are used to describe how this is to be done—in sanctification and honor (4:4). The first idea of holiness or sanctification has already been addressed by Paul. The second one of "honor" is a new term brought into the discussion. In this context it refers to respectability. A loss of respect occurs whenever a believer abandons the moral high road.

The Thessalonian believers (and by application all Christians) are not to live "in lustful passion, like the Gentiles who do not know God" (4:5). Couch explains the words "in lustful passion" (*en pathei epithumias*) this way: "The word *lustful* is sexual passion in the passive sense, an ungovernable force like a firestorm that begins all by itself. 'Passion' is active desire that can be fed and further encouraged by the individual."[9] Believers in Thessalonica were not to be identified by these acts of immorality and thus were to be different from the "Gentiles who do not know God" (4:5). The indication is that the fact of knowing God ought to preclude the actions of shameful immorality. Yet a true Christian can fall into the trap of sin, so Paul warns in his epistles about this possibility (see 1 Cor. 6:15–20). God expects more from those who belong to Him. When the apostle mentions the Gentiles who do not know God, one is reminded of his discourse in Romans 1:18–32 (see especially v. 24). People suppress the truth to their own hurt. Such people, according to 2 Thessalonians 1:8, receive retribution at the second coming of Christ.

Defrauding other believers. The apostle gives a strong warning "that no man transgress and defraud his brother in the matter" (4:6). The word "transgress" (*huperbainein*) literally means to go beyond. In this context it must mean to go beyond the boundaries that have been established for moral behavior. To "defraud" (*pleonektein*) someone is to cheat and rob them. It is a seeking after more than one should have. Thus it relates quite strongly to the area of covetousness.[10] In the context of sexual sin, it carries the idea of taking advantage of someone. To be more precise, it is one person stealing (taking) another person's spouse for sexual pleasure. In this verse the object of the transgression and defrauding is another believer. While Paul would certainly not approve of sexual infidelity involving a believer with a pagan, his primary focus is on the relationships among believers at Thessalonica. It is an especially grievous sin for a believer to take advantage of another Christian to satisfy his sexual pleasure.

The seriousness of the issue is brought out when Paul tells the Thessalonians that any defrauding will bring the vengeance of God into the picture—"because the Lord is the avenger in all these things" (4:6). The Bible teaches that believers are not allowed to take vengeance because it belongs to God (Rom. 12:17–21). In the area of defrauding another believer, the Lord will be the avenger (*ekdikos*), the one who will bring justice and righteousness. The only other occurrence in the New Testament of this word is when the apostle tells the Romans that the government minister works for God as an "avenger who brings wrath upon the one who practices evil" (Rom. 13:4). The image is quite negative. God will not refrain from judging those who commit immorality. "All these things" refers in context to the discussion of sexual impurity and heightens the thought that no one will skip punishment in these matters. The tension of the verse is confirmed when Paul reminds them that he had said these things before. In fact, he had "solemnly warned" (4:6) them when he was with them about this area of life. The expression here comes originally from the idea of testifying under oath. It is a charge or warning as Paul reminds them that they should not take his words lightly.

God's purpose for us. The calling of the believer in sanctification and not in impurity is mentioned by Paul in 4:7. The word "called" (*ekalesen*) is the normal word used by the New Testament to describe God's work in salvation. Paul views it in this verse as an accomplished fact. This highlights the certainty that the life of those who are called should be lived properly: "In the Thessalonian letters, Paul uses *called* to mean the divine, sovereign work of grace. In the early part of his Thessalonian letters, Paul writes that the believer should walk worthy of his or her calling (2:12). God, who calls us, is faithful, and He 'also will bring it to pass' (5:24). In concluding his writing to the Thessalonians, Paul reminds them that 'He called you through our gospel, that you may gain the glory of our Lord Jesus Christ' (2 Thess. 2:14)."[11]

Paul now summarizes both the negative and the positive as he gives a reason for believers to abstain from sexual immorality (4:7). Therefore, Paul begins by noting that the believer is *not* called for the purpose of impurity. The term here (*akatharsia*) literally means "uncleanness." In a general sense it can mean "dirt or impurity" in terms of refuse or garbage. When applied to ethical behavior, the concept is almost always about sexual misdeeds. On the other side, the apostle argues that believers are in a positive sense called in *sanctification* or holiness. This word has been used in 4:3. Paul has come back to the summary of what was said in the earlier verse. The will of God is for believers to lead sanctified lives in the matter of abstaining from sexual immorality. The restatement from a different angle reminds the Thessalonians that this will of God is consistent with the position they now have by virtue of their relationship with God.

The implication of the overall exhortation relative to immorality is now amplified even more (4:8). Here "consequently" (*toigaroun*) means "for that very reason." The stated principle leads quite clearly to a particular application. The one who rejects the teaching on sexual immorality is not rejecting men but God. The idea of rejection means to set aside or not recognize as correct. It is an implicit warning. Paul is no doubt aware that for the Thessalonians to reject this teaching entails to some degree that they reject him as a man. However, it is more than just the setting aside of his words. If, as he stated before, they had received his proclamation as the Word of God, the conclusion is easily made that they tread on dangerous ground to discard his teaching in any matter. The reason is that the ultimate source of the instruction is God Himself. This is one of the problems with postmodern Western culture. It generally attributes biblical teachings in most matters, but certainly in moral ones, to the prejudices of ancient people. According to this thinking, teachings forbidding immoral behavior are social conventions invented by those in control of society. This shortsightedness and wrongheaded thinking leaves itself open to judgment from God who has designed how relationships should work.

Paul depicts God in this context as the one "who gives His Holy Spirit to you" (4:8). This added reference, which emphasizes the holiness of God's Spirit, serves to suggest that believers are without excuse in the matter of immorality. To reject the plan of God in the matter is in spite of the Spirit's presence and brings to mind the possibility of grieving the Spirit (see Eph. 4:30). The word "gives" (*didonta*) is in the present tense, which implies the ongoing nature of the gift of the Spirit and the present reality of the available endowment with power that is available for the believers to use in overcoming the temptation to immorality. Morris eloquently comments on this point:

> The verb is in the present, which is unusual for Paul; he generally thinks of the Spirit as given once for all. . . . But in this passage there is a profound truth in the use of the present. Anyone who carries on an act of impurity is not simply breaking a human code, nor even sinning against the God who at some time in the past gave him the gift of the Spirit. He is sinning against the God who is present at that moment, against the One who continually gives the Spirit. The impure act is an act of despite against God's good gift at the very moment it is being proffered.[12]

The Element of Love (4:9–12)

Paul keeps coming back to the idea of love as he writes (1 Thess. 1:3–4; 3:6, 12) and will continue to do so in the Thessalonian correspondence (1 Thess. 5:8, 13; 2 Thess. 1:3; 2:10, 13, 16; 3:5).

Love the essential element. As Paul has dealt with the issue of morals, he now turns his attention to the "love of the brethren" (4:9). This is not totally distinct. It is natural that genuine love be considered in the context of morality. However, it does appear that Paul is making a slight transition to another topic. In the midst of persecution it would be vital for the brethren to love one another. The term "love of the brethren" (*philadelphias*) is different from all the other words for love used by the apostle in the letters to the Thessalonians. It is often said that the *philadelphia* kind of love, brotherly love, is a lesser love than the self-sacrificing *agapē* love. It is the *agapē* word group that is used by Paul in all other occurrences of the word *love*. However, in this context, the distinction should not be overplayed. It would be quite natural to use the first term since the context is dealing with relationships among brothers and sisters in Christ. Nonetheless, the verb *love* (*agapēn*) occurs later in the same verse, making it likely that Paul is not stressing any nuance of distinction between the words.

Throughout the epistle so far, the apostle has many times referred to the things the Thessalonians already know from his prior stormy stay with them. Now he mentions something they should know because of God's direct work in them. He notes that they do not need a letter from him to know what he is about to say, "for you yourselves are taught by God to love one another" (4:9). "Taught by God" or God-taught (*theodidaktoi*) is an expression that is used only here in the New Testament. What does this mean precisely? It would be in the realm of possibility to assume that they were taught by God through the apostolic missionary team since they had accepted their teachings as the

Word of God. If this is the meaning, the idea is that no new letter is needed. They have heard it before. However, a better interpretation is to see it as quite natural to take Paul's reference as the Holy Spirit who is mentioned in the previous section (4:8). God's love should be natural to a believer who has the Holy Spirit: "hope does not disappoint, because the love of God has been poured out within our hearts through the Holy Spirit who was given to us" (Rom. 5:5). Thus Paul is reminding the Thessalonian believers of the presence of the Spirit of God within each of them who helps to prod them toward love for each other.

Horizontal love between believers in Christ gets the attention of those who are in the world. Paul talks about love more than any other New Testament author and focuses often on the essence of "one another" living. For example, just within the book of 1 Thessalonians the apostle often highlights this horizontal bent that should be present among genuine believers in Jesus:

Love and Caring between Believers	
1 Thessalonians 3:12	*Abound in love for one another.*
1 Thessalonians 4:9	*Love one another.*
1 Thessalonians 4:18	*Comfort one another.*
1 Thessalonians 5:11	*Build up one another.*
1 Thessalonians 5:13	*Live in peace with one another.*
1 Thessalonians 5:15	*Seek that which is good for one another.*

It would seem that love is the supreme part of such "one another" living, not just because it occurs in the list more often, but because it appears to be the fountain of all right behavior between believers.

Paul is not chiding the Thessalonians for a lack of love (4:10). In wording parallel to 4:1, he acknowledges that they do currently practice love for each other, but that he wants them "to excel still more." The extent of their love is to the brethren throughout all of Macedonia, the region where they live. Apparently opportunities had presented themselves for them to demonstrate in some concrete way how they cared for believers in other locations. It is Paul's desire that this kind of attitude and action would not just continue but increase in the personal experience of the Thessalonian believers.

Living before the world. Paul now shifts focus to the relationship that the Thessalonians should have to unbelievers in their community and beyond (4:11). The term "make it your ambition" (*philotimeisthai*) is used only by Paul in the New Testament. In 2 Corinthians 5:9 he speaks of his ambition to please God, while in Romans 15:20 he aspires to preach the gospel. The word means to consider it an honor or to make it an aim to do something. What is it that Paul wants them to be ambitious to do? He lays out three separate but related expressions to describe what he wants. First of all, the believer should desire to "lead a quiet life" (4:11). Christians who practice the art of genuine love do not need to be troublemakers. Their lives should be settled down, mature, and able to adapt to the society in which they live. In his first letter to Timothy, Paul gave similar instruction while discussing prayer. Christians should pray "for kings and all who are in authority, in order that we may lead a tranquil and quiet life in all godliness and dignity. This is good and acceptable in the sight of God our Savior" (1 Tim. 2:2–3).

It seems a bit odd that the idea of having ambition is coupled in the apostle's mind with leading a quiet life. Morris thinks the idea is "to seek strenuously to be still."[13] However, the thought is not strange. Those living in modern times understand well that the world can come in upon the individual with all of its social concerns and cares, wanted and unwanted, sympathetic and conflicting. It sometimes takes a great deal of effort to maintain a quiet life in the midst of the storm. It may also seem odd that Paul's example does not seem to fit the model of life that he is encouraging for them. After all, everywhere the apostle goes he appears to be a lightning rod of opposition, overflowing excitement, and public rousing. In Thessalonica Paul's ministry had caused a firestorm of protest. That does not mean he was wrong in his methods or attitude. Elsewhere the apostle reminds us that although it is not possible to live at peace with all people, we should try ("If possible, so far as it depends on you, be at peace with all men," Rom. 12:18). He is, however, reminding the Thessalonian believers that they can strive for peace and quiet in the midst of the storm.

The second thing believers should make it their ambition to do is to "attend to your own business" (4:11). The expression "attend to" (*prassein*) means "to do, accomplish, or act." The words "your own business" means "your own things." In modern lingo, one would interpret Paul's words as "mind your own business." There is no place for a Christian to be a busybody. This would be vital in the current climate at Thessalonica. For the believers to have an attitude of intrusion into the affairs of other people would mark them for more accusation and trouble in the community, something they already had in abundance.

The third goal Paul wanted the Thessalonians to have is given by the words "work with your hands" (4:11). This is another thing that the apostle had already taught them when he was with them and reminds them of it. In reminding them, he uses the strong word "commanded." Not only had the apostle given them authoritative direction when he was with them, but he also was their example of hard work (2:9), so they would understand what he meant. He will visit this issue again in 2 Thessalonians 3:7–12, using rather strident tones. There was no way that Paul could countenance laziness, whatever the reason used to justify it. If there was any hesitation among the believers to do manual labor (remember that Paul says to work "with your hands"), they would only have to remember that their Lord and Savior had worked as a carpenter.[14]

The apostle Paul wraps up this section by noting two results that come from applying the three goals of seeking a quiet life, not intruding upon others, and working hard (4:12). The first result is that the Thessalonian Christians would have a good testimony before the world, that is, "behave properly." The word "behave" is the same as the word "walk," which Paul used earlier in the letter for how one should live life. The term *properly* (*euschemonōs*) means "decently or respectable." In Romans 13:13 Paul contrasts the concept with carousing, drunkenness, sexual promiscuity, sensuality, strife, and jealousy. In this verse the focus of decent behavior is "toward outsiders." Outsiders here would be those who are not part of the church, the Jews and Gentiles of their community who were not part of the family of God. Although most of this present chapter involved how believers were to relate to believers, Paul feels compelled to point out behavior for the larger community context. In a similar way, he notes in another letter that church leaders should have a good reputation to those outside the church (1 Tim. 3:7).

The second result of successfully meeting the three goals of godly living listed in the first part of 4:12 is that the Thessalonians would "not be in any need." The other three occurrences of the word "need" (*chreian*) in 1 Thessalonians are used by Paul to express the fact that he did not need to write or say anything further to the believers at Thessalonica (1:8: 4:9; 5:1). Here the thought is entirely different. In light of the command to work with their hands, the derived meaning no doubt involves financial matters. Bruce comments, "If all the able-bodied members worked with their hands, they would be able to support themselves and their dependents, and not fall into destitution and become a charge on the generosity of others."[15]

Study Questions

1. How different is our current society from that of Paul's day? How much alike?

2. What temptations do you and your family face in the moral realm? What steps can you take to deal with it? How does this section of 1 Thessalonians help you to deal with it?
3. How can a person control his own personal passions and desires?
4. What does it mean to defraud? How can a person be defrauded by someone else?
5. How can you recognize a loving church?
6. What steps can a believer take to have a good testimony toward unbelievers outside the church?

CHAPTER 7

The Comfort of the Rapture 1 Thessalonians 4:13–18

Preview:

Paul teaches the saints at Thessalonica that their believing loved ones who have died will not miss the rapture of the church. All true believers in Christ, whether dead or alive, can be comforted in knowing that one day Christ will come to gather them to be with Him forever.

This section covers that part of the apostle's general outline given in 1 Thessalonians 1:10: "to wait for His Son from heaven, whom He raised from the dead." Nothing has brought more comfort to the hearts of Christians for the last twenty centuries than the glorious prospect of the return of Jesus Christ. Believers have often differed over the details of how and when Christ would return, but the true heartbeat of any true child of God would be "Come, Lord Jesus" (Rev. 22:20).

There are three major views about the coming of Christ's kingdom. *Postmillennialism* says that the church will usher in a period of righteousness on earth (the kingdom of God) and present it to Christ when He returns. That is, Christ will return after (post) the kingdom is established. *Amillennialism* basically denies a future earthly kingdom and sees the kingdom promises as being applied to the church in the present time. *Premillennialism* teaches that Christ will come back before His kingdom. In fact, He will inaugurate His own kingdom by His return.

The view we espouse here is that of premillennialism, which is demonstrated largely by an appeal to Old Testament biblical covenants and kingdom promises as well as the straightforward chronological understanding of Revelation 19–20 where the Second Coming precedes a thousand-year reign of Christ on the earth. But among premillennialists there are differing views of when Christ will return relative to the seven years of Daniel's Seventieth Week (Dan. 9:24–27), which is commonly called the future tribulation period. Several views have been put forward:

> *Pretribulational Rapture:* The Second Coming is in two stages. First, the Rapture, or catching up of the church, will take place at some time prior to the future tribulation that closes out the present age. The church will escape this future wrath on planet Earth and be caught away prior to it taking place.
>
> *Midtribulational Rapture:* Here the Second Coming is also in two stages. The Rapture will take place in the middle of the future tribulation. The church will escape the great tribulation or the last three and a half years but will have to go through the first three and a half years of the tribulation period.
>
> *Prewrath Rapture:* Here the Second Coming is also in two stages. The Rapture will take place somewhere within the second three and a half years of the tribulation. This view is a hybrid using many of the arguments of the midtribulational position.
>
> *Posttribulational Rapture:* The Rapture will take place at the same time as the second coming of Christ at the end of the tribulation. These are the same event, so the church will have to endure the entire seven years of tribulation. This view holds to a single-phase second coming.[1]

The pretribulational rapture view is usually associated with a viewpoint called dispensationalism. This perspective follows a grammatical-historical approach to the interpretation (sometimes called literal interpretation) and believes that the Bible normally honors the distinctions between God's program for the church and His program for Israel.

First Thessalonians 4:13–5:11 form a unit, which is important in deciding between the above interpretive options. Paul begins by expounding on the rapture of the church (1 Thess. 4:13–18) and then expounds on the Day of the Lord, or tribulation, to follow (1 Thess. 5:1–11). As a unit they help to form a strong argument for the pretribulational Rapture. However, one must be careful not to overlook other prominent teachings in this section. The timing of the Rapture is not the only issue that is raised.

The Reunion of the Saints (4:13–14)

Grieving with hope. One question on the heart of the Thessalonian believers was what had happened to those who had died in the Lord. Apparently there was some concern that those Christians who had already died would miss the Rapture because they did not survive to see it. By dealing with the question of the Rapture, Paul answers their question and intends to provide comfort and hope as well (4:18).

In 4:13 the apostle notes that he did not wish the Thessalonians to be "uninformed" (*agnoein*), which comes from the word that forms the basis of our modern term *agnostic*. The meaning comes out clearly in Romans 11:25 where Paul tells the believers in Rome he does not want them to be *ignorant* of the mystery of the temporary blindness of Israel in the plan of God. Here the issue is different. In a positive way, one can say that Paul wanted them to know some information about the question of those who are "asleep." This statement is an interesting twist within the flow of 1 Thessalonians. So often Paul has told them that they already know something—he only wants to reinforce the notion. However, in this passage he is covering material that they have probably not yet heard. The question of those who have died has been raised. Perhaps someone in the congregation had died and their relationship to the coming of the Lord was a difficulty that naturally came to the grieving minds in the church. It is also possible that Timothy has brought back this inquiry for the apostle to answer.

The phrase "those who are asleep" (*koimōmenōn*) is an often used euphemism for those who have died. Even in modern times we use the idea of sleep to represent death. In this context the particular reference is to those who have died in the Lord.

Typical New Testament Descriptions of Death

Lazarus was said to have fallen asleep when he had died before Jesus raised him up (John 11:1–40).

The bodies of many saints who were raised from the dead after the resurrection of Jesus were said to have "fallen asleep" (Matt. 27:52).

The godly deacon Stephen who was martyred "fell asleep" when he was stoned (Acts 7:60).

At the church of Corinth, Paul announced the judgment of death upon many because of the careless way that they approached the Lord's Table. It was said of them that "a number sleep" (1 Cor. 11:30).

It is evident from a study of these and similar passages that it is the *body that sleeps,* not the soul. The doctrine of soul sleep, that the soul goes to sleep at death, is an unscriptural viewpoint. In 4:14 Paul mentions those "who have fallen asleep in Jesus." These are believers whose spirits are now in heaven with Jesus (2 Cor. 5:8; Phil. 1:21–24), but whose bodies have the appearance of sleep in the grave.

Paul gives a reason why he wants to clarify the point of those who have died in Jesus (4:13). He does not want the Thessalonian believers to "grieve" (*lupēsthe*). This term means "to be sad or distressed" or "to hurt deeply." It is a word describing enormous inner and emotional pain. Every human being who has lived long enough knows what this means by way of experience. Yet at first glance Paul surprisingly asks the Thessalonians not to grieve. To ask a person not to grieve over the loss of a loved one is like asking the sun not to shine on a cloudless day. The context makes clear, however, that Paul is not asking the impossible. He makes a contrast—the Thessalonian believers are not to grieve as "the rest" (*loipoi*). This expression means "the remaining ones." Who are they in this context? They are those who do not have a personal relationship with God through Christ. In short, they are unbelievers. Paul's meaning is that he does not want the saints at Thessalonica to grieve *in the same way* as those who do not know God.

The apostle explains his intention further when he describes the remaining ones as those "who have no hope" (4:13). This statement clarifies Paul's contrast. Those outside of Christ do not share in the good things Paul is going to enumerate in the next verses. They are not accepted by God but are under His judgment. There is no glad and future reunion with resurrected loved ones who have died.[2] In contrast to this, the Thessalonians as believers in Jesus are a people of hope (1:3) who eagerly await the coming of the Lord. For those outside of the faith, if they understood their future, they would try to postpone it as long as they could. Their grieving will not be relieved by any future changes. They have no prospective hope. In contrast, believers can take heart in knowing that their grief is only temporary and is of a different sort. It makes all the difference in the world if people know that their destiny is marked by the words "and He shall wipe away every tear from their eyes; and there shall no longer be any death; there shall no longer be any mourning, or crying, or pain; the first things have passed away" (Rev. 21:4). The Thessalonians can grieve differently because they can know that for them there are no permanent broken hearts.

Basis for hope. Paul is not just speaking generally of the large outline of things to come in order to give hope to grieving believers, although that would be part of his intention here. Specifically, he wants to shed light on what will happen individually to believers who have died. Have they missed the rapture of the church because they failed to live to see its occurrence? Paul's answer is no, and he gives two reasons in the form of a conditional statement.

The first reason is the gospel and its teaching of the resurrection (4:14). The apostle starts with the words "if we believe that Jesus died and rose again." The interpreter should not make anything out of the conditional word "if." Its form lends itself to certainty and not something that is merely potential. In this context it could be translated "because we believe."[3] The term "we believe" (*pisteuomen*) is in the present tense with the weight of "we are believing." Paul is suggesting that the Thessalonians examine their current faith in the gospel for the answer to their question. The very fact that they know to be true and have embraced to be true the historical fact of the death and resurrection of Jesus has enormous implications for all of those who have put their faith in him, even for those who are deceased.

The second reason is in the last half of verse 14. The words "even so" imply that the declaration in the second half of the verse is as sure as the pure gospel message cited in the first portion of the text. In short, Paul is telling the Thessalonians, "Because you believe in the gospel, believe also in what I am about to tell you." The content of what they are to believe is that "God will bring with him those who have fallen asleep in Jesus." The reference to those who have died is once again made using the figurative "fallen asleep," as in 4:13. Paul is also clearly talking about those who have died "in Jesus." Literally, *in* Jesus means *through* Jesus and thus does not refer to the normal thought of the apostle emphasizing the believer's position *in* Christ. Here Jesus is viewed as leading the deceased believers through the veil of death. The parallelism is that one day Jesus will be the means of their resurrection. They will not be left out. It is a guaranteed fact that the saints should embrace fully.

Paul uses the words "will bring" to describe the future act of Christ that is in view. This general word (*axei*) means variously "to lead, guide, direct, bring, take along, or go." There exist a range of possibilities for how to understand the action that is being depicted, especially in light of the fact that Christ will bring *with Him* those who have died. The major options appear to be the following:

> When Christ appears He *will bring with Him* the souls of the departed believers so that they can be reunited with their resurrected bodies to return holistically to heaven with Christ.
>
> When Christ appears He will raise the bodies of the deceased Christians now to be reunited with their souls, and He *will bring* them *with Him* back to heaven.

When Christ appears He will raise the bodies of the deceased Christians now to be reunited with their souls and immediately return to earth, *bringing them with Him* down to earth as He starts His kingdom.

The last option is in harmony with the posttribulational view of the rapture of the church. The first two options appear to be consistent with a pretribulational view of the Rapture.[4] Although Paul's main point here is not the timing of the rapture of the church, one's view of the matter is intricately tied up with how one understands the terms of the verse.

It is important not to read one's prior belief into the text, but to derive the meaning from the text. The preferred option appears to be the first one. The phrase "will bring with Him" is attached to those who have fallen asleep through Jesus. The assumption throughout the verse is that they are in their spirits with Jesus after they have died. It is quite natural then to see them in their disembodied spirits as being brought by Jesus when He comes to unite them with their resurrected bodies so that they can holistically be raptured or caught up to be with the Lord forever. Regardless of which option one believes, the larger point is still in place. Christ will not forget to deal faithfully with those who have died in Him. They will be part of God's future plan and will not be overlooked.

The Coming of the Lord (4:15–17)

The next three verses describe in order the actual events that will take place at the appearing of the Lord Jesus.

The Order of Events
1. The Lord Himself will descend from heaven
2. with a shout,
3. with the voice of the archangel,
4. and with the trumpet of God;
5. and the dead in Christ shall rise first.
6. Then we who are alive and remain shall be caught up (raptured) together with those who have been resurrected in the clouds to meet the Lord in the air.

The priority of those who have died (4:15). Paul begins by reminding the Thessalonians that his teaching comes directly from the Lord: "we say to you by the word of the Lord." The expression "word of God" is the common one for Paul. However, in the epistles to the Thessalonians, he favors the alternate phrase "word of the Lord" (1 Thess. 1:8; 4:15; 2 Thess. 3:1). That he means the same thing by either wording is made clear when he reverts to "word of God" in 1 Thessalonians 2:13. It is not clear if Paul is referring to some extra-biblical teaching of Christ that had been passed down or if he means some prophetic utterance that came through the Spirit in the name of Christ, perhaps to him or to one of the apostolic missionary team.[5] While we have records of Jesus teaching about the end-times, with resurrections of both the saved and the lost (Matthew 24–25; Luke 14:14; John 5:25–29), there is no specific teaching from Christ about the relationship of the resurrection of those who have died and those who are still alive at His coming. Nonetheless, the apostle shares what he knows is God's word on the matter and expects the readers to consider it authoritative.

The precise content of the word of the Lord on the current issue is "we who are alive, and remain until the coming of the Lord, shall not precede those who have fallen asleep" (4:15). The apostle acknowledges the obvious. When Christ returns, there will be a certain generation that he returns to. He has in mind the believers in that last terminal generation who will not have to suffer physical death. This group of believers shall be changed, that is, glorified with resurrection bodies (1 Cor. 15:51–52). He speaks representatively when he says, "*we* who are alive," perhaps with the hope that he might be part of that number. Regardless, he speaks generally of the church at large and not simply of the Thessalonians. Those who are "alive" (*zōntes*) refer to believers who are *physically* alive. Any sense of being alive spiritually would be foreign to the context of the passage. This is especially true when Paul qualifies the term as "those who remain until the coming of the Lord," that is, those who physically live long enough to see the appearing of Jesus. As stated earlier the "coming" (*parousia*), or *appearance,* of the Lord has alternately been described as a two-phase or one-phase second coming. The first approach is favored as shown above and as will be argued throughout this book.

Now Paul comes to his main point—those who live until Jesus comes will not "precede those who have fallen asleep" (4:15). The term "precede" (*psthasōmen*) is an infrequent verb that means to attain or acquire in all other New Testament occurrences. However, in this context it implies a coming before or a preceding that takes place as the ones who have died in the Lord attain a place of priority before those who live to see the Parousia. This priority is chronological (see 4:16). Consequently, the Thessalonians need not worry about their loved ones who have died in the Lord.

The parousia of the Lord. Paul portrays the coming, or parousia, of the Lord Jesus with several different elements (4:16), although the presentation is brief.[6] First, he mentions that the Lord will descend. The term "descend" is a common and frequent one in the New Testament. The focus seems to be on the Lord more than the manner of His appearance. He comes "from heaven," the place where the Thessalonians were expectantly looking for Him (1:10—"to wait for His Son from heaven"). Furthermore, the apostle emphasizes that it is the Lord *Himself* who will appear. There is no proxy or substitute. Jesus will come personally for his saints.

Second, Jesus will descend with a "shout" (4:16). "Shout" (*keleusmati*), in its only occurrence in the New Testament, refers to a signal or verbal command. The verb form *keleuō* means to give an order or command. Mal Couch notes that this "is a classical and a military term meaning to command, and is used for the purpose of gathering together. It has been used as a word of encouragement for rowers to keep up the pace."[7] The connotation is that of joining the ranks at the shout of the command. This is what the Lord Jesus Christ taught: "when the dead will hear the voice of the Son of God and those who hear will live" (John 11:25, NIV).

Third, the voice of the archangel will be heard. The only other passage in the Bible that mentions an archangel is Jude 9, which specifies Michael as an archangel. What the voice says or how it is said is not stated. Michael is mentioned by name (without the designation of archangel) in Daniel 10:13, 21; 12:1, and Revelation 12:7. In those passages the archangel is defending the nation of Israel during the time of the great tribulation (last three and a half years of Daniel's seventieth week) or doing God's bidding in general against Satan and his demons. However, in 1 Thessalonians 4:16 the archangel has a unique role to play relative to the future of the church. Some interpreters suggest that we cannot be sure that Michael is in view. The text could be taken to mean "*an* archangel" rather than "*the* archangel." If one accepts Jewish extrabiblical tradition that there is more than one archangel, then any of the archangels can be meant by Paul.[8] However, in the absence of any clear biblical indication that there is another chief angel besides Michael, his designation should be the accepted one. In light of the special role that the archangel plays as one of God's created beings, this sounding forth emphasizes the extraordinary and exceptional nature of the event of Christ's appearing.

Fourth, a trumpet will be sounded (4:16). Some see this as what the archangel uses as a voice.[9] Trumpets sound forth throughout the Bible when it speaks of future events. Other references to end-time trumpets can be found in Revelation 11:15 (the seventh and last trumpet of the trumpet judgments during the tribulation, which is around the midpoint of the seven years) and in Matthew 24:31 when Jesus spoke of His literal second coming to the earth at the end of the tribulation. It is highly probable that 1 Thessalonians 4:16 is most closely paralleled by 1 Corinthians 15:52: "in a moment, in the twinkling of an eye, at the last trumpet; for the trumpet will sound, and the dead will be raised imperishable, and we shall be changed." This is the "last" trumpet for the church and is not tied chronologically to the other trumpets just mentioned. This text speaks of the sound of a trumpet, resurrection of the dead in Christ, and the sudden transformation of those alive at the time of the Rapture. All of these same elements are found in the Thessalonians passage. In any case, the fact that the trumpet is the trumpet of God notifies the reader that God the Father is announcing this event.

In summary, the events mentioned in 4:16 give a powerful picture of what will happen when Jesus comes again for His own:

> The sounds mentioned in this verse—**a loud command, with the voice of the archangel and with the trumpet call of God**—are difficult to interpret. Who will voice the loud shout? Will it be Jesus Himself (cf. John 11:43), or the archangel Michael (Dan. 10:13; Jude 9), or another angel? Is this a literal trumpet call, or was Paul speaking figuratively in describing the call of God by which He will announce the Advent of His Son? (cf. 1 Cor. 15:52). These three phenomena may all refer to the same thing, but probably they are three separate almost simultaneous announcements heralding Christ's return. Though one's curiosity about these aspects of the Rapture is not fully satisfied in this passage, one thing is clear: Christ's return for His saints will be announced from heaven forcefully and dramatically.[10]

To be sure, all of these elements mark the parousia of Christ as an event sanctioned by heaven itself and the sovereign occupant of heaven's throne.

The rapture of the church. The end of 4:16 teaches that after the descent of the Lord with a shout, the voice of the archangel, and the trump of God, "the dead in Christ shall rise first." Here Paul repeats the sentiment of 4:15—those who have died in Christ will have chronological priority at the rapture of the church. The position of the dead "in Christ" is emphasized. Those who are believers are meant. The word "first" (*prōton*) implies a temporal sequence or chronological order. Such an interpretation is strengthened by the use of another time word, "then" (*epeita*), in 4:17 immediately after it. Paul is giving an order of events that happens in time when Christ appears.

Just as Paul had mentioned for a second time in the passage those who have died in Christ, he now comes back to "we who are alive and remain" (4:17). The meaning is no different than in 4:15. Paul has divided the church into two groups—saints who have died during the church age and saints who will be alive at the end of the church age when Jesus returns. Here the division is merely one of chronology and not equality before God. Those who have died will be resurrected and will receive their glorified bodies. Those who are alive and remain will be changed and will receive their glorified bodies. Now they stand the same in unity before the Lord who has come to receive them to Himself. This notion is accentuated by Paul's use of the words "together with" (*hama sun*), which carry the idea that the main action of the verse is for all the saints simultaneously in unity as brothers in Christ.

The heart of the appearing of the Lord is depicted as a *catching up* of all the saints. The expression "shall be caught up" (*harpagēsometha*) articulates the main thought. D. Edmond Hiebert notes the significance of the word: "The verb *caught up* . . . denotes a sudden and forcible seizure, an irresistible act of catching away, due to divine activity. It might also be rendered 'snatch up, sweep up, carry off by force.' The Latin for the Greek verb is *rapturo*, from which we derive our English word *rapture*. Here is the revelation of the bodily snatching up of the church to meet her returning Lord."[11] Hence, one must reject the notion sometimes defended that the word *rapture* is not in the Bible, and therefore the doctrine must be rejected. The Bible here speaks of a rapture, that is, a catching up of all the church saints when Jesus appears.

The saints have no decision in the matter of the Rapture. They cannot decide to stay on earth. They cannot refuse to go with Jesus. In this sense, it is a forcible action in which the objects of the action have no say. Yet it is a good thing for them and something that the Thessalonians eagerly anticipated. The word is used in such a positive way in other settings, as when the Roman commander "was afraid Paul would be torn to pieces by them [some of the Jews] and ordered the troops to go down and *take him away from them by force*, and bring him into the barracks" (Acts 23:10).[12]

The timing of this event relative to other end-time events is not made clear in this section of Scripture, although we have seen hints that the pretribulational rapture position makes the best sense of all the various facets of the text. It will remain for the discussion of the Day of the Lord in chapter 5 and its relationship to this rapture of the church to help establish the timing of the event within the framework of the end-time panorama.

All the saints are caught up "in the clouds" (4:17; *en nephelais*). This term refers to the clouds of the sky. It is a mistake to take these words as just a literary reference tying the event to passages in which Messiah comes to rule in his kingdom (e.g., Dan. 7:13–14). Christ literally brings the saints up in the sky to be with Him. This interpretation is reinforced by the fact that the saints are caught up in the clouds to meet the Lord "in the air." This coming of Christ is not to the earth. Consequently, this event cannot be the fulfillment of many of the Old Testament prophecies when Messiah would come to the earth in glory to establish his kingdom.[13] For example, in Zechariah 14 he comes to step on the Mount of Olives in Jerusalem and deliver His people. This passage in 1 Thessalonians knows no such event. Instead, this message to the Thessalonian Christians is more in keeping with Jesus' words in John 14:2–3: "In My Father's house are many dwelling places; if it were not so, I would have told you; for I go to prepare a place for you. And if I go and prepare a place for you, I will come again, and receive you to Myself; that where I am, there you may be also."

In the passage Paul gives two pleasant consequences of the rapture of the saints. First of all, the catching up is "to meet the Lord" (4:17). Literally, the expression is "with respect to a meeting with the Lord." The wording "meeting" (*apantēsin*) is used by Paul only in this passage among his New Testament books. The other two occurrences are Matthew 25:6 and Acts 28:15. In the former the watching virgins were bid to come out and meet the bridegroom when he came at midnight. In the latter, the Roman Christians met Paul outside of Rome and escorted him into the city. Some who hold to a posttribulational rapture of the church emphasize this particular thought, which fits their scheme. The Lord comes in the air where the saints meet him and then escort him back down to earth immediately. While the word allows for such an interpretation, it is by no means a necessary one. F. F. Bruce comments, "There is nothing in the word . . . or in this context which *demands* this interpretation; it cannot be determined from what is said here whether the Lord (with his people) continues his journey to earth or returns to heaven."[14] While this passage is inconclusive by itself, the one who holds to a pretribulational rapture of the church can easily suggest that, if the posttribulationalist is right in his understanding of the term, then there is no place in the timeline of the New Testament for a catching up to go with the Lord in heaven as demanded in John 14:2–3. In the midst of fine-tuning one's interpretation on various aspects of the passage, one should not lose sight of the precious idea that is meant for the Thessalonians to embrace. They are meeting their Lord for the first time by sight and not by faith.

The second pleasant consequence of the rapture of the church is that believers will from that moment on be with Christ forever (4:17). The time expression used is the word "always." This is coupled with the satisfying thought of being "with the Lord" (*sun kuriō*). Saints are together with the One who died for them and raised them from the dead. They can look into the eyes of their Creator and Savior and know that they have a permanent relationship and proximity to Him that will never end. The eager waiting of 1:10 will at that moment be worth the wait.

This entire section of Paul's letter to the Thessalonians (4:13–17) was written so that the Thessalonians would have comfort and encouragement. This encouragement came in teachings they had not yet heard. They were to take these words and use them to reassure each other. They now knew more of the story and Jesus' plan for them when He returned to rapture the church. The present tense of the imperative word "comfort" (*parakaleite*) implies that they were to continue applying these words to their lives as long as support was needed (4:18). The continuing application of these words for all generations of Christians has proven the test of time as countless ministers down through the centuries have reassured grieving believers at the graveside of a loved one by reading these precious promises and obeying the command to "comfort one another with these words."

The practical value of the teaching of the Rapture is also brought home throughout the rest of the New Testament. Not only does it bring comfort as Paul declared to the Thessalonians (4:18), but it also motivates to zealous works (Titus 2:13–14) and to a pure lifestyle: "Beloved, now we are children of God, and it has not appeared as yet what we shall be. We know that, when He appears, we shall be like Him, because we shall see Him just as He is. And everyone who has this hope fixed on Him purifies himself, just as He is pure" (1 John 3:2–3).

Study Questions

1. What does the Bible say about death? What was the major concern of the Thessalonian Christians in this section?
2. Do you have any loved ones who are now with the Lord? What will happen to them at the Rapture?
3. What precise events will happen as the Rapture takes place?
4. Who will take part in the Rapture and why?
5. How many resurrections are there in the Bible?
6. How does the doctrine of the Rapture bring comfort to believers?

CHAPTER 8

The Day of the Lord
1 Thessalonians 5:1–11

Preview:

Paul reminds the Thessalonian believers that they are exempt from participation in the future day of the Lord's wrath of God, that is, the tribulation period. That time will overtake the world like a thief in the night, but church saints cannot be caught off guard in light of God's purpose for their lives.

This section corresponds to the outline given by Paul in 1 Thessalonians 1:10: "Jesus, who delivers us from the wrath to come." In light of the chronological nature of the rest of the outline, it is clear that the previous rapture event (1 Thess. 4:14–18) precedes in time the Day of the Lord's wrath of God that is presented in this section. This truth has significance for understanding the church's exemption from this time of wrath (5:9).

The Bible predicts a time of severe judgment on planet Earth prior to Christ's coming to set up His kingdom. The Old Testament prophets were pronounced in their predictions of just such a time. It was called Daniel's Seventieth Week (Dan. 9:24–27) and the times of Jacob's distress or trouble (Jer. 30:7). The prophet Joel spoke of the Day of the Lord coming with great alarm: "Blow a trumpet in Zion, and sound an alarm on My holy mountain! Let all the inhabitants of the land tremble, for the day of the LORD is coming; surely it is near, a day of darkness and gloom, a day of clouds and thick darkness . . . the great and awesome day of the LORD" (Joel 2:1–2, 31).

Other prophets mentioned this time period as well (Isa. 2:12; Ezek. 30:3; Amos 5:18; Zech. 14:1–4; Mal. 4:5). Most of the book of Revelation is given over to a description of that future time when God will send His wrath upon the earth before the second coming of the Lord Jesus Christ (Rev. 6–19). However, we also find in the first epistle to the Thessalonians a limited but useful description of that awful time. In 1 Thessalonians 5:1–11 he gives a picture of the Day of the Lord and explains the relationship of believers in the church age to that time.

The Description of the Day of the Lord (5:1–3)

Coming without warning. Paul begins with an introductory phrase, "Now as to" (*peri de*), that marks off 5:1–11 as a new section, although he still continues the end-time discussion started in 4:13. Paul notes that he did not need to write anything to them about "the times and the epochs" (5:1). This is language similar to earlier statements in the book when he acknowledges what the Thessalonians already know. The "times" (*chronos*) make reference to chronological time according to the clock or the calendar. The word "epochs" (*kairos*) focuses on events in various seasons.[1] Used together the two words are perhaps a common formula for the end-time days (see Acts 1:7).[2] The Thessalonians were very much aware of what Paul had taught them, and his teaching included end-time events. For those who shun prophecy, it should be noted that Paul was not afraid to speak of "times and epochs."

The Thessalonian believers knew "full well" (*akribōs*) or precisely what the Day of the Lord was all about (5:2). Most likely this is because of Paul's oral instructions when he was with them. Unfortunately, modern-day readers do not have access to what Paul told the Thessalonians orally when he taught them. If such was available, there would be much less controversy about the meaning of this particular section of Scripture. He is concerned to tell them that the Day of Lord will come. There is a ring of certainty in his words that the Thessalonians could easily ascertain. The verb "will come" (*erchetai*), literally "is coming," is like a prophetic present that depicts the Day of the Lord as already on its way and will someday arrive.[3]

However, the question emerges as to the nature of the Day of the Lord itself. It is one thing to know that it is coming but quite another to know what it actually is. This topic is so important that an appendix has been supplied dealing with the meaning of the term *Day of the Lord,* a term that is used frequently in the Bible, especially in prophetic texts (see appendix A). For now, it is sufficient to note that the Day of the Lord as a general concept is a time when God breaks through in history to judge and establish. It could have a near fulfillment to the time of the prophecy and not an end-time meaning (see Joel 1:16–20). It can also refer to a specific time when God enters history in severe judgment just before the establishment of His kingdom on earth. From Old Testament texts, we know that it is a time of despair, darkness, gloom, and judgment upon the nation of Israel and the entire world (e.g., Joel 2–3; Amos 5:18–20; Isa. 13; Zech. 14:1) just before the restoration of Israel in its kingdom glory. The details, of course, must be established by each context where the term is used.

In these Old Testament texts and others like them, two major tracks of identification emerge for the meaning of the term *Day of the Lord*. It sometimes describes an *event*, such as when Christ sets his feet on the Mount of Olives in Jerusalem to deliver the city of Jerusalem and Israel while destroying His enemies (Zech. 14:1–19). This would be in keeping with the Day of the Lord as the second coming of Christ as he comes to slay his enemies (Rev. 19:11–21). Other times it is used to express a *period of time* where God judges throughout (Joel 2:1–10). Interestingly, both approaches to the term, Day of the Lord as *event* and as *period of time*, emerge within the same book of the Bible, namely, the prophecy of Joel (see appendix A for more information).

It would be hard to imagine Paul not understanding this Old Testament backdrop to the term. Thus the question must be asked: what is the specific use of the term *Day of the Lord* in 1 Thessalonians in light of this Old Testament understanding? One's answer to this question determines his view of the timing of the rapture of the church based on this passage. The reason for this is the exemption from wrath that is mentioned in 5:9. If Christians are exempt from the Day of the Lord's wrath, then a definition of the Day of the Lord will result in a particular view of the timing of the rapture of the church, which is mentioned in 4:17. Posttribulationalists normally see the Day of the Lord in 5:2 as an event—the Second Coming. Thus Christians will be spared from the wrath of that event. They will not be spared from any of the troubles of the tribulation period that precedes the Second Coming. Pretribulationalists see the Day of the Lord as a period of time, the full seven years of the Seventieth Week of Daniel. They usually argue for this based on the association of the judgments of the book of Revelation (chaps. 6–19) with the entire seven years of what has come to be called the tribulation period.[4] Thus, in this scheme, the church will be exempt from the entire time. Which option is correct depends largely on the interpretation of 5:3 to be discussed below.

At this point, the main idea that Paul wants to stress is that the Day of the Lord will come suddenly on an unsuspecting world. He uses two illustrations to make his claim: it will come like a thief in the night (5:2; cf. v. 4), and it will come like birth pangs upon a woman with child (5:3). The picture of a thief coming in the night is used in several different contexts in the Bible. Jesus tells the church at Sardis that He will come like a thief to judge them if they do not repent (Rev. 3:3). They will not know the hour when He will come. His coming will be unannounced. It is easy in this context to imagine this particular coming as a temporal one and not the end-time judgment of the Second Coming. Another use of the term can be found in Revelation 16:15–16 where the context speaks of God coming to judge like a thief in the night. Interestingly, Armageddon, the last great battle, is mentioned in the context, which helps to identify the coming, which is spoken of to be near the end or at the end of the tribulation. Jesus again uses the image of a thief in the night in Matthew 24:42–43 in conjunction with His second coming to earth at the end of the tribulation: "Therefore be on the alert, for you do not know which day your Lord is coming. But be sure of this, that if the head of the house had known at what time of the night the thief was coming, he would have been on the alert." Christ will come suddenly and unexpectedly as far as the world is concerned.

The last two examples correlate well with the Day of the Lord as the second coming of Christ at the end of the tribulation. They, therefore, fit with the notion of a posttribulational rapture of the church. In this view, the church goes through the tribulation but is exempt from the wrathful aspect of Christ's second coming. However, even though the correlation can be made in this way, it is not the only correlation possible relative to the picture of the Day of the Lord as a thief in the night. In Joel 2:9 the image of thieves coming through the windows is part of the description of the Day of the Lord. In that context, which no doubt involves the end-time scenario, it is impossible to take the term as referring to a singular event such as the Second Coming. It is a period of time. If this is the background of the image in Paul's mind, the entire duration of the Day of the Lord's wrath, that is, the tribulation, may be in view. The Day of the Lord as an awful period of time will come upon the world suddenly when people are not expecting it. This preferred interpretation fits well with a pretribulational rapture of the church. This particular approach is confirmed by an exploration of the second illustration that Paul uses to portray suddenness—the birth pangs of a pregnant woman. This illustration will be considered below.

Coming with deception. The second illustration indicating the sudden and unexpected arrival of the Day of the Lord is that it "will come suddenly like birth pangs upon a woman with child" (5:3). The term "birth pangs" (*odin*) refers to a pregnant woman's labor pains. Here it is used metaphorically and is a well-known expression for the "eschatological woes" that precede the coming of the Lord to earth.[5] The origin of this image for the Day of the Lord is found in the Major Prophets of the Old Testament. Jeremiah speaks of a horrible period in history in which Israel is to be judged (the time of Jacob's trouble) and pictures it as a woman in childbirth (Jer. 30:7). Isaiah portrays this time as an awful judgment upon not just Israel but the whole world (Isa. 13:6–16; cf. Isa. 26:17–18). Part of the imagery used to depict this period is found in the negative expression "they will writhe like a woman in labor" (Isa. 13:8).

This highly descriptive expression also occurs three other times in the New Testament. On one occasion Peter uses the term to describe Jesus' resurrection as "putting an end to the *agony* of death" (Acts 2:24). However, twice the term is used in the New Testament to refer to the period of time at the end of history prior to the coming of Christ and the messianic kingdom: "For nation will arise against nation, and kingdom against kingdom; there will be earthquakes in various places; there will also be famines. These things are merely the beginning of birth pangs" (Mark 13:8; cf. Matt. 24:8). In light of these Old and New Testament passages, it is hard to visualize the arrival of birth pangs as an event. There is a period of time in which the labor pains take place that leads to an event, namely, the birth of a child. Paul's use of the term is an echo of Jesus' use of the word when he describes several happenings that occur over time. Consequently, once again the meaning of this particular metaphor helps to support the pretribulational rapture of the church, since it is this time period that the church is exempt from according to 5:9.

Paul's illustration is consistent with the Old Testament and with Jesus' understanding of the end-times. The apostle begins to contrast the Thessalonians with unbelievers in the world who will be taken by surprise by the coming of the Day of the Lord. He describes it with words of judgment. It is called "destruction" (*olethros*), a word meaning "ruin" or "death" (5:3). This time of destructive ruin comes "suddenly" (*aiphnidios*), a word that is emphatically placed by Paul in the verse. It only occurs here and in Luke 21:34–35 where Jesus warns, "Be on guard, that your hearts may not be weighted down with dissipation and drunkenness and the worries of life, and that day comes on you *suddenly* like a trap; for it will come upon all those who dwell on the face of all the earth." In Paul's understanding, those who do not know God will be forced to face this time, since "they shall not escape" (5:3). Paul uses a double negative (*ou mē*) so that the statement can be translated, "they shall in no wise escape."[6] The term "escape" (*ekphugōsin*) carries the thought of avoiding or shunning. However, for those who are not ready for that time, there is no place to hide. Once it comes upon them, they will experience the Day of the Lord.

Finally, Paul informs his readers that the Day of the Lord will come at a time when people are deceived into thinking that there would be peace and safety: "While they are saying, 'Peace and safety!' then destruction will come upon them suddenly" (5:3). One question that arises is whether the people are crying *for* peace and safety because they do not have such security or they are shouting the words because *they think they already have* such refuge. The overall thrust of the metaphor used in the verse forces the second option. Those who think they are fine—that is, they possess peace and safety—have the opposite suddenly come upon them. That is the normal flow of the wording.

A second question that then emerges is *when* the people believe they have this peace and safety. One's answer here affects how he or she views the timing of the rapture of the church. G. K. Beale argues, "Those in the house not prepared for a thief and who think they have peace and safety will be surprised by Christ's coming . . . at which time the ungodly will be surprised by the final judgment inflicted upon them."[7] This line of reasoning fits a posttribulational view of the rapture of the church. But such an interpretation cannot be maintained. In that scheme the time of peace and safety would have to be right before the second coming of Christ to earth and would have to harmonize with the Battle of Armageddon. It is hardly likely than any earth dweller at that time would feel secure and safe, since it is one of the most, if not *the* most, unstable times in history and is a conflagration affecting the entire world (cf. Rev. 16:15–16). The general descriptions of the prophets and Jesus concerning the entire tribulation period, and especially the last three and a half years, makes it hard to visualize any single individual, much less the entire culture, crying out, "Peace and safety!" The best understanding for when unbelievers cry out, "Peace and safety," with their false sense of security is right before the seven-year tribulation period—that is, right before the Day of the Lord's wrath of seven years. Why is this so? The event that starts the seven-year tribulation period, also known as Daniel's Seventieth Week, is the signing of a peace treaty between the Antichrist and the nation of Israel (Dan. 9:27). Consequently, it is easy to visualize the people on earth speaking positively about peace and safety leading up to this event. In addition, the rider on the white horse as part of the first seal in Revelation 6 is most probably the Antichrist who comes with a false peace. So the early days of the tribulation are characterized with this notion as well. Such cannot be said of the end of the tribulation with its Armageddon and the middle of the tribulation with its intrigues of war (see Dan. 11:36–12:1). Therefore, the only solution is to see the people crying, "Peace and safety," before the start of the entire seven-year Day of the Lord's wrath. This conclusion naturally leads to the viewpoint that the rapture of the church is pretribulational since the Day of the Lord is seen as the full seven years.

The Believer and the Day of the Lord (5:4–11)

Light and darkness. Paul in this section now finishes the statement of his contrast. The Thessalonian believers are not like those in the world. He tells the saints in Thessalonica, "You, brethren, are not in darkness" (5:4). The fact that he addresses them as brethren in this context may not be incidental. They are part of the brethren, the family of God that makes up the church of God. In this way he gently reminds them that they have a different status and relationship than those outside the boundaries of God's assembly. Thus it is not a strange thing for them to have a different destiny relative to the time of the Day of the Lord's wrath.

The phrase "in darkness" also characterizes those in the world outside of Christ. The word "darkness" (*skotei*) is a general term that is frequently applied to spiritual matters throughout the New Testament (5:4). Perhaps the best parallel to what Paul means here is found in Ephesians 5:8: "for you were formerly *darkness*, but now you are light in the Lord; walk as children of light." The Thessalonians and all genuine Christians are not in darkness but in the light because they are "in the Lord" who is light (John 8:12). They do not exist in the domain of darkness but in the sphere of the light of Christ. "Nothing is plainer than that Paul regards his Christian readers as standing in a relationship to this eschatological outpouring that is markedly different from that of the unregenerate world around them. This is because they belong intrinsically to the 'light' rather than to the 'darkness.'"[8]

Paul goes on to teach the Thessalonians that they are not in darkness, "that the day should overtake you like a thief" (5:4). The clear message is that the day will not overtake believers. The word "day" in context refers to the Day of the Lord's wrath, which is the main topic of discussion throughout this section of Paul's epistle. The term "overtake" (*katalabē*), in a rare occurrence in an end-time passage, carries the idea of a hostile intent to seize. The Day of the Lord would come to seize those outside of Christ but not those who were in Him. The phrase "like a thief" continues the metaphor from 5:2. True believers will not be surprised by the Day of the Lord as if a thief has suddenly come upon them.

Awake or asleep. Paul now expands the contrasting metaphors of light and darkness to include the similar thoughts of night/day, sleeping/waking, and drunkenness/soberness (5:5–8). The continuing contrast of light/darkness or day/night lends itself powerfully to Paul's argument. In 5:5 he tells the Thessalonians that "you are all sons of light and sons of day." The two expressions "sons of light" and "sons of day" are equivalent in their basic meaning. The phrase "sons of day" occurs only here in the entire Bible. There is no justification for the view of Morris that the word *day* in the designation "sons of day" must refer the Day of the Lord in light of the context.[9] Surely the context suggests otherwise. The Day of the Lord is a time of wrath that is not for the sons of light or sons of day (5:9). Thus the word *day* in the title for believers here should not be associated with the Day of the Lord. The opposing view makes the unfortunate assumption that the Day of the Lord must refer only to the event of the second coming of Christ, which is a shining day for believers and an extremely dark one for unbelievers. However, this meaning should not be imported into a context where there are better alternatives of interpretation.

The term "sons of light" comes partly from the teaching of Jesus that had no doubt been passed down to Paul. In the parable of the unrighteous steward, Jesus comments, "And his master praised the unrighteous steward because he had acted shrewdly; for the sons of this age are more shrewd in relation to their own kind than the sons of light" (Luke 16:8). It is not clear if Jesus' distinction between *sons of this age* and *sons of light* matches Paul's distinction, but the correspondence is likely. Paul is clearly talking about the saved and the lost. Further, in a discourse in which Jesus identifies himself as the Messiah and those who accept him as children of light, Christ exhorts, "While you have the light [Christ], believe in the light, in order that you may become sons of light" (John 12:36). Thus sons of light are believers in Jesus. This is certainly Paul's understanding in 1 Thessalonians 5:5. The Thessalonian saints, as believers, are those whose domain is light and not darkness.[10]

In the remainder of 5:5, Paul switches gears slightly. He has just told the Thessalonians who they *are*. Now he tells them who they *are not*. It is interesting that in doing so, the apostle changes from second person ("you") to first person ("we"). It is possible that this change is merely stylistic, but more than likely he means to communicate that what he says of the Thessalonians is universally true of all believers in Jesus including himself. The particular statement is that "we are not of night nor of darkness" (5:5). It is the thief who comes at night and surprises those who are not alert (5:2). *Night* then characterizes those outside of Christ.

Interestingly, there are no other Bible texts that use the terms *children of night, children of darkness, sons of night,* or *sons of darkness*. Nonetheless, the concept is a prominent one throughout the Old Testament, although its association with the word *night* does not usually occur. In the Psalms, while followers of God come to Him as the One providing and being light and salvation (Ps. 18:28; 27:1; 119:105), the wicked are associated with darkness (Ps. 11:2). Isaiah gives a suitable warning from God using the light and dark distinction: "Woe to those who call evil good, and good evil; Who substitute darkness for light and light for darkness" (Isa. 5:20). It is highly appropriate for Paul to use similar images in his words to the Thessalonians about the Day of the Lord. Zephaniah had centuries earlier described the Day of the Lord with these words: "A day of wrath is that day, a day of trouble and distress, a day of destruction and desolation, a day of *darkness* and gloom, a day of clouds and thick *darkness*" (Zeph. 1:15). Because the Thessalonians are sons of day, they will not be overtaken by the dark night of the Day of the Lord's wrath that is coming upon the world.

Next Paul gives a conclusion ("so then") that must follow (5:6). The conclusion is given in the form of an exhortation stated in a negative way ("let us not sleep as others do") and in a positive way ("but let us be alert and sober"). The word *others* is the previous term for "remaining ones" (see 4:13). It has already been shown that this term refers to those who do not know God, the ones who remain after believers are removed from consideration. The call not to sleep adds another descriptive word to the mix of Paul's contrasts. He has talked about light and darkness along with night and day. Now he adds to the list the concept of being asleep versus being alert. Christians ought to be alert and not like the world, which is sleeping. The imagery of sleeping here in 5:6 is different from that in 4:13–14 where sleep euphemistically depicts the death of believers. The exhortation for Christians to be alert is given by the apostle to three other churches besides the Thessalonians (1 Cor. 16:13; Eph. 6:18; Col. 4:2). The term for "let us be alert" (*grēgorōmen*) means to keep awake or be watchful. Again, Paul shows that his thoughts are rooted and grounded in the teachings of Jesus. The Lord had told his disciples to watch and be alert for His return (Matt. 24:42–43; 25:13; Mark 13:34–37; Luke 12:37). Here Paul tells the Thessalonians to be alert concerning the period of judgment that precedes the Lord's return to earth. This is not so they would recognize the tribulation when it comes and act appropriately, for they are exempt from that time (5:9) and will not be around to endure it since they have been raptured (4:13–17). They are not those who will be overtaken by the darkness of the Day of the Lord (5:4). This is a fact and not something Paul hopes is true of them. In 5:6 the apostle wants them to live in this world before that dark time in light of who they are—a common Pauline theme.

In 5:6 the apostle also wants the Thessalonians to be *sober* (*nēphōmen*). The word can mean being vigilant and alert, thus making it a synonym for the previous verb (be alert; cf. 1 Pet. 5:8).[11] If this is so, at some level this could mean that unbelievers "do not hear nor understand spiritual truth" as do believers who live a different way in light of a different understanding of the truth.[12] However, one should not lose sight of Paul's basic intention to contrast being sober with being drunk (*methuskomenoi*): "For those who sleep do their sleeping at night, and those who get drunk get drunk at night" (5:7). The only other time that Paul uses the word is when he teaches the Ephesians to be filled with the Spirit instead of being drunk with wine (Eph. 5:18). The images of being drunken and not being watchful for His return are combined by Jesus in His teaching in the Olivet Discourse (Matt. 24:48–49). Concerning the language of drunkenness, Bruce comments, "The language here is not figurative but factual: night is the time when people sleep; night is the time when people get drunk (and therefore reckless)."[13] The picture is similar to poor Belshazzar, the last king of Babylon, who in drunken stupor was vanquished suddenly and unexpectedly by the Persians (Dan. 5). However, the overall contrast of being sober versus being drunk appears to be used figuratively for spiritual alertness as the explanation of the next verse will show.

The apostle now summarizes with a repeated exhortation: "But since we are of *the* day, let us be sober" (5:8). Paul continues to use the first person "we" to suggest the universal nature of his statement for all Christians. The opening part of this verse is the same thought as that at the end of 5:6: "let us be alert and sober." A believer is to take matters seriously and be alert to what is happening. His practice in this area should match his position. He is of the day. Therefore, he should act like he is of the day.

At this point it will be useful to recap the various contrasts that Paul has made in 5:4–8. On one hand are the terms "darkness," "night," "sleeping," and "drunkenness." These describe the world—those who do not know God. These are the ones upon whom the darkness of the Day of the Lord shall come suddenly like a thief in the night. On the other hand, one sees the expressions "light," "day," "alert" or "awake," and "sober." These terms describe those who are followers of Christ who will not experience the negative judgment of the Day of the Lord. The four contrasts set up by these terms—light and darkness, day and night, awake and asleep, sober and drunk—demonstrate that Paul believes that there are two kinds of people. He writes to let the Thessalonians know which group they belong to and to ask them to live in light of that membership.

The armor of a soldier. The alertness that is spoken of in 5:8 is pictured by warfare imagery, specifically a soldier in military dress. Two parts of the warrior's uniform are mentioned. First, there is the *breastplate* of faith and love.

One is instantly reminded of the earlier verses of the book where Paul bragged on the work of faith and labor of love the Thessalonians exercised (1:3). Even though they already possessed and practiced these qualities, they were urged by the apostle to continue to grow in their use (3:2–13). Now he repeats essentially the same message using the warfare imagery. They are to be alert by using their faith and love just as a soldier in battle would use a breastplate to protect him in battle.

Second, there is the *helmet,* which is called the hope of salvation (5:8). This reference completes the reminder of the earlier triad of "work of faith," "labor of love," and "steadfastness of hope" (1:3). Similarly, the Christian should stay alert as a soldier who has made himself ready for battle with his helmet for defense. Taken together, the breastplate and the helmet give a small glimpse of the soldier's task, not the complete picture. Paul's purpose is simply to keep the Thessalonians alert by way of the analogy to warfare, something he speaks of in Ephesians 6:10–17 with more comprehensive terms. There the helmet is also the helmet of salvation, but the breastplate is the breastplate of righteousness. In that passage his goal is to get Christians to stand against the devil and his deceit. In 1 Thessalonians 5:8 Paul's purpose is to convince the Thessalonians to be alert in light of God's overall plan for history including the Day of the Lord's wrath coming at the end of the age.

One remaining question is the nature of the salvation that is mentioned. MacArthur says, "The salvation in view here is not the past aspect of salvation (justification), or its present aspect (sanctification), but rather its future aspect (glorification)."[14] The context of 1 Thessalonians 4:13–5:11 would seem to support such an interpretation for a couple of reasons. First, the word "hope" in the book seems to push the reader to future prospects and not just past accomplishment. Second, this futuristic bent is supported by the fact that deliverance from the Day of the Lord's wrath is considered part of the salvation that is in mind. This is the thrust of the next verse, which is taken up below.

Deliverance from wrath. Paul now proclaims the major truth that he has been anticipating: "For God has not destined us for wrath, but for obtaining salvation through our Lord Jesus Christ" (5:9). The word "destined" (*etheto*) means "to set, put, place, or appoint." The Thessalonian believers were destined to the realization of God's purpose for them that they would not experience the wrath of God.

However, one must at this point entertain the question of what particular wrath of God is in view. The idea that Paul is strictly speaking of the wrath of God in eternal hell does not fit well with the context. It is the Day of the Lord's wrath of God that the apostle has in mind (v. 2), although it is clear from other biblical texts that the unsaved will experience eternal hell. Thus the question comes back to the identification of the Day of the Lord.

D. Michael Martin, who appears to hold a posttribulational view of the rapture of the church, seems to limit the Day of the Lord's wrath and judgment to the event of the second coming of Christ to the earth. Thus he argues for the singularity of the rapture event of 1 Thessalonians 4:13–18 and Christ's second coming to earth. Throughout his discussion Martin appears to assume that the Day of the Lord is the event of the Second Coming and not the severe judgment of the tribulation period that precedes it.[15] Deliverance from wrath in this scheme is simply the exemption of the saints from judgment at the Second Coming.

Contrary to this view is the teaching of the Scriptures that sometimes suggests that the Day of the Lord is a period of time, not a singular event.[16] Jesus teaches that the tribulation saints would not survive unless this time period was shortened (Matt. 24:22). The events associated with this time include the abomination of desolation (Dan. 9:27; Matt. 24:15), thereby making it reasonable to discuss this time in terms of Daniel's Seventieth Week (Dan. 9:24–27). Furthermore, the correlation of the seal judgments with the descriptions in Matthew 24:4–14 shows that the seals of the book of Revelation begin in the first half of the seven-year tribulation. This is important since it is relatively easy to show that the seals of Revelation 6 are in fact the wrath of God in light of the divine unleashing of the seals through the Lamb of God and a detailed examination of the seal judgments themselves. In addition, Paul's description of the man of lawlessness (Antichrist) and his activities in 2 Thessalonians 2:3–4 helps to frame the interpretation in favor of tribulational events and not just the end of the tribulation. All of the above facts, with some associated common terminology, mesh nicely with many Old Testament passages (alluded to earlier) that teach that the Day of the Lord is a time period when Israel and the nations of the world face severe temporal judgment from God. It is a time of cleansing for Israel before the nation receives its kingdom when Messiah comes again (see appendix A).

Consequently, the deliverance spoken of in 5:9 would not be deliverance from eternal hell or from the judgments of the Second Coming event, but exemption from the entirety of the future horrors of the earthly tribulation period. Of course, whether one has this end-time exemption depends upon his status as a believer in the gospel of Christ; that is, he has eternal life or salvation through faith in Him—probably the reason Paul alludes to the death of Christ at the beginning of verse 10. However, Paul's general argument would be, first the Rapture (1 Thess. 4:13–18), then the tribulation of the Day of the Lord (1 Thess. 5:1–9). The chronological nature of the passage and the correct understanding of the Day of the Lord as the tribulation wrath of God lead to a belief in a pretribulational rapture of the church.

In 5:10 the apostle gives an enigmatic explanation about the deliverance from the Day of the Lord's wrath. It involves this truth: "that whether we are awake or asleep, we may live together with him." One might be tempted to interpret the words "awake or asleep" in terms of the earlier contrasts that Paul has made between believers and unbelievers in 5:4–8. While this approach might be attractive initially, the interpretation cannot be made. The contrast of 5:10 is simply different. At the end of the verse, both those who are awake and those who are asleep "live together with Him [Christ]." In other words, both those who are awake and those who are asleep are believers whose destinies involve living with Christ and avoidance of the Day of the Lord's wrath. In 5:4–8 those who are asleep are unbelievers upon whom the Day of the Lord's wrath would come suddenly without warning. Hodges further explains:

> Special attention should be directed to the contrasting tenses employed in the last part of verse 10. Whereas the words for "awake" and for "asleep" are in the present tense, the word for "live" is in the aorist tense. This contrast imparts to "live" a touch of what the grammars call an "ingressive" force. That is, the Greek verb *zēsōmen* may be taken to imply "we shall commence to live." But this subtle nuance is not strictly necessary for gleaning the transparent force of Paul's declaration. "When the day of the Lord arrives," Paul means to say, "whether we are watching or sleeping, we will live with Him."[17]

Then, what is the contrast that Paul is now making? One does not have far to look in the context. In the previous section on the rapture of the church, Paul answered the question about those believers who had already died and referred to them as those who were asleep (4:13–14). He concluded that both those who had died and those who were still alive would be caught up together to be with the Lord forever, a notion closely resembling the words "live together with Him" in 5:10. Thus in 5:10 those who are awake are believers who are physically alive, and those who are asleep are believers whose bodies lie in the grave. So 5:10 is simply a recap of 4:13–17.

Such an interpretation is reinforced by the next verse (5:11), which ends this section on the Day of the Lord in the same way that Paul ended the section on the rapture of the church. While the truth of the Rapture was to bring comfort (4:18), its corollary truth of being freed from the horrors of the future

Day of the Lord's wrath ought to cause the Thessalonians to "encourage one another" and "build up one another" (5:11). They were already doing this as Paul was so fond of saying, but in the light of the current situation of persecution that the church at Thessalonica was experiencing, an increase in such encouragement would be a good thing.

Study Questions

1. What is the Day of the Lord? Is it a single event or is it a period of time? Is it good or is it bad?
2. What does the phrase "thief in the night" (5:2) imply for the unbelieving world? For the believer?
3. Will the church have to go through the future tribulation? Why or why not?
4. What kind of wrath is referred to in 1 Thessalonians 5:9?
5. What aspect of salvation is referred to in 1 Thessalonians 5:9?

CHAPTER 9

A Church in Harmony
1 Thessalonians 5:12–22

Preview:

The apostle Paul teaches the Thessalonians the need to have a proper attitude toward church leaders and other believers. Struggling believers are to be the recipients of special care from the church members. Believers are to rejoice, give thanks, follow the Holy Spirit, and abstain from evil activities.

A dysfunctional family is a difficult thing to watch. When people do not get along, when marriages crumble, and when kids are on drugs or involved in all kinds of vices, it becomes clear that the family is on the verge of collapse. In the same way a church family can be in sinful dysfunction as well. Throughout church history there have been church splits over major and minor issues that have damaged the testimony of the church. In many churches disunity seems to be the rule rather than the exception. For those who know their Bibles, these things ought not to be.

When pressures come and people are squeezed, what comes out is what is on the inside. Paul understood that the pressures the church at Thessalonica faced would cause them to be tempted to fight among themselves. Therefore he gives them instruction on how to live in harmony in the church.

Proper Attitude toward Church Leaders (5:12–13a)

The apostle begins this section teaching on the proper relationship church members should have to their church leaders. He makes a "request" (*erōtaō*) of the Thessalonians, pleading with them to have the right attitude. Unlike in 4:1, Paul appears to use the word to make a simple request without emphasizing his own authority.[1] The apostle does not directly say what occasioned this exhortation. Some suggest it had something to do with people who refused to work, whom Paul indicts in 2 Thessalonians 3:10.[2]

Paul's exhortation starts with the need for proper *appreciation*. He wants them to "appreciate those who diligently labor among you" (5:12). In context this refers to church leaders. The KJV rendering to "know them" may be closer to the mark than "appreciate those." The Greek word is *oida*, which leads to the interpretation of Paul's thought here as the "realization . . . of how much others are laboring among you."[3] If the rank and file members of the Thessalonian assembly adopted an adversarial attitude toward their leaders, the lack of unity would be devastating.

Paul identifies church leaders in three ways. First, "they are those who diligently labor among you" (5:12). The kind of labor spoken of is "diligent" toil or work that is done until someone is weary. It is important to note that the leaders labor *among* the people, not over them in some ownership capacity. This neither diminishes the oversight function of leaders, as will be shown below, nor does it make everyone in the assembly a leader. However, Paul has already bragged on the *entire church* as hard workers for the cause of Christ (1:3). The leaders were part of that mix as partners in ministry with the entire local body.

Second, the apostle describes church leaders as those who "have charge over you in the Lord" (5:12). The word for "have charge over" (*proistamenous*) literally means to stand before the group. The general thought is that the leader rules or gives direction. It is the concept of oversight. However, the word sometimes carries the notion of caring for someone or something. This idea would not preclude but perhaps go beyond the thought of ruling and oversight. Though not mentioned directly in the Thessalonian epistles, this must be a reference to the elders of the church. The Bible uses three distinct words concerning the rulers of the church. These are brought together in Acts 20:17–28 where the Scripture uses the words "elders," "overseers," and "shepherd" (which here is the verb form for "pastor") to refer to the same office. The word "elder" speaks of the character of the man. "Overseer" defines his function of oversight and administration of church affairs. "Shepherd" or "pastor" represents the nurturing and protective relationship he must bear with the people as he ministers to them. Perhaps all three are in the apostle's mind when he says they "have charge over you." Also, Paul adds the qualifier "in the Lord" when giving this portrayal of the oversight of church leaders. This probably helps to prevent the impression that the leaders somehow possessed inherent authority of their own accord. Their oversight function is proscribed by the Lord Himself for the benefit of all.

Third, Paul depicts church leaders as those who "give you instruction" (5:12). The term *nouthetountas* is used only by Paul in the New Testament, including when Luke records Paul's farewell sermon to the elders of Ephesus (Acts 20:31). This instruction comes as admonition and warning, which carries the idea of "putting sense into the heads of people."[4] Leon Morris, in referring to the word, notes: "While its tone is brotherly, it is big-brotherly. There is often the notion of some tie between the admonisher and the admonished, and there is the thought of blame attaching to some wrongdoing that is being rebuked."[5] Therefore, to admonish or warn people is a difficult business. People do not like to be told they are wrong or to be warned. But this was and is the task of pastors and, in some cases, the job of the entire church (see 5:14). Paul's request is that the people in the church follow the admonition and instruction and not rebel against it.

In addition to appreciating the work of church leaders, Paul tells the Thessalonian believers to "esteem them very highly" (5:13). The word *esteem* (*hēgeisthai*) means to consider, think, or regard. Church leaders are to be thought of in the highest regard with a proper attitude. One can easily see how this must be true for church leaders to be appreciated as requested in 5:12. The expression "very highly" (*huperekperissou*) is the strongest way to compare something (5:13)—meaning "beyond all measure." The term forces the readers to treat church leaders in an extremely high position of respect. Paul adds two qualifiers to explain how this is to be done. First, he says they are to be esteemed highly "in love." While love is to be shown to all, leaders are to be the special focus of love in the congregation. The reason for this is given next, thus providing the second qualification: leaders are to be highly esteemed and loved "because of their work" (5:13). It is not that they are to be treated like royalty for their sake as if they are worshiped. No, because of the strategic and difficult nature of their ministry, they are to be shown the respect that is due their office and calling. One is reminded of Hebrews 13:17: "Obey your leaders, and submit to them; for they keep watch over your souls, as those who will give an account. Let them do this with joy and not with grief, for this would be unprofitable for you." The work for Christ and the church are the most important work on planet Earth. Therefore, the church should show proper appreciation for those who lead them: "The ropes that bind Christians together should not be simply a nod of approval or casual recognition but a deep and meaningful holy affection. To harbor such feelings requires the work of the Holy Spirit within that brings forth honest appreciation."[6]

Proper Attitude and Actions toward Others (5:13b–15)

After dealing with a proper attitude toward church leaders, Paul now shifts to focus on the church itself. How are members to view themselves? How are they to react to one another? How do they deal with different situations? His first statement is simple to understand—"Live in peace with one another" (5:13b). The verb translated "live in peace" (*eireneuete*) is a rare word appearing four times in the New Testament, three times by Paul. In addition to this occurrence, Paul tells the Corinthian church to "be like-minded, live in peace; and the God of love and peace shall be with you" (2 Cor. 13:11). He further tells the Romans to "be at peace with all men" (Rom. 12:18). Such thoughts are once again grounded in the teachings of Jesus. He told his followers, "Have salt in yourselves, and be at peace with one another" (Mark 9:50). To live in peace means to live without quarreling. It does not mean the absence of all disputes, but it surely means that disagreement does not characterize the nature of the relationship among believers. This is the apostle's first goal for the Thessalonians.

In the next verse, the apostle gives four short commands to encourage and counsel the Thessalonian saints to the right behavior and thoughts. First, they are to "admonish the unruly" (5:14). *Admonish* is the same word as that used for "give you instruction" back in 5:12. It bears here also the meaning of confrontation. The term "unruly" (*ataktous*) as an adjective occurs only here in the New Testament. It describes a man as insubordinate, disorderly, and undisciplined. Paul uses the related adverb, meaning "in an unruly manner," in 2 Thessalonians 3:6 and 11, where he spends much time discussing people who live that way. In that context those who live in an unruly manner are those who live in idleness with no discipline. They are not hard workers. The unruly were those whose lives needed to be placed in order. Such disorderly people in the church were "those who were out of step with the direction everyone else was headed. . . . They may have been unsupportive because they did not care, or because they were angry, rebellious, and contentious. Such people, if not dealt with, tend to become bitter."[7]

The second command Paul gives the Thessalonian believers in 5:14 is to "encourage the fainthearted." "Fainthearted" is the compound of two words—"little" and "soul." This combination comes out in its meaning as "little-souled" or "little-hearted." In other words, it describes the person who is faint-hearted or discouraged, perhaps easily discouraged. Paul uses the term to depict those who lose heart or do not have courage. The stronger among the brethren were to assist those in the church who were weak-hearted. The expression "encourage" (*paramuthoumenoi*) is a narrowly defined word meaning to comfort or cheer the heart (cf. 2:11). As stated earlier, this would be extremely appropriate in light of the persecution familiar at Thessalonica. Some of the believers at Thessalonica would need the strongest of encouragement since they would be sorely tempted to give up and quit on their Christian experience. The persecutions and afflictions they were facing were probably causing great discouragement. Therefore the more courageous among them would be needed to help the weak.

The third command Paul issues in 5:14 is for the Thessalonian saints to "help the weak." The word "weak" (*asthenōn*) is the basic word for ill or sick when applied to the physical realm. Some interpreters see the word as imprecise and referring to those who were without moral, spiritual, physical, or economic strength.[8] In light of the context here, it is doubtful that the apostle is telling the Thessalonians to tend the physically ill. While Paul does on occasion use the term that way (see 1 Cor. 11:30), most of the time he uses the word to speak of some form of moral weakness, such as weak faith (1 Cor. 9:22) or a weak conscience (1 Cor. 8:7). So it is here. All of the other commands in the verse apply to the spiritual realm. Thus the word here must refer to a weakness in faith. Even though as a whole the church had done well in the matter of strong faith (1:3), Paul knew that not everyone in the congregation stood at the same level in their strength of faith. The term "help" (*antechesthe*) is used by Paul in Titus 1:9 to refer to "*holding fast* the faithful word." Here it is individuals who need to be held fast or upheld or helped. The expression "help the weak" in this way is virtually synonymous with the phrase "encourage the fainthearted," which occurs immediately before it.

The fourth and final command of 5:14 is for the believers at Thessalonica to "be patient with all men." The expression "be patient" (*macrothumeite*) implies a willingness to wait, that is, be longsuffering toward someone. The command is for believers to be this way toward *all*. While this probably should not be limited to all within the assembly of believers, it certainly should start among God's people. The idea is to be longsuffering and to endure the missteps of the others in the church (and without the church). This would require endurance on their part, but it would produce a peaceful church and harmonious relations. They would be following the example of the Lord who certainly has been longsuffering with His people down through time (Exod. 34:6; Ps. 86:15; Rom. 3:25). By being longsuffering, or literally, long-tempered, they would also exemplify the Christian graces and fruit of the Spirit (1 Cor. 13:4–5; Gal. 5:22).

The last issue that Paul deals with in this section on attitude and actions toward others is the subject of vengeance. He teaches the Thessalonians to "see that no one repays another with evil for evil" (5:15). The word "see" (*orate*) carries here the idea of "see to it." Thus it is a way of making imperative what is being said. The term "repays" (*apodō*) means "to give back, return, render, or recompense." It can apply to *repaying* with a bad undertone (2 Tim. 4:4) or with a good connotation (2 Tim. 4:8). The word "evil" in this context carries the idea of doing harm to someone else, a temptation the Thessalonians would no doubt face in the midst of severe oppression. The expression "evil for evil" reminds one of the identical teaching of Paul found in Romans 12:17: "Never pay back evil for evil to anyone." As Bruce notes, this is "basic Christian teaching," which goes back to the instruction of Christ (see Matt. 5:39–48).[9] Vengeance is not the Christian way. Especially as the church faced persecution from without, it did not need any fighting on the inside.

While Christians are to avoid vengeance, on the positive side they are to "seek after that which is good for one another" (5:15). The idea of "seeking after" (*diōkete*) means "to run after, pursue, or strive" for something. What needs to be pursued is what is good; it is not the abstract notion that is in view, but "that which is helpful and good to others" in concrete action.[10] The fact that Paul exhorts the Thessalonians "*always* seek after that which is good" rules out any exceptions. At the personal level vengeance is never an option for the believer. By laying aside any vengeance, church members remember harmony and the higher standards of Christ are fulfilled: "In order to throttle human nature, the Law called for an 'eye for eye, tooth for tooth' (Exod. 21:24). The Jews abused this letter of the Law and they used the Law to take revenge upon each other. But Christ set forth a higher standard when He said, 'But whoever slaps you on your right cheek, turn to him the other also' (Matt. 5:39b)."[11] Paul encourages the believers at Thessalonica to treat "one another," that is, other believers, with this higher Christlike standard. However, he also expands the teaching—"for all men"—so that the universal nature of this behavior would not be lost on the Thessalonians. In the teaching of this verse, Paul is in agreement with his apostolic brother Peter—"not returning evil for evil, or insult for insult, but giving a blessing instead" (1 Pet. 3:9).

Various Instructions (5:16–22)

The next set of verses features clear commands, mostly short and to the point. The presentation comes across as a bit choppy, as if Paul randomly listed some thoughts as they came into his mind. However, at closer scrutiny, all of the guidelines are necessary if the church is to maintain a spirit of unity and harmony in its midst.

Rejoicing in the Lord. The first of these is the command to "Rejoice always" (5:16). The idea of rejoicing is a frequent one in the Bible. To rejoice is to be filled with gladness and cheerfulness as opposed to sadness and melancholy. It would be natural not to rejoice in the face of the severe persecutions the Thessalonians encountered, but Paul nonetheless gives it as a command. This is as it should be and is everywhere confirmed throughout the Bible. Praise and rejoicing were the battle cry of Israel when facing Moab and Ammon. King Jehoshaphat sought the Lord and organized them for rejoicing to face the battle, and they were victorious (2 Chron. 20:20–23). Nehemiah told the people of Israel not to be grieved, "for the joy of the LORD is your strength" (Neh. 8:10). The psalmists gave voice to choruses that have served as the songbook for the people of God down through the ages, with many emphasizing joy and strength in the Lord (Pss. 27:13–14; 145–150). Paul encouraged the church at Philippi to "Rejoice in the Lord always" (Phil. 4:4), the identical command to the one here. Earlier in his first epistle to the Thessalonians, Paul had told them that he was rejoicing greatly because of them. Now he tells them to join him in the exercise of gladness along with him.

The present tense of the imperative implies that the rejoicing should be an ongoing attitude and action on the part of the Thessalonians (5:16). This idea is reinforced by the insistence that it is to be done *always*. Such a thought was probably a bit strange to the Thessalonians in the light of their current predicament of oppression. Is it really possible to rejoice in the midst of a severe and discouraging environment and daily attack? Paul is not promising or asking them never to have a discouraging thought. However, the Thessalonians were very well aware of the story of Paul and Silas singing with joy in the Philippian jail (Acts 16:25) just prior to their visit to Thessalonica. Morris comments on this verse (and its preceding context) that "the emphasis is on the truth that by and large the way of Christians is a happy way. Their spiritual resources are so great that earthly things cannot disturb their composure, and they go on their way with a song in their hearts."[12]

Praying without ceasing. The apostle goes on to exhort the Thessalonians to "pray without ceasing" (5:17). The concept of prayer occurs in Paul's New

Testament letters about fifty times. The specific idea of prayer is simply to speak to God. The qualifier "without ceasing" (*adialeiptōs*) means to unceasingly or constantly do something. This word is used only by Paul in the New Testament. Of its four occurrences, three are in 1 Thessalonians. In both of the earlier passages in the epistle where Paul talks about doing something constantly or without ceasing, he mentions that he was constantly giving thanks in prayer to God for the Thessalonians (1:2; 2:13). Thus in 5:17 he is merely inviting the believers to follow his apostolic example, although he emphasizes praying in general and not just the giving of thanks.

What does it mean to pray without ceasing? It surely does not mean that an individual must always remain in a posture of prayer. The idea of continual prayer implies something deeper. It is not "prayer that prevails without any interruption, but prayer that continues whenever possible."[13] Such prayer as Paul envisions involves an unbroken fellowship with God that can and will go to Him at a moment's notice due to need or love in spite of the circumstances of a busy day. Thus the concept requires a lifestyle of fellowship with God so that the believer will not have anything hindering that communication (cf. Eph. 6:18). This teaching, as in the case of so many others found in Paul's writings, proves the apostle's grounding in the teaching of Jesus (Luke 18:1).

Thanking God for everything. Some verses in the Bible give clear reference to what constitutes the will of God. Paul dealt with such a statement about the will of God and sexual purity in 4:3. Now we find another specific statement about the will of God concerning the attitude of thanksgiving: "in everything give thanks; for this is God's will for you in Christ Jesus" (5:18). The phrase "in everything" means in every circumstance of life and applies to every believer for all times in his or her life. The command is based on the fact that the Thessalonians were "in Christ Jesus." This may imply that gratitude comes partly from knowing we are identified with our Messiah.[14]

Paul did not ask the church at Thessalonica to do something he was not willing to do. To give thanks in everything followed the pattern that Paul himself had given in his own life toward the church (1:2–3; 3:9). No matter what their problems, afflictions, trials, troubles, or persecutions, they could cry out to God and give thanks. This attitude was made possible only through the work of the Holy Spirit as He filled their lives (Eph. 5:18–21).

However, Paul's example would not necessarily eliminate the difficulty of giving thanks in all things or in every circumstance. Is it right to thank God for our sins? Would it be correct to thank God for all disasters? Just what is the content of the thanksgiving that is meant by the apostle? Even if the desire would be there for the Thessalonians and all believers, there is still the question of what reasons gratitude is offered. Martin argues well when he says, "Paul never instructed the church to thank God for evil events but to thank God that even in evil times and circumstances our hope remains, and God continues to work in our lives (Rom. 8:28)."[15] Beale tackles the question with more detail: "True, we do not thank God for bad events narrowly viewed in and of themselves, but we should thank him for such events as they are viewed in the 'wide-angle lens' as part of his plan to sanctify us and to glorify himself."[16] In the end believers should not thank God for sin or evil and should hate evil that is found in any event or behavior. However, Christians can by faith have a bird's-eye view of all of life that allows them to thank God for the big picture in spite of any evil events or intentions, including their own, that unfortunately seep into life's story.

It is interesting to note that the last three commands of Paul—to rejoice, pray, and give thanks (5:16–18)—have some connections between them. Rejoicing and expressing gratitude seem to be cousin concepts. If a person shows gratitude, rejoicing seems to be taking place. In addition, as we have already seen, Paul articulated his own thanksgiving in the context of prayer. Prayer seems to be a natural undertaking in which to demonstrate both joy and gratitude. Finally, in all three of the commands, the apostle calls for an ongoing vigilance—"rejoice *always*," "pray *without ceasing*," "*in everything* give thanks." All three of these actions (rejoicing, praying, and giving thanks) are to be part of the characteristic practice of believers that help them to rise above the potentially discouraging circumstances of life that emerge in a fallen world.

Quenching the Spirit. The next command in the apostle's list is "Do not quench the Spirit" (5:19). "Quench" (*sbennute*) means "to extinguish, put out, stifle, smother, or suppress." Paul uses the same term when he presses the Ephesians to take up "the shield of faith with which you will be able to extinguish all the flaming missiles of the evil one" (Eph. 6:16). In Ephesians believers must suppress Satan's work in their lives. In 1 Thessalonians 5:19 believers must not suppress God's work through the Spirit. What God is trying to do in their hearts they must allow.

Now precisely what aspect of the Spirit's ministry the Thessalonians might be stifling or have the potential of smothering is not mentioned by the apostle in this terse exhortation of five words in English. Some have considered the idea that the problem in Thessalonica was the opposite of that in Corinth. In Corinth Paul had to deal with excesses involving the manifestations of the Spirit, particularly in the area of tongues (1 Cor. 12–14). Perhaps in Thessalonica he was forced to deal with an assembly that was too reserved in these matters and needed to be more accepting of outward workings of the presence of the Holy Spirit.[17] In favor of this view would be the fact that the next verse (5:20) tells them not to despise prophetic utterances, which could be a reference to a manifestation of the Spirit. However, the work of the Spirit is much broader in Paul's overall New Testament teaching, and the Thessalonian verse is too sparse of content to go in that direction with any confidence. Since sanctification is also in the context (5:23), it could be that other passages such as Ephesians 5:18–21 and Romans 8 need to be invoked as aids in piecing together a possible interpretation of Paul's meaning. Thus a prohibition of quenching the Spirit in this light would entail a general appeal by the apostle Paul asking the Thessalonians to allow the Spirit to have his way in all aspects of their lives in which He is working. In this light 5:19 would be a prerequisite for Christian growth. Lewis Sperry Chafer notes that a "Christian is a Christian because he is rightly related to Christ; but 'he that is spiritual' is spiritual because he is rightly related to the Spirit, in addition to his relation to Christ in salvation."[18] Understood in this light, a prohibition of quenching the Spirit is a positive assertion to stoke the flames of right Christian living aided by the Holy Spirit.

Despising prophetic utterances. Next the apostle gives another negative command to the church—"do not despise prophetic utterances" (5:20). The word "despise" (*exoutheneite*) means "to set down as of no account, to set at naught, to reject with contempt."[19] An example of it elsewhere in the New Testament is when Herod treated Jesus with *contempt* (Luke 23:11). Usually in Paul's letters the expression "prophetic utterance" (i.e., prophecy) refers to direct revelation from God that is given to an individual. This was a spiritual gift that Paul possessed and exercised (2 Cor. 12:7). In the early church during the time of the apostles, a believer with this gift would bring forth a declaration from God that would be tested as to its genuineness (1 Cor. 14:23–40). Such examination and approval were necessary, which may be the point of the next verse (5:21). Paul's main thought is to encourage the Thessalonians to be open to such revelations from God given in their midst, probably through their own members.

The appropriateness of the use of prophetic utterances in modern times is, of course, a highly debated topic in Christendom. There does seem to be something unique about manifestations of the Spirit with respect to the apostles (2 Cor. 12:12). Although others besides the apostles practiced various manifestations of the Spirit, it seems that only apostles could actually grant to others the ability to perform the manifestations of the Spirit (e.g., Acts 8:14–19; Rom. 1:11). Since the apostolic office ceased at the close of the apostolic age near the end of the first century, there was no one who could give such abilities to others. In addition, Beale comments with application about the connection between the gift of apostleship and that of prophet: "If the gift of apostleship ceased by the end of the first century, then it is possible that the gift of prophet likewise came to an end. If this were the case, which is greatly debated, then it would emphasize all the more that the point of 5:19–22 for the modern church is that it guard the truth of prophetic scriptural revelation and reject false teachings purportedly grounded on this revelation."[20] His point is, if there is no direct prophetic revelation from God today, then only by way of application can we use these verses (especially v. 20) for the church today. The revelation we do have directly from God is in the Bible, which we should vigorously exposit and defend against all deceivers. However, the verses are written to a first-century audience for whom the manifestations of the Spirit were still a reality and should be interpreted in that manner. Those who are cessationists (those who believe the manifestations of the gifts of the Spirit have ceased for the remainder of the church age) should not be accused of violating this verse. When Paul commanded the Thessalonians not to despise prophetic utterances, such speech was still available for a response.

Examining all things. Paul now says, "But examine everything carefully" (5:21a). This command has a relationship in the text to what went before it and what comes after it. The Thessalonians were not to despise prophetic utterances (5:20), yet neither were they to accept all claims to prophetic utterance. Instead, they were to study and check out any claims being made. The next phrase—"hold fast to that which is good" (5:21b)—is the expected action that should result after everything is examined.

The word "examine" (*dokimazete*) is the usual word for "testing" or "proving." Paul uses it in 2:4 to express the ideas that God both tested the apostolic team and approved them. Whether dealing with prophetic utterance or preaching in general, there is a tendency toward substitution of our own thoughts in place of God's revelation. Thus any subjective feelings or thoughts must be carefully weighed, then as well as now, because "the temptation to put the ideas of men on an equal footing with the Word of God is still present."[21] Paul continues his penchant for all-encompassing words in this section, when he says that the Thessalonians should examine *everything*. Thus every word preached, proclaimed, or prophesied was to be put to the test and examined. If it did not agree with already given revelation in Scripture, it was not to be followed (cf. Acts 17:10–15).

Holding fast the good. The apostle tells the Thessalonians to "hold fast to that which is good" (5:21b). He has just used the expression "that which is good" for something that they were to seek in their relationships with each other (5:15). Here the expression "that which is good" may refer to various teachings or alleged revelations that have been determined to be valid as a result of the examination of all things according to the previous words (5:21a). Taken in this way, the idea is that once the message is proven correct it can be embraced.[22] The phrase "hold fast" (*katechete*) means "to retain or keep or hold on to" something. It is used by Paul in speaking of "holding fast the word" he preached (1 Cor. 15:2). The Thessalonian believers, once truth was clearly known, were to embrace it completely. If the entire expression is taken to go with what follows ("abstain from every form of evil"), the statement is more general, as it provides a contrast to wrong behavior. Paul would then be instructing the Thessalonians to hold fast to good things in the sense of right behavior, something he has already told them to do.

Abstaining from evil. The last appeal or exhortation given by Paul in this section is to "abstain from every form of evil" (5:22). Three key words make up this verse: "abstain," "form," and "evil." "Abstain" (*apechesthe*) means to hold at a distance or keep away from something. The word was used earlier by Paul when he told the Thessalonians to abstain from sexual immorality (4:3). The idea is that Christians should want to keep their distance from evil.

The second word, "from" (*eidous*), "points to the external form in which evil presents itself."[23] It is not a correct interpretation or application to suggest that the verse carries with it the idea that Christians should avoid appearing to be evil as if appearances are what is meant. Even if the visible form is meant by the word, it is the actual evil that is to be avoided based on this passage. Otherwise, Paul might be teaching contrary to the example of Jesus who at times did things that appeared to those around him to be wrong (cf. Matt. 11:19). The point of the verse is not to set some legalistic barrier, which in this case would be quite vague. The adjective "every" yields a broadness and universality to Paul's injunction as various expressions have done throughout this section of the epistle. Christians are to have absolutely nothing to do with any form of evil. The final major word, "evil" (*ponērou*) is a strong term that may stand in contrast to "that which is good" in 5:21.

Study Questions

1. What is your attitude toward the pastors in your church? Is it a biblical attitude? If not, how can you change to match what God wants?
2. How can you encourage others in your church to be at peace?

3. Are you a rejoicing Christian? How can a believer rejoice in hard times?
4. How does an individual pray without ceasing? Is this difficult to do?
5. How difficult is it to give thanks in everything? Do you find it difficult to obey this exhortation? Why or why not?
6. What does it mean to quench the Spirit? What are the ways a Christian can quench the Spirit?

CHAPTER 10

The Faithfulness of God
1 Thessalonians 5:23–28

Preview:

Paul prays that the God of peace will allow the Thessalonian believers to stand before Him one day fully set apart to Him. The apostle fully expects God to be exhaustive in his preparation of individual saints, leaving no part of the believer's life untouched. This hope can be guaranteed because of the faithful character of God.

A benediction is defined as an expression of good wishes or the invocation of a blessing, especially the short blessing with which public worship is concluded. It could be also be the blessing bestowed at the end of a letter.

Paul gives a closing benediction in most of his writings (e.g., Rom. 16:24–27; 1 Cor. 16:23–24; 2 Cor.13:11–14; 2 Thess. 3:17–18). 1 Thessalonians is no exception (1 Thess. 5:23–28).

The God of Peace (5:23)

The apostle begins his benedictory prayer focusing on "the God of peace" (5:23). One must ask, however, what aspect of peace does the apostle have in mind? Does Paul intend the reader to understand the reconciling work of God for humankind (2 Cor. 5:18–21) that appears to be applied especially to the believer at the moment of conversion? This is a peace with God that is closely related to justification (Rom. 5:1). This would be a legal or position al peace. Paul explained this to the Colossian church with these words—

"through Him to reconcile all things to Himself, having made peace through the blood of His cross; through Him, I say, whether things on earth or things in heaven" (Col. 1:20).

Another option is that the apostle wants the Thessalonians to think about the aspect of peace that is God's working in the heart of believers as they live day to day in this complex and testy world. This aspect of peace would be the "peace of God" which God gives along life's journey. Paul encouraged the Philippian church to lay aside anxieties and to seek this kind of peace: "Be anxious for nothing, but in everything by prayer and supplication with thanksgiving let your requests be made known to God. And the peace of God, which surpasses all comprehension, shall guard your hearts and your minds in Christ Jesus. . . . The things you have learned and received and heard and seen in me, practice these things; and the God of peace shall be with you (Phil. 4:6–9).

F. F. Bruce notes that there is another option. The word "peace" (*eirēnēs*) could refer to the "sum total of gospel blessings," with the phrase "God of peace" "pointing to God as the source of them all."[1] Even so, Bruce concludes that, if this were so, the particular application that goes with the larger context would still be part of Paul's meaning in the use of the expression.[2] In other words, the God of all peace who grants a form of peace in justification, sanctification, and glorification would be by nature and capability able to answer the prayer given in the verse. While the apostle may not be precise in his use of the expression "God of peace," the context does show that Paul's main concern is not the peace of justification but ongoing sanctification and ultimate presentation to Christ at his return.

In this light, while peace was a common theme in all of Paul's epistles and was already addressed in 1:1, it would have a special meaning to the Thessalonian believers who were facing stern persecution. The experience of peace would be a sincere desire on their part as they faced hardships and trials. To remember that the God they had received through Jesus Christ is a God characterized by peace would be of great comfort to them. The text goes on to say "the God of peace *Himself*." In the original language the reference to *Himself* stands at the first of the sentence and emphasizes that only God brings about the necessary peace and sanctification that Paul encourages. This peace of God is not a legal peace, but an emotional peace or assurance in the midst of trials and troubles. Believers are to deal with their anxieties by bringing prayers of thanksgiving with their petitions to God. This kind of peace is beyond human comprehension and can come only by the power of God through prayer. The benediction of Paul at the end of 1 Thessalonians is that kind of prayer.

A Complete Sanctification (5:23)

The goal of Paul's prayer for the Thessalonians is that God would "sanctify you entirely" (5:23). "Sanctify" (*hagiasai*) has as its basic meaning "to set apart from sin, or to consecrate." The term *sanctified* is synonymous with the word *holy* and has many applications in the Scriptures just like the word *peace* discussed above. Sanctification can refer to the initial salvation experience (justification) as sinners are set apart for God and from sin *positionally* (Heb. 10:10–17; 1 Pet. 1:2). It can also refer to the *practice* of believers as they live apart from sin in their day-to-day lives (1 Pet. 1:14–16). The third way *sanctify* can be used is of our future deliverance from sin when the Lord returns and deals with the curse of sin (Rom. 8:18–30; Phil. 3:20–21).

The particular thought behind the term *sanctify* is partly determined by its earlier use in the book and partly by the immediate context. Previously, sanctification was discussed in terms of day-to-day life in the avoidance of immoral behavior (4:3–5). In addition, the next part of the verse (Paul's prayer for preservation) lends itself to a view of life that leads up to the second coming of Christ. Thus it is doubtful that the apostle is emphasizing any positional truth about sanctification, but is praying for results in the Christian experience of the Thessalonians from now and until Jesus comes.

The word "entirely" (*holoteleis*) occurs only here in the New Testament. It comes from a "compound of *holos*, 'whole, entire,' and *telos*, 'end.' Its basic connotation is 'wholly attaining the end, reaching the intended goal,' hence has the force of no part being left unreached. The prayer is that the divine sanctification may extend to every part of their being, leaving no area untouched by the pervasive power of divine holiness."[3] In other words, it means "completely" or "totally."

Some theological viewpoints have used this particular expression of entire sanctification to assert that it is possible in the Christian life to attain to a certain status of perfection.[4] In a sense, this would involve an eradication of sinful tendencies within the individual believer or at least the elimination of willful sin. Others have not gone so far but have suggested that the terminology of entire sanctification in this context does suggest such a pervasive influence of the Spirit's work that the individual believer is completely transfigured as to his or her character: "it is the full suffusion by the Holy Spirit, in which the believer's continuous abiding in Christ is answered by the Holy Spirit's continuous renewing of the believer's moral nature—heart, mind, soul, contemplations, reactions, aspirations, aims and urges. It is the fullest present *abiding* in Christ, accompanied by the fullest spiritual *abounding* in Christ, and resulting in truest *character-likeness* to Christ."[5] It is not clear that Paul means by the term to invite speculation about details involving the nature and means of sanctification. Furthermore, the verse overall seems to suggest that he desires progress in the present experience of the Thessalonians, but their entire sanctification may await the second coming of Christ. At any rate Paul wanted the Thessalonians to experience God's best in their lives now and did not want them to settle for anything less. His prayer is an expression of that desire.

Preservation at the Coming of Christ (5:23)

Paul continues his benediction—"and may your spirit and soul and body be preserved complete" (5:23). A question often raised by interpreters of this verse is, "Does Paul view man as a three-part being or a two-part being?" Some hold to the dichotomist view that man should be viewed as composed of two parts, the material and the immaterial. Others, because of this verse, support the idea that man is made up of three parts. This is called the trichotomist or tripartite view. Scholars have debated this throughout church history. Some believe that the tripartite view comes from Greek philosophy and has been read into the New Testament. As Mal Couch points out, the

> early Church Fathers, however, also spoke of body, mind, and spirit. But in no way were the prophets and apostles simply copying worldly thinking. It is more likely that the Gentile world, in far-off ancient times, had been touched by the truth of the Old Testament Scriptures. Too, before one rejects what seems so plain in Paul's writing, one must remember that these descriptions of human nature are found in the Old Testament. The wisdom and revelation of ancient Hebrew Scripture probably spread out and influenced, even in a small degree, the Mediterranean civilizations.[6]

According to the trichotomist view, man is comprised of spirit (God-consciousness), soul (self-consciousness, or personality), and body (world-consciousness, or the physical). Spirit and soul would be the higher and lower sides of the immaterial part of man. One other Scripture is often cited to support this: "For the word of God is living and active and sharper than any two-edged sword, and *piercing as far as the division of soul and spirit,* of both joints and marrow, and able to judge the thoughts and intentions of the heart" (Heb. 4:12).

However, the dichotomist view is probably the best way to describe the actual constitution of a human being. Among the arguments for a dichotomy of man are the following: (1) God breathed into man just one principle of life (Gen. 2:7). (2) "Soul" and "spirit" are used interchangeably throughout the Bible (Matt. 20:28 ["life"]; 27:50). (3) "Body and soul" are said to constitute the whole of man (Matt. 10:28). (4) The consciousness of man can testify of a material and an immaterial part but cannot discriminate between soul and spirit.[7] One can also point to similar passages, such as Luke 10:27, where four aspects of man are mentioned (heart, soul, strength, mind) to show that statements such as these may not be dealing with the basic constituent elements of man. Instead, such passages may give functional aspects of man. Of course, when Christ comes, glorified humans will exist holistically without any possibility of separation of their parts. In the end there is still much mystery as to the constitution of human beings.

It is important to remember that Paul's intent here is not to teach a full-orbed theology of the constitution of man. Whatever view is taken, it is clear that Paul is praying that the entire person be "preserved" (*tērēthein*). Often Paul uses the term to mean "keep from" or "maintain." For example, he tells Timothy to "keep yourself free from sin" (1 Tim. 5:22). There the idea is that Timothy would keep himself from sexual immorality but also that he would maintain, remain in, or continue the practice of purity. However, in the context of 1 Thessalonians 5:23, the word carries with it the idea of protection. Furthermore, this protection will be made "complete" (*holoklēron*). The only other occurrence of the word in the New Testament is found in James 1:4 where the term is translated "perfect" but is coupled with another word meaning "complete." By these terms Paul is making clear in his prayer that he is asking God to preserve intact and undamaged every facet of their lives.

Consequently, Paul was confident that God would preserve the believers at Thessalonica "without blame." The expression here (*amemptōs*) is "the same word archeologists have found on Christian tombs from ancient Thessalonica."[8] It was used in 2:10 to describe his own behavior in the matter of working hard in the midst of the saints at Thessalonica. In 5:23 the apostle does not specify in detail the means that God will use to preserve believers in this blameless state. The emphasis in the previous two verses forces one to consider that progressive sanctification is in view. The believer's growth in practical, everyday holiness would then be included in the apostolic prayer of the passage.

However, Paul's understanding elsewhere is that some Christians will not automatically continue to grow as believers (e.g., 2 Cor. 11:28–30), although his wish for this not to be so for the Thessalonians is evident. Coupled with the somewhat unconnected nature of the list of exhortations at the end of 1 Thessalonians 5, it is probably best to see Paul as pointing believers ahead to their ultimate status before God, although it is preceded by the journey of the Christian walk. This would fit the end-time focus that dominates both of Paul's epistles to the Thessalonians. In particular, the coming of the Lord is once again mentioned as it has been in every chapter of 1 Thessalonians (1:10;

2:17–20; 3:13; 4:13–18; 5:23). This coming is the same as the appearing when Jesus will rapture the church before the Day of the Lord's wrath or tribulation period (1 Thess. 4:13–18). Therefore, one must be careful not to focus on Christian growth as the *only means* to produce the ultimate blamelessness that is implied in the verse. The body is also included. An entire blamelessness of the body can only take place when the day of resurrection arrives and there is glorification of the believer.[9]

The Faithfulness of God (5:24)

The apostle now calls attention to the whole purpose of the benediction. While Paul is certainly wanting to pray for their sanctification and preservation (5:23), he knows the only reason this is possible is God's faithfulness: "Faithful is He who calls you, and He also will bring it to pass." Paul uses the word *faithful* in his writings to speak of the faithfulness of people (ten times), the faithfulness of the Word of God (once), and the faithfulness of God (six times). The term refers to what or who is trustworthy. It is a description of a person who will always be there. In this verse it is God who is described in this way.

God is also portrayed as "He who calls you" (5:24). Paul had already told the Thessalonians that God had called them to sanctification and not immorality (4:7), an idea in keeping with the context here at the end of the book. This calling or summons by God to salvation covers the entire spectrum of the believer's life. In Romans 8:28–30 the apostle makes clear that those who are called are also justified and glorified, the latter term in keeping with the focus on the appearing of the Lord just mentioned in 5:23. The point that can be made strongly is that what God starts he finishes. Similarly, Paul's terse statement to the Thessalonians is that "He also will bring it to pass." The expression "bring it to pass" (*poiēsei*) means that God will accomplish what He set out to do in the lives of the Thessalonian believers. In another place the apostle summarizes well for the Philippians, "For I am confident of this very thing, that He who began a good work in you will perfect it until the day of Christ Jesus" (Phil. 1:6). This is the essence of the faithfulness of God as Paul is expressing it at the end of 1 Thessalonians. The saints can rest secure and with full assurance that God will see them through whatever it is they must face. They can face it with a holy lifestyle and victory over the world while knowing their ultimate destiny is in God's faithful hands.

Final Requests (5:25–28)

Praying for us. In the closing four verses, Paul gives some final requests and instructions for the church. The first is "Brethren, pray for us" (5:25). Some may at first consider this request odd. Morris comments on how we sometimes view the apostolic life: "It is easy to picture for ourselves Paul as a very great apostle ceaselessly occupied with his work of issuing directives to other people on how they should live out their faith, while he himself sits above the storm or calmly proceeds along on his undisturbed way."[10] Morris goes on correctly to note that such a view does not reflect the real world and Paul's actual circumstances. Paul had his own troubles and ministry needs, of which the Thessalonians were well aware. So here in the benediction, without any details, he simply asks them to pray for him.

Such prayer was something Paul frequently requested from the churches. Often he wanted his ministry of outreach to be supported in prayer (Eph. 6:19–22; Col. 4:3–4). The apostle had told them of his prayers for the Thessalonians throughout the letter (1:2; 2:13; 3:9–13) and had generally told them to pray without ceasing (5:17). Now he asks them to return the favor and pray specifically for the missionary team and presumably its success.

Greeting the brethren. Paul also tells his readers, "Greet all the brethren with a holy kiss" (5:26). The word "greet" (*aspassasthe*) can mean "to bid welcome" or "to bid farewell."[11] It is a common ending in Paul's letters, especially in Romans 16:3–16 where the term occurs sixteen times. Here the apostle does not list all of the names he wishes to greet as he did with the Romans. Instead, he includes them in a general statement that *all* of the brethren were to be included. Such a statement shows that Paul wanted no one to be left out in his greeting.

The greeting also included the familiar "holy kiss" (5:26). That this kiss is *holy* implies that no sensuality is involved. It is a special kiss made so by custom to demonstrate love among the brothers and sisters. The word *kiss* (*philēmati*) is used outside of Paul's writings in a few ways. Jesus refers positively to the kissing of his feet by the sinful woman who washed his feet with her hair (Luke 7:45). The word is used negatively of the kiss that Judas gave to Jesus to betray Him (Luke 22:48). Peter probably uses the word with the same meaning as Paul when he asks the saints to greet each other with a kiss of love. It would be hard to distinguish Peter's kiss of love from Paul's holy kiss. The other occurrences of the term are all Pauline references to the same greeting (Rom. 16:16; 1 Cor. 16:20; 2 Cor. 13:12). D. Edmond Hiebert helps to frame the idea behind the holy kiss as a Christian greeting:

> While defining its spirit, there is no indication that these words were intended to inaugurate a new Christian practice. The kiss upon the cheek was a common form of Oriental greeting among friends. . . . The custom, common in non-Christian circles, was taken over by the Christian church, but purified and sanctified. It was exchanged among believers as they assembled for worship. Apparently at this time, the sexes were segregated in the assembly, and the men kissed the men and the women the women. The kiss was exchanged on the basis of brotherly love among the members of one spiritual family.[12]

In Western culture, the closest approximation to the holy kiss would be the handshake. In many church worship times, there is a time of fellowship in which the brothers and sisters will shake hands with those around them. This is the custom that is similar to that in the Oriental nations.

Reading the letter. Paul wants the letter read by all, and he puts it in the form of an adjuration: "I adjure you by the Lord to have this letter read to all the brethren" (5:27). "Adjure" (*enorkizō*) is a strong word used only here in the New Testament. It refers to the taking of an oath and indicates the requirement the apostle of God is placing on the church. The language in certain circumstances would invoke or ask someone to place himself under oath. He wants the Thessalonians to promise, not just to him, but before God, that they will read his letter to all the brethren when they receive it. The envisioned reading is a public one where every believer would have a chance to hear it.

It is not clear if Paul is speaking in general terms or if he really does have some concern about the possibility that something or someone will prevent the reading of his letter to the entire church. We know that later he had the problem of someone potentially using his name on a letter that he did not write (2 Thess. 2:2). How early on such kinds of things were intruding into the mind of the apostle is hard to say.

Another issue in the verse is the nature of an adjuration as an oath and that it is further reinforced by the expression "by the Lord" (5:27). Has Paul not heard of the teaching of Jesus that encourages not to make oaths (Matt. 5:33–37)? Is Paul's adjuration by the Lord in violation of what Christ taught? Bruce responds, "Paul's use of adjuration need not imply that he was unaware of Jesus' ban on the use of oaths by his followers. . . . This is not a strengthening of a statement of his own by the invocation of the divine name . . . but an appeal to those addressed to act in this matter as responsible to the Lord himself."[13] Furthermore, it must be pointed out that to fault Paul here is to oversimplify the content of Jesus' teaching. Jesus was not prohibiting the making of a promise or even an appropriate use of an oath as in a court of law.

Instead, he was reacting to the flippant rules applied to such actions that were often appealed to by many rabbis in the Jewish tradition.

The grace of God. The apostle then closes where he began. In 1:1 the apostle had opened with a greeting of "grace to you." Here his closing greeting is the same: "The grace of our Lord Jesus Christ be with you" (5:28). The expression here is elevated somewhat by the use of the full name of the Lord Jesus Christ, commonly used by Paul (including fourteen times in 1 and 2 Thessalonians). In this way the conclusion of the letter "brings grace and the source of God's grace to center stage and reminds the readers that it applies to them."[14]

Study Questions

1. Do you have peace *with* God? Have you become a Christian through faith in the Lord Jesus Christ?
2. Do you have the peace *of* God? How does it differ from peace *with* God? What affects your sense of peace?
3. How many parts does a human being have? Is this an important issue? Why or why not?
4. What does it mean to be without blame at the coming of the Lord?
5. What does it mean for God to be faithful? How do we know that He is faithful? Can you list five ways that God has been faithful to you in the last year? Does God measure faithfulness the same way we do?
6. What is a holy kiss, and how could it be applied in the Western church and culture?

Section 2

The Book of 2 Thessalonians

Introduction

Background of 2 Thessalonians

Authorship

Only in recent times has the authorship of 2 Thessalonians actually and unfortunately been doubted. The internal evidence of the book itself argues strongly for Paul as the author of 2 Thessalonians on several counts: the mention of Silvanus and Timothy (1:1), the fact that the letter addresses the question of forgeries in Paul's name (2:2), and the personal identification by Paul as a benediction for the epistle (3:17). External evidence also casts its vote in favor of Paul as the author of 2 Thessalonians. Polycarp, Ignatius, and Justin (all early to mid-second-century sources) seem to know about the letter and its author. The book is in early lists of canonical books (e.g., Marcionite and Muratorian) and is also quoted by Irenaeus and other church fathers.[1] The church has traditionally received this book as from the pen of the apostle Paul and has associated it with the first letter to the Thessalonians.

It is somewhat dubious that the authenticity of 2 Thessalonians has been questioned on the basis of both its similarities to 1 Thessalonians and its differences. Apparently, in the minds of some interpreters, 2 Thessalonians is too much like 1 Thessalonians, providing a redundancy that is not fitting for the great apostle Paul.[2] D. Michael Martin, in summarizing this view but not holding it, states, "Where the letters are similar, it is argued they are too similar, indicating a likeness born of imitation, not common authorship."[3] In a rebuttal to this notion, Leon Morris comments: "It is very difficult to envisage a forger who could imitate Paul's language so very closely. Pauline words and phrases and constructions are everywhere. So are Pauline ideas. If Paul wrote 2 Thessalonians not so very long after 1 Thessalonians, it would not be surprising if sometimes words and phrases were repeated."[4] Consequently, most of the questioning of Paul's authorship of 2 Thessalonians has come from a perception of differences between 1 and 2 Thessalonians, which, in the minds of those doing the questioning, is sufficient to see two different authors.

One difference between the two epistles to the Thessalonians that has sometimes been used to argue for a different author in the second epistle is the focus in the first on a coming of the Lord before the Day of the Lord with eager waiting urged for believers (1 Thess. 4:13–18). This allegedly contradicts the focus in the second epistle on a series of signs the believers are told to anticipate (2 Thess. 2). However, several factors speak against this complaint. Some pretribulationalists note that a two-phase second coming fits extremely well with the outline of both books. It is also true that watchful language ("be alert," "thief in the night," etc.) is sometimes used elsewhere in the Bible of events that could not happen at any moment (see Rev. 16:15–16). In the end the second letter actually complements the teaching of the first. Therefore, all sensible interpreters have dropped any concerns that the two letters have different end-time scenarios. On this point there is no basis to dispute Paul's authorship of the second epistle.

Another sample of an argument based on the dissimilarity of the two books is the difference in tone between the two. The first epistle is considered more personal and warm. After all, in the first chapter of the first letter, Paul uses a lot of verbiage to tell the Thessalonians how much he thinks about them when he talks to God (1:2) and to praise them for their great faith, love, and hope (1:3ff.). This is followed by a second chapter that highlights Paul's memory of the personal encounter he had when he first came to them. By contrast, the second epistle has less personal terminology and at some points strikes a posture of hostility, such as the strongly worded statements against unruly and lazy believers that are found in the third chapter. Such differences are easy to exaggerate and abuse. There are still extremely personal statements, such as the section at the end of chapter 1 when the apostle holds them up as trophies of God's grace at the time of Christ's second coming, something to warm their hearts in light of present persecution.[5] Consequently, there are really no strong arguments for discounting Paul's authorship of 2 Thessalonians. It is better to accept the received tradition in the matter.

Date

The date of 2 Thessalonians is clearly within a few weeks or months of the penning of 1 Thessalonians. It makes little sense to see a delay in its writing until after Paul's soon visit to Macedonia stated in Acts 20:1–2. Paul would have covered the areas of concern in person at that time. Moreover, Silvanus and Timothy were with Paul only during the stay at Corinth (Acts 18:5) based on the available information.[6] Thus 2 Thessalonians was probably written in AD 50 or 51, soon after the first letter of Paul to the church. Such a conclusion is probably reinforced by the common focus on end-time events. Many of the arguments for the date of 2 Thessalonians would flow from the same chronology established for the date of 1 Thessalonians (see earlier discussion on the date of 1 Thessalonians). In addition, the sequence of the letters, that is, the issue of which came first, plays some role in deciding any particular window of time for the date of each book (see below). However, in almost any serious scheme, the dates are so close together, there really is little difference that is worth mentioning.

Sequence of 1 and 2 Thessalonians

One of the more interesting debates concerning introductory issues for 1 and 2 Thessalonians is the chronological order of the two books. While the evidence from the church fathers supports the order we have in our New Testament, some modern scholars have suggested that the order of the books should be reversed based on internal evidence in the books themselves. Second Thessalonians, on this view, was written first and followed by 1 Thessalonians. Several arguments have been put forward to justify this nontraditional conclusion.

First, the description of the timing of persecutions is thought to support a reversal of the order of the books. Persecutions mentioned in 1 Thessalonians are spoken of as in the past (1:6, 2:14–15; 3:2–4). In 2 Thessalonians the afflictions are clearly a present concern and reality for the believers (1:4–10). Hence, the first book actually follows the second in time. However, this argument is weak. In 1 Thessalonians the discussion of persecution is within a larger context of Paul's treatment of the past. Thus the context lends reason to the past frame of reference without any resort to a change in order. Paul elsewhere treats persecution as the normal and expected lot of Christians (2 Tim. 3:12). As Martin notes, "A scenario of recurring persecution in Thessalonica, if valid, would make it impossible to determine the sequence of the letters on the basis of the use of past- versus present-tense verbs describing persecution."[7]

Second, the signature of Paul in 2 Thessalonians 3:17 ("I, Paul, write this greeting with my own hand . . . ") is believed to be more appropriate for a first letter than a second, follow-up epistle. If this were true, however, why do so many other Pauline first letters in the New Testament not contain such a statement?[8]

Third, an alleged problem for the traditional order involves the fact that 1 Thessalonians deals with the issue of believers who had died. The question arises, "How can there be a problem with how to view the death of believers (1 Thess. 4:13–18) since 1 Thessalonians is written so soon after Paul makes his first converts at Thessalonica?" A later date after 2 Thessalonians, the reasoning goes, would make Paul's statements more realistic. However, this is pure conjecture. Only one death in the congregation would be necessary to raise this issue for apostolic comment. Also, it is not a stretch to see death as coming from persecution in light of the Thessalonian experience. As D. Edmond Hiebert remarks, "The acknowledged interval between the departure of the missionaries from Thessalonica and the return of Timothy with his report of affairs there provides ample time for this problem to arise."[9]

Fourth, some scholars claim that 2 Thessalonians was written first because it demonstrates less church organization than that found in 1 Thessalonians. For example, the first epistle speaks of the need to be obedient to church leaders (1 Thess. 5:12–13). The second letter does not refer to church leaders at all. Thus the conclusion is drawn that 2 Thessalonians was written first to allow for this development.[10] The assumptions here are legion and demonstrate extrabiblical attitudes that govern thinking. Does it really make sense to be dogmatic about what the apostle would or would not have said in short letters to a congregation? Perhaps there was no need to address the question of leaders in the second letter since it had already been addressed. Furthermore, it might make as much sense to see a first letter encourage the leadership, especially after Paul's abrupt departure from Thessalonica.

Similarly, it has been suggested that a view of ministry is advanced in 1 Thessalonians. In 2 Thessalonians 3:7, the believers are instructed by Paul to follow his example in behavior. In 1 Thessalonians 1:6–7, the saints at Thessalonica were already examples for others. The natural progression, therefore, goes from the second epistle to the first, not following the traditional order. However, this kind of thinking avoids careful scrutiny of the context. In the first letter, the issue is the example of conversion the Thessalonians provided. In the second letter, the issue is continuing growth by imitating the apostolic team in day-to-day behavior as those who had already embraced Christ. The progression actually fits more closely the traditional order of the books as we have them in our New Testament.[11]

Likewise, a fifth reason sometimes cited for the reversal of the two books is the general understanding that the shorter book (2 Thessalonians) must come first. In this scheme the second book chronologically (1 Thessalonians in this view) is understood as naturally giving an elaboration and expansion upon the themes of the earlier book. This reason serves as a type of summary of some of the other explanations that can be cited for the nontraditional approach. However, this view is entrapped in the worldview of evolutionary thinking. Development is seen as only in one direction, expanding rather than summarizing, streamlining, or providing further details of whatever volume. This is not at all an assured result in any area of biblical studies. Furthermore, Hiebert has pointed out that when the two books deal with the same subject matter, the content in 2 Thessalonians is slightly longer.[12] This can be seen when comparing 1 Thessalonians 4:13–5:11 with 2 Thessalonians 1:6–2:14. Therefore, the argument holds little weight.

Sixth, some interpreters think that the passages touching on the topic of idleness or loafers in each book make better sense if 2 Thessalonians was written first. Second Thessalonians 3:6–15 reads as if Paul is addressing a new issue of idleness for which a form of church discipline is necessary. Instruction on the topic of loafers is mentioned briefly, almost in passing, in 1 Thessalonians 5:14. The conclusion is drawn that the instructions of 2 Thessalonians came first and the comments in 1 Thessalonians are only a reminder of prior apostolic commands. However, the comparison or contrast is only cursory. Paul does not address loafers directly in 1 Thessalonians except through his thoughts about the "unruly," which can be a generalized statement that goes in any number of directions. Martin wisely points out that "it is also possible that a minor problem mentioned first in 1 Thessalonians escalated and became a major problem that required church discipline by the time 2 Thessalonians was written."[13] Therefore the so-called problem of idleness does not present itself as a major difficulty for the traditional order of the books.

Paul's statement in 1 Thessalonians 5:1, which implies that the believers had already been instructed about the "the times and the epochs," provides a seventh reason given to prove that 2 Thessalonians was written first. It is assumed that the end-time material recorded in the book constitutes the information that Paul says they had already received. But the text of 1 Thessalonians clearly points out that Paul had a major teaching ministry among the people (1 Thess. 2:1–13) so that oral instruction is most likely behind the statement in 1 Thessalonians 5:1. As Morris notes, "On any showing Paul spoke about the Parousia and attendant happenings during his preaching while he was yet in the city, and this is sufficient to explain any reference in 1 Thessalonians."[14] This conclusion is probably strengthened by the fact that Paul refers to the Second Coming at the end of each chapter in the first epistle. This whole area of doctrine had been a point of major exposition when Paul was with them. Consequently, there is no need to assert that 2 Thessalonians was written first to make sense of 1 Thessalonians 5:1.

Besides the above responses to those who favor the priority in time of 2 Thessalonians, a positive case can be made for 1 Thessalonians being written first. Second Thessalonians refers to a prior letter which has been written by Paul. The natural view would lend itself to see this as the first letter in the traditional order. If it is not, then an unknown letter was previously written by Paul to the Thessalonian Christians. Yet the short time frame involved makes this highly unlikely. Beyond this argument, there is clear intensification as one moves from 1 Thessalonians to 2 Thessalonians relative to the idea of persecution, the issue of the loafers, and the details about Christ's coming.[15] It could also be said that the lengthy and somewhat introductory material about Paul's visit to the church in Thessalonica cited in the first two chapters of 1 Thessalonians is more like that of a first letter, not a later epistle.[16]

Beale suggests that the arguments for both views are somewhat subjective and notes that "the two epistles mutually illumine one another."[17] Yet the evidence for the traditional order seems strong enough to agree with Hiebert that one can see clear logical progression if one accepts the traditional view of the order of the books.[18]

Purpose of 2 Thessalonians

The purpose of the book of 2 Thessalonians follows closely the discussion of the structure and argument of the book as a whole (see below). Paul addresses three major questions in his letter. First, he wants to encourage the Thessalonians in light of the continuing and severe persecution they are enduring (1:4–10). They would continue to persevere if they came to understand the larger picture of God's end-time plan in which they would overcome and be vindicated over against those who oppressed them.

Second, Paul writes to counter some identity theft. Someone had masqueraded as Paul, either by letter or prophetic message (2:2). The false teaching that the Day of the Lord had already come was put forward in his name. In this way the Thessalonians were open to being deceived (2:3). Paul wants to make sure that the believers will not be taken in by any charlatans, especially involving such important matters as those related to the Day of the Lord tribulation and the subsequent second coming of Christ to earth.

Third, the apostle wants to deal with evil men who might be in the presence of the congregation (3:2). His focus seems to be on unruly brothers in Christ (3:6) who are undisciplined (3:11). This lack of discipline is demonstrated by a poor work ethic, which is contrary to the apostolic example and teaching (3:7–11). The believers at Thessalonica were to avoid such lazy and unruly men.

In reviewing these three major questions, it is clear that two-thirds of the epistle deals with end-time issues. Paul's concern about persecution involves external pressures on the church. The other two issues, the misrepresentation concerning the Day of the Lord and the loafers in the congregation, involved internal pressures the believers must face successfully. Standing out by way of introduction is the thought that Paul's charge to oppressed Christians is not based primarily on any present reality but on future hope. The message for believers who are being persecuted is that they should take heart precisely because Jesus is coming to make all things right. A focus on the Second Advent was, in the mind of the apostle, not an emphasis that would make believers get off track in their present lives. On the contrary, it was a necessity for wholesome attitudes in troublous times.

Structure and Argument

The structure of 2 Thessalonians follows the three questions discussed above under the discussion of the purpose for the book. The three questions follow the chapter divisions.

Outline of 2 Thessalonians	
1:1–3	*Introduction*
1:4–12	*Responding to Persecution*
2:1–17	*Responding to Wrong Claims about the Day of the Lord*
3:1– 15	*Responding to Unruly Loafers in the Congregation*
3:16–18	*Concluding Benediction*

In Paul's instructions for responding to persecution, we find perhaps the most difficult section to follow. However, in the end the apostle's point has two aspects. The Thessalonians could endure their persecution because one day Christ was going to return both to judge those who were bothering them and to vindicate their place as rightful children of the living God.

In Paul's correction concerning mistaken notions of the Day of the Lord, he argues that it was impossible for the tribulation period to have begun, because certain events must happen first. First, a departure must occur, which either refers to the departure of the church in the Rapture or to a declension from the true faith (2:3). Second, the man of lawlessness (the Antichrist) must appear on the scene to be part of the tribulation period (2:3). The Antichrist cannot come on the scene until a certain restraining of sin is removed.

In Paul's admonition about unruly loafers in the congregation, he teaches the Thessalonians to "keep aloof" from such believers who are lazy and bothersome to the body of Christ (3:6, 14). This means, at the least, a refusal to eat with or give food to these weak brothers (3:10) or to associate with them (3:14). They are also to follow the apostle's own example of hard work (3:7–9).

CHAPTER 11

Encouraging the Church 2 Thessalonians 1:1–5

Preview:

Paul boasts about the enduring faith of the Thessalonians in the midst of severe persecution. Their posture toward God is evidence that they are worthy of the coming kingdom of God. Their persecutions should not be understood as evidence of God's disfavor.

Salutation (1:1–2)

The second epistle to the Thessalonians begins in much the same way as the first epistle (cf. 1 Thess. 1:1–2). The letter is said to be from Paul, Silvanus (Silas), and Timothy. The recipients are called "the church," or assembly, at Thessalonica. The church is said in the salutations of both epistles to be "in God." The details are virtually the same, giving a formulaic feel to the apostle's salutation. The complete expression is "in God our Father and the Lord Jesus Christ" (1:1). The only difference is that in 1 Thessalonians the formula reads, "in God *the* Father" while in 2 Thessalonians it appears as "in God *our* Father." The interpreter should not read too much into the difference, for the Thessalonian believers would have understood they shared with the apostle a relationship to God as *their* Father when he wrote the first letter. In the first letter there is an appeal to "*our* God and Father," although it is not in the salutation (1 Thess. 3:11). The possessive pronoun "our" is placed differently, but the personal meaning of the entire expression is still the same. In addition, in 2 Thessalonians 1:2 Paul alludes to God the Father and the

Lord Jesus Christ a second time in the span of two verses, but this time without the personal pronoun so that it matches the way the reference to God is given in 1 Thessalonians 1:1.

Several observations can again be made concerning these words of Paul. First, the close connection of the Father and the Lord Jesus by way of this formula implies the deity of Christ. The Thessalonians are in both, and both seem to be equally the basis and authority for the content of much of the two letters. The teaching of the full deity of Jesus Christ is not popular in some circles due to a dependence on a somewhat modernistic and Unitarian mind-set in which the incarnation is considered to be an unreasonable doctrine. However, man's experience or mind is not the measure of all things. In a theistic universe, miracles are possible. The idea that God could become incarnate in man is a small thing for a Creator who made everything out of nothing by the words of His mouth. Paul's words here leave no room for a less than infinite and powerful God.

Second, the full formula for Christ's name is given once again—"the Lord Jesus Christ" (1:1–2). It could be that by this time in Paul's Christian pilgrimage the terms had combined to be virtually a proper name. However, it is doubtful that all theological meaning has disappeared from the apostle's mind. There are hints of deity in the expression "Lord." There may also be hints of humanity in the name Jesus, the one born of Mary, although the designation surely refers to him most clearly as Savior. The word *Christ* is of course the standard Greek term for Messiah or Anointed One, who was the promised King of Israel. Leon Morris notes that the "combination of the three terms into one impressive title gives us compactly a view of a Person who alone can be ranked with God."[1]

Paul's expression "Grace to you and peace" (1:2) is equivalent to the opening in the first epistle. Appended to it is a repeat of the expression from 1:1—"from God the Father and the Lord Jesus Christ," the only difference being the possessive pronoun "our" in front of the word *Father* in 1:1 as discussed above. Here the repeat of the strong statement bringing together Father and Son appears to accentuate more than usual the divine source of grace and peace as Paul invokes it for his readers. The same lengthy formula as a greeting is virtually the same as that in Romans 1:7.That Paul so frequently makes such appeals in his letters is not incidental. Grace and peace are two necessary ingredients for daily Christian living, which have their origin in God Himself and emanate from Him (1 Cor. 15:10; 2 Cor. 12:9). To have a relationship with the One who provided these things would be a big comfort and encouragement to the believers at Thessalonica.

Encouragement and Commendation (1:3–5)

Paul continues another theme found in his other epistles and in 1 Thessalonians, that of thanksgiving (see 1 Thess. 1:2). Here he tells his readers, "We ought always to give thanks to God for you" (1:3). "Ought" (*opheilomen*) implies a special responsibility on the part of the apostle and his party to maintain a grateful spirit toward the Thessalonians during their prayers:

> "We ought" appears only here and in 2:13 in connection with his thanksgiving and gives a glimpse into how Paul conceived of his duty to God. This unusual reference to responsibility, thought by some to be prompted by the readers' remarkable progress or by a special need among them . . . should be limited to a special personal duty to God (Rom. 1:14; 1 Cor. 9:16, 17), because the Greek verb (*opheilō*, "ought") implies an exclusive personal responsibility.[2]

This focus on obligation is somewhat different from Paul's matter-of-fact statements in 1 Thessalonians telling them that he was frequently giving thanks to God for them. Here the apostle goes deeper with his thoughts. Not only does he give thanks, but the giving of thanks emerges as a necessity in his soul. Some, taking the difference a little more pessimistically, have suggested that there is a loss of the personal touch from the first epistle to this one. In the first, there can be detected a certain amount of warmth in the wording while here the idea of mandated duty perhaps comes across as impersonal. However, this would be overstating the case. The apostle's sense of duty should cause no damper on the highly personal nature of his fatherly relationship to his converts. After all, he calls them by the personal designation brethren (1:3) and will shortly tell them that he speaks proudly of them (1:4). Therefore, any so-called view of Paul's second letter as impersonal should be rejected.

Next, Paul speaks of giving thanks to God for the Thessalonians "as is only fitting" (1:3). Here the word "fitting" (*axion*) means that something is proper or worthy to be associated with whatever is being mentioned. Here Paul suggests that it is quite proper for the apostolic team to give thanks always to God for the Thessalonian believers. To dispel any doubts the saints would have about the necessity for this in Paul's thinking, he gives them two reasons why this is so. First, he says, "your faith is greatly enlarged" (1:3). The term "greatly enlarged" (*huperauxanō*) means "to grow or increase beyond."[3] Paul had applauded the faith of the Thessalonians early on in his first epistle but encouraged them to continue on in that faith. Whether the apostle received any further news of their developments along those lines between the first and second letter is unclear, although we know that some news about the Thessalonians had come to Paul (2:2).

The second reason Paul gives as to why it is fitting for him to give thanks to God for the Thessalonians is the growth of their love for one another. Just as with faith, here also, Paul had written in the first epistle praising them for the public testimony of their great love, while praying for them to continue and increase in the same (see 1 Thess. 1:3; 3:12). The love that the apostle approves here in his second letter is love among the brethren for the brethren: "the love of each one of you toward one another" (1:3). Such love could be commended in them especially since it "grows ever greater" (*pleonazei*), a term implying an increase or a growing rich.

It is useful to compare and contrast Paul's two epistles on these points. Here in the second letter, Paul has praised the Thessalonians for their vast faith and great love. These are only two of the three concepts that made up the triad in the first epistle: faith, love, and hope. Hope is not mentioned here in this context in 2 Thessalonians as a word. However, one should not be too hasty to see Paul making any reduction in what he says. The word "hope" does occur in 2 Thessalonians at a later point when the apostle speaks of God's granting of "good hope by grace" (2:16). However, even if the word has not been used, the thought is everywhere present in the following context of the first chapter. Beginning in 1:5 and going to the end of the first chapter, the apostle lays out the hope that is before them and indirectly asks them not to give up. This hope the Thessalonians possess is something that is produced by God Himself partly through the promises of his future work at the coming of Christ.

Boasting in the Brethren in their Persecution (1:4–5)

Because of the growing faith and love of the Thessalonians, Paul can tell them that "we ourselves speak proudly of you" (1:4). The expression "speak proudly" (*egkauchasthai*) is a superlative form of boasting; it is boasting in the highest degree—"to boast forth." Mal Couch comments, "Often used in the negative sense, Paul here makes it a legitimate word."[4] Paul is in overdrive in his pride and public boasting about the Thessalonians. The Thessalonians could also look to the emphasis of "we *ourselves*" to highlight the great apostolic encouragement they were receiving. An apostle of God was boasting about them. When someone boasts in themselves, you know that a proud spirit prevails. The Bible warns, "Let another praise you, and not your own mouth; a stranger, and not your own lips" (Prov. 27:2). However, there is no indirect self-praise on the part of the apostle since he is partly responsible for their growing condition. There is no puffing of the self here and no encouragement in that direction: "This boasting is never self-glorification which says what the *churches* are doing while meaning what *Paul himself* has done. The credit is given wholly where it belongs. And the aim is always to encourage and strengthen those to whom the boast is made, to stimulate their consciousness that they are not a long handful standing by themselves but are bound together with so many others in other cities and provinces."[5]

Paul's great boast in Thessalonian faith and love reminds of 1 Thessalonians 1:8 where the example of the Thessalonian believers and their own ministry was enough to produce boasting by others. As Paul says in that letter, "we have no need to say anything." However, even if there is no need, the apostle here joins the chorus of praise uttered in their direction. To whom does Paul verbalize such boasts? He brags about the Thessalonians "among the churches of God" (1:4). It is possible that Paul has only been in one church during the time that he has been hearing about the Thessalonians and writing to them. That would be the church at Corinth. If this is so, how could Paul say that he was boasting about the Thessalonians among more than one church? Several answers are possible. First, understanding that Paul's view of the church is people, there were no doubt believers from other congregations in various places in the empire who traveled through Corinth. Aquila and Priscilla are a case in point (Acts 18:2) and were probably not alone. In this way, Paul is sharing his pride in the Thessalonians among those from various churches and not just the church at Corinth, although his location is limited to that city. Second, it is possible, although unlikely, that Paul is on the move again when he writes 2 Thessalonians, so that it would be possible to have shared the story of the Thessalonians with more than one church. Third, it is a possibility that the apostle is using the expression "churches of God" as a general one to cover any sharing he does anywhere within the growing realm of Christendom. The first option is the preferred interpretation because it has the least number of assumptions. Regardless, Paul is not exaggerating when he tells the Thessalonians of the breadth of his boasting about what God is doing in and through them.

What motivates Paul to brag about the believers at Thessalonica is their "perseverance and faith" (1:4) as they faced severe trials. Here "perseverance" (*hupomonēs*) carries the thought of patience, endurance, steadfastness, or fortitude, especially when going through trying circumstances. Paul had noted this quality of the Thessalonians in his first epistle when he mentioned their "*steadfastness* of hope" in Jesus (1 Thess. 1:3). In the last chapter of the second epistle, the apostle prays that the Lord may direct their hearts into the "*steadfastness* of Christ" (3:5). This again shows the apostle's constant teaching that there was always room for growth in the qualities that he acknowledged in the

Thessalonians. "Faith" (*pisteōs*) is thought by some interpreters to refer to the faithfulness of the believers under duress rather than to the faith in Christ that they possessed.[6] In this way *perseverance* and *faith* are virtual synonyms in this context. However, the thought of continuing to trust in Christ or continuing in the faith, in spite of events, is the more likely and precise way to portray its meaning.

The circumstances that allow the Thessalonians to demonstrate perseverance and faith are described by Paul as "persecutions and afflictions which you endure" (1:4). "Persecutions" (*diōgmois*) communicates the idea of organized harassment. Such harassment against Christians once characterized Paul's own behavior and actions (Acts 8:1–3). The complete idea is illustrated by the persecution of Paul and Barnabas by Jews and others at Pisidian Antioch to the point of expelling the missionaries from their district (Acts 13:50). The notion is severe and does not refer to any trifling or small difficulties along the way. "Afflictions" (*thlipsesin*) comes from the usual word for tribulation, which refers to direct suffering or trouble. This word is broader than the concept of persecution. All persecutions are afflictions, but not all afflictions are persecutions. However, in this case, Paul uses both terms to express the same suffering caused by the evil intent of others. Such persecutions are those that the Thessalonians endure. The term "endure" (*anechesthe*) implies a patience with or bearing up under something. Its present tense implies that it is an ongoing patience exercised by the Thessalonian believers.[7] Coupled with the phrase "persecutions and afflictions," this easily leads one to draw the conclusion that there were several incidents of persecution and a continuing pressure against the church. However, at the time of Paul's letter, the Thessalonians were handling things well.

The persecutions and trials mentioned in this verse are different from the horrors of the Day of the Lord mentioned by Paul in 1 Thessalonians 5:1–11 and 2 Thessalonians 2:2–12. Christians will face trials of persecution in every age (2 Tim. 3:12), but the awful time of what is called the tribulation will be far greater than anything people have faced on planet Earth (Dan. 12:1; Joel 2:2; Matt. 24:21; Rev. 3:10). Whatever it is the Thessalonian believers are facing, it is not the great end-time tribulation. Sometimes those who believe Christians will go through the seven-year tribulation period on earth insist that since affliction is the lot of Christians, the church must go through that time of tribulation. However, such an argument is not logically compelling. If God in His sovereignty chooses to exempt believers from the end-time Day of the Lord, such exemption does not disavow the fact that during the church age affliction is the lot of Christians. Furthermore, the word *tribulation* or *affliction* is not a technical term that allows the interpreter to link all passages in the Bible where the term occurs.

As to the exact nature of the afflictions and the identity of the persecutors the Thessalonians were facing in their day, Paul remains silent. The Thessalonians knew, perhaps more than Paul, all about them without need of further elaboration. All that can be surmised would be a similarity to the original situation when Paul was with them. That would mean that some Jews were doubtless involved. However, one cannot rule out the regular pagan population of Thessalonica, which could most likely be easily aroused.[8]

Evidence of God's Righteous Judgment (1:5)

Paul shockingly describes the persecutions against the Thessalonians as "a plain indication of God's righteous judgment" (1:5). It has been common but wrong thinking throughout history that calamity should *always* be viewed as a sign of God's judgment. With respect to this section, Morris notes, "It is at first sight somewhat difficult to follow the apostle's train of thought. To us the fact of suffering seems to deny, rather than to prove, that God is working out his righteous purpose."[9] Paul insists, however, that in some way the suffering of the Thessalonians was a reminder of something good—the Thessalonians could be "considered worthy of the kingdom of God" (1:5).

"Plain indication" (*endeigma*) is a word used only here in the New Testament and means "a thing pointed out, a thing proved."[10] It is a word conveying the thought of verification or evidence of something. But what precisely is the proof that Paul mentions? One possibility is that it is the persecution itself. In this view the existence of suffering should be used by the believers as evidence of their status as those going into God's coming kingdom rather than believing that God had abandoned them.[11] A different view is given by Charles Ryrie when he notes, "Not suffering itself but their attitude of faith and constancy in suffering" is the proof that Paul cites.[12] In other words, this perseverance of the Thessalonians in their faith before God in spite of suffering is one pointer to their true status before God. In either case, the existence of suffering is part of the mix as proof of God's genuine work in the Thessalonians.

The word *judgment* (*kriseōs*) in the expression "righteous judgment" (1:5) carries the notion of verdict or assessment. Furthermore, it is *God's* appraisal that is in view, not another human perspective. This verdict or judgment is also described as "righteous" (*dikaias*). This term depicts that which is right, proper, or fully justified. The same word is used in the next verse where Paul tells them that "it is only *just* for God to repay" their persecutors (1:6). The basic understanding is that God is right in his decision to allow the Thessalonians to undergo persecution to give them a chance to express continuing faith.

In what way could such a predicament and setting be considered a positive development? Paul states plainly that the Thessalonians' faith under oppression indicated a right verdict from God that the Thessalonian believers could be "considered worthy of the kingdom of God" (1:5). The descriptive expression "considered worthy" (*kataxiōthēnai*) means to be regarded as valuable. Using this word, a similar idea is found in Acts 5:41 where Peter and the apostles are literally flogged by Jews opposing their preaching and then go on their way "rejoicing that they had been considered worthy to suffer shame for [Christ's] name." Such a focus on suffering as a positive experience should not be seen in the same way that Islam understands affliction. In that false religion people actually seek suffering thinking they have a larger reward ahead of them simply because of the experience. That is not the teaching here, nor is it consistent with biblical Christianity. While God calls some to suffer in life's circumstances (such as the Thessalonians), there is no unseemly coveting of suffering to prove that one is numbered among the elect. To be considered worthy of the kingdom of God does not mean the Thessalonians were saved because of their performance under persecution. Salvation is a free gift of God that cannot be earned (John 1:12–13; 3:16–18; 5:24; Rom. 3:28; 4:4–5; 5:1; 6:23; 10:8–13; Eph. 2:8–10; Titus 3:5). In light of the later context of the chapter, Paul is beginning his argument that God will vindicate the Thessalonians even if events currently do not make them feel up to their true standing.

Another question that emerges at this point is the meaning of the "kingdom of God" (1:5). It is certainly true that God reigns over all things at all times. This sovereign reign of God is a kind of universal kingdom as God rules always and in every way at the highest level. However, it is also true that specific reigns or specific kingdoms are mentioned as well. For example, Jesus as God certainly reigns over the church as its head (Eph. 1:22). However, that is not the kingdom that is mentioned in this particular verse. In light of the end-time scenario that is prominent throughout the first two chapters of the book (and also of 1 Thessalonians), the kingdom that is mentioned is the coming, earthly messianic kingdom that is inaugurated at the Second Coming when the Antichrist is destroyed (Dan. 7:11–14; Rev. 19–22). This kingdom begins the ultimate fulfillment of the kingdom promises to David in the Old Testament (e.g., 2 Sam. 7; Ps. 89). Such a kingdom is future from the vantage point of the Thessalonians even though they live in the light of its coming. They should rejoice, Paul implies, because present circumstances point to their future hope.

Study Questions

1. Why did the apostle Paul feel it important to give thanks for the church at Thessalonica?
2. How does a person's Christian faith and love grow?
3. Is it ever right to be proud? Is there a difference between good pride and bad pride?
4. Is the evidence of God's righteous judgment the persecution the Thessalonians were going through or their response to the persecution? How does the answer affect your life today?
5. What does it mean to be "worthy of the kingdom"?

CHAPTER 12

The Judgment of God 2 Thessalonians 1:6–12

Preview:

Paul tells the Thessalonian Christians to take heart because Jesus is coming to make all things right. There will be a role reversal at the Second Coming. The Thessalonians, who are now suffering, will be vindicated and elevated in status. Their persecutors who currently enjoy an upper hand will be judged and destroyed by Christ.

The judgment of God is not a popular topic today. The dogma of our society is *tolerance*. The postmodern outlook argues that all beliefs are valid and no one should judge another because of his or her philosophical ideas. In essence, there is no right or wrong, so everyone's thoughts should be accepted. Of course, when the Christian view is presented, many of these "tolerant" people hypocritically recoil at the thought of having to entertain any kind of biblical view.

To the postmodern mind, God, if He exists at all, must be a God of love, accepting any and every lifestyle. He cannot be a God of judgment, only mercy. Justice cannot be pursued, because that just would not be fair. The topic of this chapter shows how God's Word runs counter to what permeates our present culture. Every Bible believer must take great care to accept the authority of the Scriptures (Matt. 5:17–19; 24:35; John 10:35; 2 Tim. 3:16) and not allow the culture to dictate what he or she believes.

The Justice of God (1:6–7a)

In 2 Thessalonians 1:5 the apostle Paul writes of God's righteous judgment, or correct verdict, about believers today. In this section he begins to unfold the doctrine of retribution or judgment and to relate it to unbelievers at the second coming of the Lord Jesus Christ. He uses several words ("repay," "retribution," "eternal destruction," and "flaming fire") that convey the doctrine of divine retribution when the Lord returns.

Paul begins with an emphatic statement: "For after all it is only just for God to repay with affliction those who afflict you" (1:6). The expression "for after all" in this context presents the idea of "since" and therefore states a certainty. The entire sentence from verse 6 to verse 8 is in this way tied to the previous verse. Thus Paul teaches for the first time in the epistle a role reversal. While those who rejected God were afflicting the Thessalonians, one day the believers would be the ones elevated while the persecutors would themselves be afflicted. In a sense, it is a clear case of reaping what one sows. The word "just" is the same term as "righteous" in verse 5. Paul is reminding the Thessalonians that it is only rig ht for God one day to reward his followers and punish the wicked.

The meaning of the word "repay" (*antapodouvai*) in 1:6 is "to pay back" or "pay in return." The idea in this context is clearly vengeance, something that is forbidden for Christians because it is the prerogative of God alone (Rom. 12:19). Paul uses the term in a good, nonvengeful sense when he rhetorically asks the Thessalonians in his first letter what thanks he could repay God for all the joy that is in his heart because of the them (1 Thess. 3:9). The content of the repayment in 1:6 is simply affliction—"it is only just for God to repay with affliction those who afflict you." This concept is identical to what the Thessalonian believers were enduring according to 1:4. The recipients of the repayment are specifically "those who afflict you"—the Jewish and pagan persecutors in Thessalonica. That Paul means to apply this sentiment to all Christians versus all believers may be surmised from the following context, for relief comes to Paul as well as to the Thessalonians (v. 7), and retribution comes upon all those who do not know God (v. 8).

The Thessalonians could take solace in knowing that the "Lord keeps perfect and infallible records. Someday those records will be opened and the unsaved dead, including the pagan persecutors of Thessalonica, will be resurrected" and judged.[1] A perfect retribution upon evil men in the end is to some degree expected by most people. What do you do with someone like Joseph Stalin or Adolf Hitler who is responsible for murdering millions of people? In this life their lives could be taken only once. But in eternity the true retribution and judgment will be realized: "This principle of just requital lies at the basis of our belief in a moral universe. Our sense of justice demands such a requital. Not good but evil creates a moral problem for us. In the face of present injustices, our conscience tells us that there must be a future retribution. A world in which justice was not done at last would not be God's world at all."[2]

The flip side of God's action to afflict the persecutors is His act to bring relief upon the afflicted—"and to give relief to you who are afflicted and to us as well" (1:7). "Relief" (*anesin*) technically refers to a release of tension as the slackening of a bow on a string.[3] Rest and relaxation from the persecution will come to the Thessalonian believers in the future. The future expectation is not some immediate or localized deliverance but a look forward to the end-time scenario predicted by God: "God used the tribulations of His people to cause them to realize that retribution only begins to operate in this life and that its perfect fulfillment is to be looked for in the world to come. Seeing great injustice in the world, but convinced of the justice of God, the Holy Spirit convinced them that God would vindicate His cause in the eternal future."[4] Thus ultimate rest, envisioned in the form of complete role reversal at the second coming of Christ is the meaning of the relief or rest promised to the Thessalonians. However, the promise is to more than them. Paul adds "and to us as well." At the time, Paul was enduring persecution, although in a different venue than the Thessalonians (Acts 18:12–17). The general thought is that all genuine Christians will be part of the role reversal that will take place when Jesus returns to earth.

Some interpreters have suggested that the rapture of the church is the rest that is promised by Paul in this passage. It would certainly be a removal of the saints from the troubles they are facing as long as the saints are the ones alive when Jesus comes to rapture the church. However, the Thessalonians died centuries ago. There is no real way that the rapture of the church is the promised rest for them. They have been in heaven resting from persecution for almost two millennia. For the promise to have genuine application to the Thessalonians, something else must be involved, namely, the idea of role reversal and ultimate vindication. Consequently, those interpreters who try to use this passage to argue against the pretribulational rapture of the church will not be successful. Rest does come to all believers at the same time as the affliction of unbelievers, although such rest is much more than simply the absence of persecution. Since this is such an important theological issue, the significance of the nature and timing of the relief or rest for believers in this passage will be given a more complete discussion below in the section on the timing of the Rapture.

The Timing of Role Reversal (1:7b)

The end-time role reversal highlighted by God's retribution of the persecutors of God's people will occur "when the Lord Jesus shall be revealed from heaven with His mighty angels in flaming fire" (1:7b). First, notice that the future reprisal will take place when Christ is "revealed from heaven." The word "revealed" (*apokalupsei*) implies that something is disclosed, made known, or unveiled. In this case it is the Lord Jesus who is disclosed or made known. This is the only passage in Paul's New Testament writings that uses the term for the second coming of Christ in which Jesus is personally made known at the time he comes to earth. But Paul is not alone is using the term in this way. Peter likewise describes the coming of the Lord in glory by means of this particular word (1 Pet. 1:7, 13; 4:13). This coming is at the end of the seven-year tribulation period and prior to the establishment of His earthly kingdom centered in Jerusalem.

The text says that Jesus will be revealed "from heaven" (1:7b). This revelation of the visible and personal Christ can be understood partly from the event of His ascension. He went upward into the sky as he ascended to the right hand of the Father in heaven, the abode of God (Acts 1:9–11). This same Jesus will come again from heaven in like manner. This occurrence will be an unveiling or revelation. This event is not the same as the rapture of the church when the Lord comes for His own. Here every eye shall see him as he comes all the way to earth (see Rev. 1:7).

Not only is this unveiling of Christ going to be from heaven, but it will also be accompanied "with His mighty angels" (1:7b). The word "angels" could generically refer to messengers of any kind (even human) and not to the created beings that are often associated with the word. However, such an interpretation could not be justified in this case. Too many other passages in the Bible associate the appearance and involvement of angelic beings at the end of the age and the coming of Christ. Jesus Himself spoke of angels coming with Him at His return: "But when the Son of Man comes in His glory, and all the angels with Him, then He will sit on His glorious throne" (Matthew 25:31; cf. Matt. 13:41). The angels are described as "mighty" (*dunameōs*) or "powerful." Angelic beings are considered to be powerful elsewhere in Scripture (Ps. 103:20; 2 Pet. 2:11). Nevertheless, their power should not be thought of as something they have in and of themselves. Their power stems from God, and it is His power on display at the return of Christ.

Christ will also be revealed "in flaming fire" (1:7b).[5] The word "flaming" (*phlogos*) is actually a noun so that the phrase roughly reads, "in fire, a flame," or "in fire of flame." The term intensifies the idea of fire. Perhaps "in fiery fire" or "in blazing fire" best expresses the intense nature of the expression. Once this meaning is established, one must ask what the description means within the given context of the Second Coming. Is the phrase to be taken in a woodenly literal way so that there is some outward manifestation of fire at the Second Coming, or does it mean something else? Fire is a fitting symbol to display the glory of God. It could help picture the presence of God. Many theophanies (physical manifestations) of God in the Old Testament were accompanied by images of fire (Exod. 3:2; 19:18; 24:17; Isa. 30:27–30; Dan. 7:9–10). In fact, the similarity to Old Testament imagery regarding Jehovah implicitly, if not explicitly, speaks of the deity of Christ as He returns.[6]

Most likely in this context the image of fire pictures Christ's majesty and His righteous anger toward sin. Christ returns from heaven with His powerful angels in flaming fire *dealing out retribution,* the following text reminds us. Thus the fire relates to the judging activity of God at the Second Coming. Not surprisingly, then, in one of the greatest images given in Scripture of the return of Christ, He returns on a white horse as a judge and with eyes that are a "flame of fire" (Rev. 19:11–12; cf. Rev. 1:14).

Final Retribution (1:8)

The apostle Paul declares that one facet of the second coming of Christ is "dealing out retribution to those who do not know God" (1:8). The expression "dealing out" (*didontos*)—often used for the idea of *giving*—in this context means "to grant, bestow, impart, or inflict something" on someone. "Retribution" (*ekdikēsin*) refers to punishment or even vengeance. The term "denotes infliction of full justice on a criminal, giving him all, but no more, than his guilt deserves."[7] Thus the entire statement refers to the meting out of deserved punishment even to the point of suffering. Those who experience this wrathful event will receive affliction, something they had dealt to others who did not deserve it.

God does not inflict judgment in an unrighteous way (Rom. 3:5), but He does deal out retribution. This theme can be seen throughout the Bible. It can be found in the imprecatory Psalms of the Old Testament with the use of severe language (Pss. 7, 35, 40, 55, 58, 59, 69, 79, 109, 137, 139, 144). It will not do to complain that the God of the Old Testament is a mean, vengeful God while the Jesus of the New Testament is a sweet, kind God. The teaching of Jesus in the Gospels clearly reveals that He taught the doctrine of retribution (Matt. 5:38–48; 10:28; 23:13–36; Mark 14:21; Luke 21:22; John 5:29). It is to Christ Himself that the Father has delivered all judgment: "For not even the Father judges anyone, but He has given all judgment to the Son" (John 5:22).

The recipients of God's retribution are described in two ways. First mentioned are "those who do not know God," and second, "those who do not obey the gospel of our Lord Jesus" (1:8). Some see in these descriptions two classes of people, Gentiles who are ignorant of God and the Jews who rejected the Messiah. It is certain that both Jews and Gentiles shared in the persecution of the Thessalonians, although the Jews appear to be the instigators (Acts 17:1–10). These two separate groups could be in the apostle's thinking by means of separate statements. In favor of this interpretation is the fact that both phrases are definite: "*those* who do not know God" and "*those* who do not obey the gospel." In addition, in Paul's first letter to the Thessalonians he refers to the "Gentiles who do not know God" (1 Thess. 4:5). Furthermore, there is Old Testament wording similar to the first phrase that is applied specifically to the Gentile nations (Pss. 9:17; 79:6).[8] In both of the Psalms passages, the Gentiles are the ones who do not know God and are judged accordingly. Thus it could be in light of such arguments that Paul is pointing to two specific groups of people. It is also possible that both statements are simply the same idea stated in two different ways. Leon Morris objects to the view that these are two distinct expressions characterizing two different people groups: "The distinction is not made clearly enough, for the verse can be readily understood as an example of synonymous parallelism. If Paul meant Jews and Gentiles, there seems to be no reason why he should not have inserted another word or two to make the meaning clear."[9] Moreover, the language of the first part of the expression is applied to the Jews elsewhere in Scripture (John 8:54–55) and the last part to the Gentiles (Rom. 11:30).[10] Thus it is best to see both statements as referring to both Gentiles and Jews.

When the text describes the recipients of God's retribution as those who do not know God, it does not mean that they have never heard of the existence of the one true and living God. In this setting, to "know" (*oida*) God is to have salvation knowledge—to be a justified believer (1:8). Paul wrote to Timothy later that God "desires all men to be saved and to come to the *knowledge* of the truth" (1 Tim. 2:4). Job describes the one who does not know God by the term "wicked" (Job 18:21). The apostle Paul uses the term several times to distinguish between those who are saved—who know God—and those who are lost—who do not know God (1 Cor. 1:21; Gal. 4:8–9; 1 Thess. 4:5; Titus 1:16). In this way "know" is not referring to mere intellectual content but is expressing a bond with God in keeping with the Hebrew use of the concept of knowing as personal relationship initiated by God (see Amos 3:2).

The second description of the recipients of God's retribution helps to explain further the first idea of not knowing God—"those who do not obey the gospel" (1:8). The same precise expression "obey the gospel" or "obey the good news" is used by Paul in Romans 10:16 where the context is clearly individual redemption. There Paul sadly comments that not all who heard the good news of the message of salvation through Christ believed. In doing so, he depicts such unbelievers as those who do not "heed the glad tidings" ("obeyed the gospel," KJV). The same sentiment echoes in Romans 1:5 where Paul reminds the Romans that his ministry is to "bring about the obedience of faith among all the Gentiles." In this expression Paul means that they were to respond in the right way, that is, by faith or belief, to the truth about Christ. He does not have in mind a good work or deed (cf. Rom. 4:1–5). The same is true of the text before us. To obey the gospel is the same as believing the truths of the gospel by receiving them. To trust the death, burial, and resurrection of Christ is to receive salvation of the soul (Rom. 10:8–10). Of those who do so, it can be said he has "obeyed the gospel." Mal Couch concludes that the two descriptions should be taken together: "It is better to refer to both clauses as pointing to the same general class, that is, all who live willfully ignorant and disobedient to God and the gospel. Not knowing God is, as spelled out in Romans 2:14–16, willful, guilty ignorance. Not accepting the gospel of Christ is to refuse what God has historically confirmed and testified with the first coming of His Son."[11] Interestingly, in this passage it is the *Lord Jesus* who comes (1:7) and the gospel of the *Lord Jesus* that is rejected by those who are judged. The lack of the formal title here may indicate the highly personal nature of the event and the reinforcement that what is being rejected is the idea behind the meaning of the name *Jesus*—that he died to be our *Savior*. However, the full title for Christ is used at the end of the chapter to summarize the entire episode (1:12).

The Penalty of Retribution (1:9)

Next, Paul reminds the Thessalonian believers that those who do not know God or do not obey the gospel will "pay the penalty of eternal destruction" (1:9). The word "pay" (*tisousin*), used only here in the New Testament, means "to pay or settle up" a debt. The term "penalty" (*dikēn*) entails a punishment that is meted out. About the expression, Morris comments, "The word 'punishment' . . . is another word from the same root as 'righteous' and 'vengeance' in the earlier verses. It brings us the idea of a just penalty, of a punishment meted out as the result of evenhanded assessment of the rights of the case."[12]

The apostle depicts the penalty as "eternal destruction" (1:9). "Eternal" (*aiōnion*) is the common word used throughout the New Testament in the expression *eternal life* (John 3:15–16; Rom. 6:23; Titus 1:2; 1 John 5:11–13). In this passage what is eternal, or of lasting duration, is not life but *destruction*: "*Olethros* ('destruction') does not refer to annihilation, but to ruination. It does not mean the cessation of existence but rather the loss of all that makes existence worthwhile (cf. 1 Tim. 6:9). The lost will not cease to exist but will experience forever a life of uselessness, hopelessness, emptiness, and meaninglessness, with no value, worth, accomplishment, purpose, goal, or hope. They will be ruined forever."[13] A couple of other uses of the word by Paul help to support the notion that destruction in this passage is an everlasting duration and not simply annihilation of the wicked person. Paul uses the term in 1 Timothy 6:9 to speak of the ruin and destruction that come within a person's life due to a covetous attention to money and riches. Also, in 1 Thessalonians 5:3 the apostle uses the expression to describe the destruction of the coming Day of the Lord's wrath, which comes suddenly upon the unsuspecting. As seen earlier in comments on that verse in 1 Thessalonians, this destruction is not a time of immediate annihilation, but a period of time in which God pours out his wrath on the earth. Thus, here in 2 Thessalonians 1:9 the time period is not finite but eternal, thereby making the destruction much more terrifying. Finally, it is appropriate to ask how annihilation can be the meaning of the term for eternal destruction if the opposite expression "eternal life" means everlasting life. Therefore, taken together, the terms "eternal destruction" refer to a punishment of the wicked that lasts forever.

Such eternal destruction is further explained by Paul in two ways. First, the apostle pictures it as "away from the presence of the Lord" (1:9). The meaning here is the exact opposite of the description of the Rapture in 1 Thessalonians 4:17. There at the rapture of the church believers are caught up to live with the Lord forever. Here those who do not know God are kept away from the life of the Lord. The word "presence" (*prosōpou*) literally means "face," following the Hebrew way of saying the concept. To be in the presence of the Lord is to be before His face. To be lost is to be outside of His presence and not to see His face. Although orthodox Christianity argues for the omnipresence of God—he is everywhere—for the unbeliever there will be no *favorable* presence of Jesus in eternal hell. To be cut off from the favor of God is the worst retribution a person could experience.

Second, the apostle depicts the eternal destruction of unbelievers as away "from the glory of His power" (1:9). In this context, the common word "glory" (*doxēs*) refers to splendor or greatness. The lesser used term "power" (*ischuos*) carries the connotation of "might" or "strength." While the idea of physical strength may provide an apt analogy, the teaching here is far from the notion of the physical, although there are ramifications within the real world. Paul gives us a glimpse into his thought process here and in two other passages from Ephesians. He wants the Ephesian Christians to know about "the surpassing greatness of His power toward us who believe. These are in accordance with the working of the strength of His *might*," the last word being the same as the word here (Eph. 1:19). Later he exhorts the Ephesians to "be strong in the Lord, and in the strength of His *might*" (Eph. 6:10). The strength of the Lord is operative for the believer. However, in 2 Thessalonians 1:9 the apostle warns that at the Second Coming separation from this might is permanent.

The entire phrase "away from the presence of the Lord and from the glory of His power" may have its roots in the Old Testament wording of the prophet Isaiah. Isaiah, when speaking about judgment upon idolaters, describes them as attempting to hide themselves "from the terror of the LORD and from the splendor of His majesty" (Isa. 2:10, 19, 21). If this is so, Beale is quite right when he says, "Isaiah's phrase underscores that idolaters will be forced to separate themselves from God's presence at the time of judgment."[14] This does not mean that unbelievers in the totality of their beings are sent to the lake of fire at this point. The bodies of unbelievers who have died before the Second Coming will continue to lie in their graves while their spirits are consigned to hades (see Luke 16:19–31). Those unbelievers who are alive when Christ returns will be killed by Christ as he slays His enemies (Rev. 19:17–21). Similarly, their bodies are in graves while their spirits are in hades. At the end of the millennium, at the Great White Throne judgment, there will be a resuscitation of the bodies of the lost and a reunion of those bodies with their spirits. Then due to the implementation of the fair, just, and legal sentence that is due them, unbelievers will be cast into the lake of fire (Rev. 20:11–15).

We must pause here and say a few words about the harshness of these verses in 2 Thessalonians or in any of the cross-references that deal with the judgment of God upon unbelievers at the Second Coming and beyond. Christians should not shrink from the sternness of the apostolic message. In our postmodern culture, there is a tendency to elevate tolerance as the greatest good, contrary to all evidence in society. No one lives as if everyone is right or that all views should be tolerated. Yet there is an insistence that philosophically we must think this way about the real world. The picture of reality and truth given by the biblical documents, including Paul's letters to the Thessalonians, leaves no room for such soft thinking that tolerates no judgment.[15] Paul was an absolutist. Regardless of people's thoughts and feelings, Christ is returning, and those who do not believe will be punished as rebels against the God of the Bible. The harshness of the view will never disappear, but it will be better understood when it is recognized that there is no greater sin than not being or doing what the Creator intended one to be and do. The cure for the ailment of sin is the cross of Christ. Those who reject the cure will suffer the consequences. The fairness of God's entire plan for judgment is supported by every drop of blood Jesus shed for the sin of the world.[16]

The Glorification of Jesus in the Saints

Paul now goes back to the importance of the Second Coming for believers. Earlier he had stated the meaning of this event in terms of rest or relief (1:7). So in 1:10 the apostle reminds his readers of the great reversal that is the main point of the section. The ones who were persecuting the Thessalonians for their faith, certainly numbered among the unbelievers, are going to be persecuted by God at the Second Coming while the Thessalonian believers will be the ones without trouble. While the specific situation of the Thessalonians is primarily in view, Paul appears to generalize so that the role reversal that is anticipated is for all believers versus unbelievers.

Paul expands the content of the rest or relief that is envisioned in 1:7 to include the ultimate expression of God's love for the saints, namely, their public vindication in the eyes of the whole world (1:10). The apostle begins this presentation with the words "when He comes to be glorified in His saints on that day." The words "when He comes" are identical in time with the revelation of Jesus from heaven cited in 1:7. The expression "to be glorified" (*endoxasthēnai*) here in verse 10 means "to be honored or lifted up" (this word will be repeated in v. 12). Jesus is the chief One who is glorified or honored on that day.

However, Jesus is glorified "in his saints." The word "saints" (*hagiois*), meaning "holy ones" has been interpreted as either His angels or human believers. In favor of the first option is a potential parallel with the expression "His mighty angels" in 1:7. Since 1:10 repeats the statement of the coming of Jesus, there may be a repeat of the mention of angelic creatures as well. However, the chief point of the passage is diminished if this interpretation is accepted. Believers are mentioned in the next part of the same verse ("among all who have believed"). Then in 1:12 Paul mentions that Jesus would be glorified "in you, and you in Him." Such language, made clear by the second person pronoun *you*, makes it impossible to view the saints in the passage as angelic beings, since Paul is writing to flesh-and-blood human believers.

Consequently, Jesus at the Second Coming will be honored in believers. One must inquire at this point into the nature of the idea of being glorified *in* someone (1:10). The Greek preposition translated "in" (*en*) can at times carry the force of "among." If this is the sense, then Jesus is glorified *among* the saints. That is, He stands among them on that day as the One who receives honor. If this interpretation is correct, the passage does not emphasize any honor directed to believers. This is highly unlikely. One must again mention 1:12 and the statement that Jesus would be glorified "in you, and you in Him." Both uses of the word "in" must be taken as parallel and identical. The idea of "you *among* Him" is nonsensical in this setting. In addition, the positional truth of believers being in Christ is found everywhere in Paul's writings and should get the benefit of the doubt in any explanation (e.g., Rom. 3:24; Eph. 1:6–7). Thus the notion of "in" as "among" must be jettisoned. Morris correctly summarizes Paul's intent: "It seems that he is saying that those who are in Christ and in whom Christ dwells will by virtue of that fact share in his glory. On the great day it is not only the Lord himself who will be glorious, but his glory will also be seen in the saints . . . the idea is that of the Lord's glory being shared with or mirrored in his people. They are one with him and they will share his glory."[17] Notice that this is the exact opposite of how the antagonists were treating the believers in Thessalonica at the time of Paul's writing.

Not only will Jesus come to be glorified on that day, but he will also come "to be marveled at among all who have believed" (1:10). The entire statement is largely parallel and identical with the preceding one. The word "marveled" (*thaumasthēnai*) means "to be astonished, amazed, to wonder at."[18] It mirrors the idea of being glorified. The intent of it is clarified by many uses throughout the Gospels when people marveled at the miracles of Jesus (e.g., Matt. 8:27; 9:33). The word "among" should be translated "in," since the same ideas discussed above must be in place here as well. The phrase "all who have believed" gives the identity of "His saints." The use of the word "all" shows that Paul is speaking generally of all believers even though the circumstances of the Thessalonians would be uppermost in his mind. Those Thessalonian who had accepted the testimony of Paul and his associates would experience all the blessings of that day. When this Second Coming would happen was not certain. What was definite was that they would enter into all that God had promised for the saved. This would include many things, but the apostle's focus here is that Christ's glory will be mirrored in all the saints when He returns.[19] Right now "the creation waits eagerly for the revealing of the sons of God" (Rom. 8:19). The great intervention of God's work of redemption experienced at the second coming of Christ will be a time in which God will cause the entire universe to marvel in astonishment. The reason was given by Paul to the church at Ephesus: "in order that in the ages to come He might show the surpassing riches of His grace in kindness toward us in Christ Jesus" (Eph. 2:7).

The Debate over the Timing of the Rapture

First Thessalonians 1:6–12 has often been used as justification to reject the doctrine of the pretribulational rapture of the church. To be sure, a cursory reading of the passage could lend itself to a posttribulational rapture instead. If the relief of the Thessalonians and the punishment of their persecutors take place at the same time (Second Coming) as the passage may be taken to teach, some suggest that a two-phase second coming cannot be held with any confidence. Robert Gundry echoes this sentiment when he notes, "The resultant difficulty for pretribulationalism is that Paul places the release of Christians from persecution at the posttribulational return of Christ to judge unbelievers, whereas according to pretribulationalism this release will occur seven years earlier."[20]

Similarly, amillennialists like Vern Poythress also make use of this first chapter of 2 Thessalonians to support a single-phase second coming.[21] It is pointed out that relief comes to the Thessalonians at the Rapture according to 1 Thessalonians 4:13–18. However, this relief also comes about at the coming of Christ to earth to judge unbelievers as shown in 2 Thessalonians 1:5–8. Therefore, there is no two-phase second coming.

Various proponents of a pretribulational rapture have approached 2 Thessalonians in three different ways. First, some have argued that the passage speaks of the pretribulational Rapture and not Jesus' second coming to earth. In this view, to say that Christ is revealed (v. 7) is not a technical description for his coming to earth. Instead, the passage can be construed as a pretribulational rapture that begins the fiery judgment of the tribulation period. However, this way of looking at the passage is probably not best. The fiery language of this section harmonizes more easily with the posttribulational return of Christ. The mention of eternal destruction in verse 9 reinforces this notion.[22]

A second option attempts a more holistic approach. The revelation of Christ mentioned in verse 7 is believed to refer to a complex of events, which include the rapture of the church, the tribulation, and the events associated with the second coming of Christ to earth. The assumption is that such groupings are common in Scripture and that interpreters have voiced such combinations for kingdom events. Thus there is no reason to prohibit such an approach here.[23] The weakness of this view is that the passage reads as if a singular moment is in view rather than a complex of events.

A third and better option advanced by pretribulational rapturists is the simple realization (put foreword by Ryrie) that the pretribulational Rapture is not in the passage at all.[24] They would agree with the postribulationalists that the coming of Christ to earth at the end of the seven-year tribulation is what is described in the passage. However, in this view the pretribulational proponent would disagree with the posttribulational contention that the main topic under consideration is deliverance from persecution. Instead, the chief point is the vindication of the saints as the passage unfolds. This approach allows direct application to all believers in all generations, not just the last generation that sees the Second Coming.

In support of the idea that the relief of verse 7 is more than the absence of suffering is the overall structure of the passage. The later verses in the chapter expand upon the earlier ones. To repay the oppressors in verse 6 is expanded to refer to eternal destruction in verse 9. In the same way, the rest or relief of verse 7 is expanded in verse 10 to refer to the ultimate vindication of the saints when Christ is glorified through them. In this way the pretribulationist view can make perfect sense of the passage without abandoning a two-phase second coming.

Study Questions

1. What is the world's concept of God? Does it include the idea of retribution?
2. What does the word *retribution* mean? What are some synonyms?
3. When will Christ be revealed from heaven?
4. What part do angels play at the second coming of Christ?
5. Who are the recipients of the retribution of God? Why? What is the penalty of retribution?
6. What is the reward for the saved at the coming of Christ?
7. How does this section of 2 Thessalonians help us to understand the timing of the rapture of the church?

CHAPTER 13

The Focus of Paul's Prayer 2 Thessalonians 1:11–12

Preview:

Paul prays that the Thessalonian believers will realize who they really are and what God is doing through their work. He wants their experience of service to match their position, or calling, in God. The ultimate desire of the apostle is that the Lord will be glorified in them and they in Him when Jesus comes.

Prayer is one of the mainstays of Christian experience. Many of the statements of prayer have already been seen in Paul's writings to the church at Thessalonica (1 Thess. 1:2–3; 3:11–13; 5:23–25; 2 Thess. 1:3). Now he closes the first chapter with a purpose for prayer that is tied to the topic of the previous verses concerning the second coming of Christ.

The Purpose and Constancy of Paul's Prayer

Paul begins this section with the words "to this end also we pray for you" (1:11). The words "to this end" have the idea of "with this in mind."[1] This introductory saying is similar to that found in Romans 14:9 and 2 Corinthians 2:9. The apostle refers back to 1:5–10, the coming of the Lord and the glorification of the saints, longing for the realities of their experience at the future Second Coming to have an impact here and now. It is one thing to look ahead with a kind of escapist mentality during trying times. It is quite another to live earnestly in the now in the light of one's ultimate destiny. So Paul brings the Thessalonian believers back to the present time with his prayer. Mal Couch summarizes the shift in this way: "The apostle is developing a continuous thought and he has not yet finished with it. He is developing his thought, progressing from glory to what is happening now on earth, moving from positional truth ('your calling') to experiential truth ('God may count you worthy') of that calling."[2] Paul's method is often to go from positional truth to practical and experiential truth (e.g., see Eph. 1–3 with 4–6). However, in many of those cases, the positional truth is a present position in Christ based on what He has done for the believer. Here the focus is different. There is an emphasis on the position believers have in Christ on the basis of what He will do for believers, namely, their ultimate vindication. By combining both of these approaches, it is easy to see that the apostle Paul's belief is that believers are to live both in the shadow of the cross and in the light of the Second Coming. Both advents and the associated provisions provide impetus for living properly in the present time.

The constancy of Paul's prayer for the Thessalonians once again is seen when he says that the missionary team prays for them *always* (1:11). This is an echo of the introductions to both epistles to the Thessalonians. In 1 Thessalonians 1:2, the apostle writes, "We give thanks to God always for all of you," followed by the similar statement, "We ought always to give thanks to God for you" in 2 Thessalonians 1:3. Paul will repeat the same exact sentiment in the next chapter following his lengthy discussion of the Day of the Lord (2:13). As in the other cases, he in no way means a never-ending practice of talking to God in behalf of the believers. He means that they are on his mind, and when he prays he remembers them regularly. The fact that Paul inserts the term "also"—"to this end *also* we pray"—probably implies that he is adding the prayer to the list of all of the things that he thinks about and does in behalf of the Thessalonians (cf. 1:3–4).

The Content of Paul's Prayer

The first part of the petition is "our God may count you worthy of your calling" (1:11). "*Our* God" is emphasized to demonstrate the shared nature of the relationship with the Lord. This matches the frequent mention of "our God" or "our Father" throughout the two epistles to the Thessalonians, including the very next verse (1 Thess. 1:3; 2:2; 3:9, 11, 13; 2 Thess. 1:1, 11, 12; 2:16). The idea "count worthy" (*axiōsē*) has been challenged by some who see its meaning as "make worthy." If this is the sense, the request is stronger with ethical overtones. In that case Paul's wish is that God will transform the Thessalonian believers so that their experience matches their standing before God. However, the sense of "count worthy" better fits the earlier context. This shows that Paul's prayer is that God will *consider* the believers worthy. The implication of Paul's statement in 1:5 is that they *are* worthy of the kingdom (using a similar word). Their continued faith under fire confirms this status. Paul's prayer is that the Thessalonians will continue the display of their true standing.[3]

Of what are the Thessalonians to be considered worthy in verse 11? The answer is their "calling." This term (*klēseōs*) implies an invitation and summons into a relationship with God. It is a frequent concept in the writings of Paul, including his two epistles to the Thessalonians (1 Thess. 2:12; 4:7; 5:24; 2 Thess. 2:14). Examination of all of these uses shows that Paul often thinks of calling in the context of the wider scope of what is in store for the one who is called (e.g., Rom. 8:28–30). Earlier in verse 5 the believers were counted worthy of entering the coming eschatological kingdom. Here the focus is slightly different although connected: "The divine call is a prominent theme in Paul's writings. Usually it refers to the initial gospel call that results in the conversion of those called (Rom. 8:30; Eph. 4:1; 1 Thess. 4:7)."[4] In order to be a member of the coming eschatological kingdom, one must be born again (John 3:7), thereby standing in a posture of acceptance before God (Eph. 1:6).

However, several factors in the following context show that the apostle's intention in his prayer is to go beyond merely affirming the status of the Thessalonians. The second part of the content of Paul's prayer in this verse is that God would "fulfill every desire for goodness and the work of faith with power" (1:11). Note that the apostle is asking God to do something, although his words convey human responsibility as well. The word "fulfill" (*plērosē*) here means "to complete or accomplish." There are two effects that Paul wants accomplished in the lives of believers. The first outcome is "every desire for goodness." The term "desire" (*eudokian*) refers to an inner purpose or choice in individual believers.[5] Such choosing stems from a wish for something that leads to satisfaction. The adjective "every" implies that the apostle wants nothing to be left out in God's work for the Thessalonian saints.[6] "Goodness" (*agathōsunēs*) is a general term that usually carries the notion of a state of doing good deeds in the behalf of others—one is *good* to people. It is not a static quality that inheres only in the believer but works itself out in life in the form of positive action that is unselfish. Paul captures the thought of the entire expression when he tells the Romans that he is confident they are full of goodness (Rom. 15:14). The apostle also considers goodness to be a fruit or effect produced by the ministry of the Holy Spirit in believers (Eph. 5:9; Gal. 5:22).

The second effect that Paul wants accomplished in the lives of believers is the "work of faith" (1:11). Paul uses this expression in 1 Thessalonians 1:3 as a positive description of the outward activity spurred on by the faith of the believers as he fondly recalls them and prays for them. There it is already a fact in their experience. Here he wants them to continue in their activity for God to the fullest extent possible.[7] However, his prayer is necessary because only God can produce the desired result. Thus the work of faith is "with power" because it can "come about only when the power of God is operative in human lives."[8]

The Ultimate Goal of Paul's Prayer

One of the major themes of Scripture is the glory of God (Matt. 6:13; Luke 2:14; John 9:24; 2 Cor. 4:4; Heb. 2:7). Glory speaks of God's worthiness to be extolled and worshiped. So as Paul sees Christ being "glorified in His saints" (1:10) he also sees the saints as being "counted worthy" (1:11). Therefore, Paul's prayer focuses on the connection between Jesus' glorification and the saints of God. The words "in order that" imply the purpose of Paul's prayer with its desired result (v. 12). The "every desire for goodness" and "the work of faith with power" of verse 11 should lead to the outcome that "the name of our Lord Jesus may be glorified in you" (v. 12). Several elements emerge from this text and highlight the significance of Paul's overall prayer.

First, priority is given to the *name* of the Lord (v. 12). It is the name of the Lord that is glorified in the wording of the apostle at this point. Of course, this means that the Lord himself is glorified, but there is probably some particular significance to the use of the word "name" in this context. Some see the reference to the name of the Lord as language similar to specific occurrences in the Old Testament. In this way a link is made to Jesus as Yahweh of the Old Testament.[9] One then could argue for the deity of Christ from this vantage point and see the glorification and exaltation in the verse as that due to God Himself in the person of Christ. Others suggest that the use of the word "name" alludes "to his character being reflected in people and that character being glorified, since *name* in both Testaments often connotes the character of a person, which others may share."[10] Probably the best summary of the intended thought is that "to glorify the name of the Lord is to show the world what the person of the Lord is like."[11]

Second, the concept of glorification must be examined. "To glorify a name is to praise and/or enhance the reputation of the person represented by that name."[12] The word translated "glorified" in verses 10 and 12 of this chapter is also used later in the epistle as Paul prays for the written Word of God to be glorified (2 Thess. 3:1). However, in Paul's prayer at the end of the first chapter, he is focusing on the glorification of Christ and indirectly the saints of God. As in verse 10, here the thought is that the name of the Lord as well as the Lord behind the name are honored and lifted up.

A third issue in this verse is the expression "in you" (1:12). Paul's petition is not simply that the name of the Lord will be glorified. It is *how* the apostle wants the Lord to be glorified that is emphasized. Part of that hope is that the name of the Lord will be glorified *in* the saints. Such a concept is not limited to Second Thessalonians. Paul is no doubt steeped in the message of Isaiah. In a context concerned with the redemption of Israel (national and individual overtones), the prophet shares God's thoughts about Israel's deliverance: "Shout for joy, O heavens, for the LORD has done it! Shout joyfully . . . for the LORD has redeemed Jacob and *in Israel* He shows forth His *glory* (Isa. 44:23, emphasis added). Later in Isaiah 49:3, God Himself says "You are My Servant, Israel, *in Whom* I will show My *glory*" (emphasis added). The clear meaning is that Israel is the instrument by which God's name is elevated and honored.[13]

The demonstration of the Lord's glory and greatness through His people is a mystery manifested to the saints, a display of riches from God, and a certain expectation described as "Christ in you, the hope of glory" (Col. 1:27). One of the first groups ever to hear the hopeful message that Christ would be glorified in them (especially in an ultimate sense when Jesus returned) was the Thessalonians. In fact, the fulfillment of this promise should remind the reader of Jesus' statement to the Father about his disciples, "I have been glorified in them" (John 17:10).[14]

A fourth element in the text that needs to be observed is the flip side of the one just described. Not only is Paul's prayer for the name of the Lord to be glorified in the Thessalonians; it is for the saints to be glorified in Christ ("you in Him," v. 12). On one hand, the lives of the Thessalonians were to demonstrate and would display the greatness of the Lord Jesus. His perfect majesty and character would be made known through their own work of faith. On the other hand, the status of the Thessalonians would be revealed through Christ. Just like Christ, they, too, would be honored and elevated through Him.

Again, this teaching mirrors that found elsewhere in both the Old and New Testaments. Isaiah notes that the Holy of One of Israel has glorified Israel (55:5). Paul gives a similar message. Romans 8:17 asserts the teaching of the apostle: "if indeed we suffer with Him in order that we may also be glorified with Him." Such a message, given years later after the Thessalonian correspondence was sent, resonates well with what is being said here, especially in light of the persecution the Thessalonians were enduring. In 1 Corinthians 2:7–8 Paul reminds the believers that his words were the wisdom of God "predestined before the ages to *our glory*" (emphasis added) and that Jesus is the "Lord of glory." Although not quite the same concept, the wording is similar when Paul tells the Colossians that they have been made complete *in Him* (Col. 2:10).

Thus the Thessalonians could be encouraged by the end desire of Paul's prayer. Both Christ and His followers would be elevated and honored in each other. But when would this honoring take place? The focus of Paul's prayer is the present behavior of the saints according to verse 11. However, the larger context of the chapter shows that there is a coming day when, in an absolute and undeniable sense, Christ will come to be ruler of the earth and the saints will take their honored places by His side. In fact, living in the present often requires the knowledge and hope that better days are yet to come. The entire chapter, with Paul's prayer as a capstone, tells the Thessalonians that there is a role reversal coming. In the present they are afflicted, but later they will get relief, vindication, and honor. In the present their enemies flourish, but later those enemies will be afflicted by the judgment of God. This is the reality that allows the saints to live day by day as they desire goodness and do the work of faith. In the end this can only be imagined and carried out by the enabling grace of God as Paul notes in closing his prayer.

The Structure of Paul's Argument

Now that all of the pieces of chapter 1 have been put in proper place, the flow of Paul's argument can be clearly outlined.

The progression of the negative and positive tracks in the passage is clear as Paul sketches out the issues. The enemies of that day are flourishing. A general statement is given that they will be repaid. The specifics of this repayment are the rather serious and expanded notions of Jesus pouring out fiery judgment as retribution, which is labeled as eternal destruction. On the positive side, the followers of Christ presently experience the negative occurrence of persecution. A general statement is given that they will receive relief. The relief is couched in terms of future glorification when Christ will come to be glorified and will elevate the saints above their enemies. In both tracks the progression moves to more detail.

The Flow of Paul's Argument

		Enemies of Christ	Followers of Christ
NOW	*1:4–5*	*Implied flourishing of Christ's enemies who are afflicting the saints*	*Enduring persecutions and afflictions*
FUTURE	*1:6–7a*	*Repay those who persecute you*	*Give relief, rest to you [Thessalonians] and to us [the apostolic missionary team]*
	1:7b-12	*When the Lord Jesus shall be revealed from heaven . . . in flaming fire, dealing out retribution to those who do not obey the gospel . . . the penalty of eternal destruction*	*When he comes to be glorified in His saints. . . . To this end we pray . . . in order that the name of our Lord Jesus may be glorified in you and you in Him*

Study Questions

1. What is the basic purpose of prayer? How did Paul pray for the Thessalonian church? How does this prayer compare to others in 1 and 2 Thessalonians?
2. What does it mean to be counted worthy of your calling?
3. How is the name of Jesus ultimately glorified?
4. What does it mean for the saints to be glorified, and how is that done?
5. How does a Christian live today in light of what God is going to do in the future?

CHAPTER 14

Prophetic Issues about the Day of the Lord 2 Thessalonians 2:1–12

Preview:

The apostle responds to a false message given to the Thessalonians that says that the Day of the Lord's wrath of God—that is, the tribulation period—has already started. He asserts that the tribulation cannot begin until a special apostasy occurs and the man of lawlessness (Antichrist) is revealed. The Antichrist will not arrive on the scene until the restrainer no longer holds back his appearance.

The second chapter of 2 Thessalonians provides one of the keys for understanding the reason for Paul writing the letter. One of the chief truths Paul had taught the believers when he was in Thessalonica and later in his first epistle to them was the truth about the Rapture and the Day of the Lord (1 Thess. 1:10; 2:19; 3:13; 4:13–5:11). These truths were delivered in the midst of persecution (Acts 17:6–10; 1 Thess. 1:6), and there seemed to be some misunderstanding on the part of the Thessalonian believers about whether they were in the future tribulation called the "day of the Lord."

Issue of the Presence of the Day of the Lord

The first two verses of chapter 2 mark a transition in Paul's second epistle to the Thessalonians. The first chapter had been taken up mostly by the topic of the role reversal at the Second Coming when Christ will come back to judge all unbelievers (especially those persecuting the Thessalonians) and to vindicate and honor the true saints of God. Leading into the second chapter, Paul moves from the prayer to God at the end of the previous chapter to a request now given directly to the Thessalonians (2:1). This transition is reinforced by his acknowledgment that he has heard some false beliefs on their part, which require correction (2:2).

Coming of the Lord and our gathering together. Paul approaches the Thessalonians at the beginning of this chapter by making a new request (2:1). The word he uses means "to plead, implore, or beg."[1] Moreover, Paul speaks with endearing terms, once again calling them "brethren," a highly personal expression used twenty-five times in his two epistles to the Thessalonians (2:1). This request involves "the coming of our Lord Jesus Christ, and our gathering together to Him." The word "coming" (*parousia*) is the same word found several times throughout the two epistles (1 Thess. 2:19; 3:13; 4:15; 5:23; 2 Thess. 2:1, 8, 9). The term "gathering together" (*episunagōgēs*) paints the picture of an assembly coming together. The only other occurrence of this exact word in the New Testament is in Hebrews 10:25 where the writer tells the readers not to forsake the assembling of themselves together.

The next question is the identity of the event Paul has in mind. The first thing one can say is that these two events refer to the same event: "The government of the two nouns under one article makes it clear that one event, viewed under two complementary aspects, is the thought. It is a summary statement of the teaching given them in 1 Thessalonians 4:13–18."[2] In addition, most interpreters, regardless of their view of the timing of the Rapture, see these words as a reference to the Rapture that is mentioned in 1 Thessalonians 4:13–18. I showed earlier that the *coming* (*parousia*) of the Lord referred to in the first epistle is consistently the rapture of the church, when Christ will come to catch up believers to be with Him. The likely thought at the outset is that the first occurrence of the word may refer to the same event.

Those who follow the interpretation that the Rapture follows the tribulation often believe these words in 1 Thessalonians 2:1 are referring to a one-phase second coming. In this view believers meet Christ in the air for the purpose of immediately escorting Him to earth when He establishes His kingdom.[3] For proof of this approach, appeal is made to the use of the phrase "gathering together" to refer sometimes to the arrival of an important dignitary to a city. The city leaders go out to meet the dignitary and escort him back to the city.[4] This reliance on the terminology, however, depends on the word being a technical term. The expression does not contain within it the idea of an immediate return. Only the context of the passage could provide that information. Therefore, one cannot assume a posttribulational rapture on the basis of this word alone. The word simply implies a gathering together. Later context, to be discussed below, points in the direction of a two-phase second coming, thereby opening up the possibility of a pretribulational rapture in the passage.

At this point a couple of other objections to a pretribulational rapture in this passage are sometimes mentioned. First, it is pointed out that the previous chapter of 2 Thessalonians talks about the coming of Christ to the earth at the end of the tribulation and not the beginning. Why would the first verse of chapter 2 go back to an earlier rapture? If the same subject matter is in view—that is, end-time events—then there would be a continuation of the same topic, which would be quite natural. In response to this objection, the pretribulational rapturist refers to the outline of 2 Thessalonians with its three distinct subjects of persecution, Day of the Lord questions, and unruly believers. Since the second chapter has a unique topic, even if still about the end-times, there is no need to expect a continuation of the same subject matter in verse 1. Even those holding a posttribulational rapture view have agreed that the second chapter is an entirely new section.[5]

A second objection against a pretribulational understanding of the coming of the Lord in 2:1 involves the use of the same word *parousia* for a *coming* of the Lord mentioned later in 2:8. All interpreters agree that the slaying of the Antichrist in 2:8 occurs at the *coming* of Christ to earth at the end of the tribulation period. This objection claims that it would be highly likely for the two verses to be talking about the same coming of Christ.[6]

However, two responses can be made to this argument. To begin with, 2:8 does not have the qualifier "our gathering together to Him." In addition, Paul's argument in 2:1–2 makes perfect sense if the problem at hand is that the Thessalonians were wondering if the tribulation period had already started. If this is the meaning of 2:1–2, then an allusion to a pretribulational rapture would be appropriate, especially in light of Paul's earlier discussion of the church's exemption from the Day of the Lord's wrath in 1 Thessalonians.

Those today who hold to a rapture prior to the tribulation often speak in the same paragraph of their own writings of a coming of Christ in a pretribulational rapture and a coming of Christ to earth at the end of the tribulation. In doing so, they see themselves in harmony with Paul's own language. While the language of 2:1 and 2:8 can fit a posttribulational rapture, it does not demand one. It can just as easily be seen to demonstrate a pretribulational rapture. The debate is not really solved in 2:1 but must be dealt with in the context of the entire chapter.

A disturbing message. As the apostle brings their attention to the rapture of the church, he requests "that you may not be quickly shaken from your composure or be disturbed" (2:2). Something had indeed shaken their poise, so he urgently requests that a spirit of calm prevail. This may have been just a simple misunderstanding of something Paul had taught. Or it may have been the work of false teachers and preachers who had contradicted Paul after he had departed.

To be "quickly shaken" indicates that the church at Thessalonica was hastily being agitated over the issue of the Day of the Lord. "Quickly" (*tacheōs*) pertains to something that is a short amount of time (i.e., soon) or the manner in which something takes place (i.e., suddenly). Potentially both thoughts could be in mind based on the context. For example, Paul told the Galatians that he was amazed at how soon or how suddenly they had adopted a different gospel (Gal. 1:6). Here in 2:1 Paul does not want the Thessalonians to move hastily from their solid foundation to spurious questions. The term "shaken" (*saleuthēnai*) pictures something moving back and forth. The word was used in the language of that day to refer to the "motion produced by wind and wave" and of "a ship driven from its mooring."[7] In this context it conveys the notion of wavering or tottering. The word "composure" (*vous*) means "mind." R. C. H. Lenski points out that Christians are "to keep their heads against error and fanatic notions."[8] Apparently Paul had heard that the Thessalonians were facing some beliefs or questions that threatened to push them away from their faithful standing before God, so he encourages them to remain on solid ground.

In addition, Paul describes the predicament of the Thessalonians with the word "disturbed." Mal Couch explains how this word drives home the truth:

> This is the most emotional word Paul uses in this discussion. *Disturbed* (*throeō*, present passive infinitive) is a strong and powerful word in Greek that is used only here and in two other places in the New Testament (Matt. 24:6; Mark 13:7). It means "to cry aloud" as in pain or tumult. . . . It is interesting that the word *throeō* is used in Matthew 24:6 and Mark 13:7 in the same context about the Tribulation or the Day of the Lord, with the same warning by Christ that Paul uses.[9]

What exactly was disturbing the Thessalonian believers? Paul mentions three possible things. First, Paul refers to a "spirit" (2:2). This may have been a demonically inspired false prophecy. Paul had given the instruction in 1 Thessalonians 5:20: "Do not despise prophetic utterances." Of course Paul did not mean that every person claiming to prophesy in the name of the Lord would be proclaiming truth. Every prophecy had to be checked and examined

(v. 21). Someone may have claimed to have a direct word from God that the church at Thessalonica must be experiencing the tribulation because of all the persecution they were facing (cf. 1 John 4:1–6). It is also possible that there was a genuine prophecy that was simply misunderstood, although the earlier idea seems to fit the context more easily.

The second possible source was a wrong "message" (2:2). "Message" (*logos*) simply means a verbal teaching or a truth presented. What had disturbed them did not have to come through some supposed supernatural revelation, but may have been some message brought by a false teacher. The Bible warns believers to be cautious and to test everything they are taught (Matt. 7:15; Acts 17:11; Eph. 4:14; 2 Pet. 2:1; 1 John 2:19; Jude 4).

The third source that Paul mentions as a possible cause of the disruption of the church was a "letter" (2:2). Someone had potentially claimed that Paul had written a letter "to the effect that the day of the Lord has come" (2:2). Paul could be speaking of his first letter to the Thessalonians or another one written to them that we do not possess. In either case, if this is the letter that is meant, Paul's concern is wrapped up in his intent being misconstrued by the Thessalonians. More likely, however, is the notion that someone was using Paul's name without his authority, and he wanted the Thessalonians to be cautious about any letters supposedly from him. In fact, the claim may have been made that the spirit, message, and letter all came from Paul. The false notion that Paul wants them to discard is that "the day of the Lord has come." The Day of the Lord's wrath is the same as that in 1 Thessalonians 5:1–11. It refers to the Seventieth Week of Daniel, commonly called the tribulation period. The options for the verb "has come" (*enesteken*) are that the Day of the Lord had already come and the Thessalonians were in it or that it had come and gone and they missed it. It is also grammatically possible that the Day of the Lord had come in the sense of being at the door or impending. This latter sense cannot be maintained by the context, because Paul's answer beginning in 2:3 suggests one of the first two options. Whatever it is, there was a false claim or understanding, as Paul points out: "Let no one in any way deceive you, for it will not come unless . . . " (2:3). The apostle emphatically states that certain things have to be true before the Day of the Lord comes.

Before examining those certain things in 2:3, this is a good place in the discussion to summarize and frame the overall argument that is generated by the controversy mentioned in 2:2. One's understanding of the argument directly affects one's view of the timing of the Rapture. If the posttribulational view of the Rapture is assumed, the Day of the Lord refers to the judgment events associated with the actual second coming of Christ to earth along with the resurrection of believers. In this scheme, the Thessalonians are disturbed that the return of Christ and the resurrection has already happened.[10] The saints at Thessalonica were worried that somehow they missed the experience of these major end-time events. However, does it really make sense that the promises of 1 Thessalonians 4:13–18 would have been that misunderstood? If they believed that Jesus had come to earth, the kingdom would be under way. They would be in the kingdom with Christ present on earth and not know it. Is this really the concern that is on their hearts?

The much better approach is to understand the Day of the Lord as a period of time rather than a singular event. The teaching of the passage would then be that the Thessalonians had mistook the persecution they were suffering (chapter 1) and believed it to be the Day of the Lord's wrath or tribulation. The question would be more about missing a pretribulational rapture, which harmonizes well with some of the questions they seemed to have in 1 Thessalonians.[11] Many of them believed their persecution placed them squarely in the middle of the tribulation period Paul had predicted when he was with them and in his first letter.

In that light one can then look at 2:3. Paul teaches that two events must take place before the Day of the Lord, or tribulation, arrives. Something called "apostasy," followed by the revelation of the man of lawlessness, must occur before one could say he was in the tribulation. If these two things have not been seen, then the Thessalonians were not in the Day of the Lord. Thus each one must be examined closely.

Issue of the Apostasy

The apostle does not want the Thessalonians to go astray in this matter, so he warns them, "Let no one in any way deceive you" (2:3). The phrase "in any way" means "in any manner" and probably harks back to the three options that Paul gave in 2:2 of a prophetic utterance, verbal teaching, or letter supposedly from him. They are to be alert on all fronts. The word "deceive" (*exapatēsē*) is used only by Paul in the New Testament. It means to mislead or lead to error. Paul uses the term to describe the deception of Eve by the serpent (2 Cor. 11:3). In particular the apostle wants them to know that there are two things that must happen before the Day of the Lord comes. The Thessalonians should not let others sway them into different thinking.

Paul declares that the Day of the Lord will not come "unless the apostasy comes first" (2:3). Much debate has centered on the meaning of the word "apostasy." Whatever it means, it has to come before the Day of the Lord. The context also suggests that it may also be connected in some way to the revelation of the man of lawlessness mentioned next in the passage

Apostasy simply means "departure." The word usually "denotes a deliberate abandonment of a formerly professed position or view, a defection, a rejection of a former allegiance."[12] The word in its noun form is used only twice in the New Testament, here and in Acts 21:21. In the Acts passage, Jewish accusers charge Paul with abandoning or forsaking the Law of Moses, hence a religious defection. In the Greek translation of the Old Testament, all occurrences of the noun refer to religious unfaithfulness and defection (Josh. 22:22; 2 Chron. 29:19; Jer. 2:19) or to political rebellion (Ezra 4:12–15). In light of this usage, *rebellion* would be a good synonym for *apostasy* in 2 Thessalonians 2:3.

Another possible interpretation of the word that has been put forward is that it does not mean a departure in the sense of religious defection, but departure in the sense of "removal" or "change of location." It is usually then applied to the rapture of the church as a removal. In this view one of the things that must occur before the Day of the Lord comes is the rapture of the church. This fits nicely with the pretribulational Rapture before the tribulation period.

To support such a notion, one could emphasize that the verb associated with the noun for *apostasy* is used fourteen times in the New Testament and almost always speaks of departure in this sense of removal or change of location. Examples would be Anna the prophetess not "leaving" the temple (Luke 2:37) and the devil "departing" from Jesus after the temptations (Luke 4:13). In addition, the identification of the restrainer later in the passage (1 Thess. 2:6–7) is often given as the Holy Spirit. The special relationship of the Spirit to the church then comes into the argument. In this view, if the restrainer is taken away (not a religious defection), the passage is probably suggesting that the church is taken away (not a religious defection). Wayne House argues passionately for a reconsideration of the particular interpretation in 2 Thessalonians 2:3 of apostasy as removal or change of location.

> I have sought to demonstrate that the departure of the church may be the proper understanding found in the Greek word *apostasia* in 2 Thessalonians 2:3. Certainly the case is not conclusive, but it should not be dismissed out of hand as many have done. If *apostasia* means departure, in the context of the departure of Christians before the Day of the Lord, then the word corresponds with Paul's other terms to describe the deliverance of Christians from this world and their gathering to Jesus Christ. The meaning of *apostasia* in Greek literature, the grammar of the passage, and contextual considerations found in the Thessalonian epistles fit well with this interpretation

and may provide hope and comfort to Christians today, even as it did to the Thessalonian Christians of the first century.[13]

Couch points out that most conservative interpreters agree that *apostasia* refers in this context to religious defection.[14] John Walvoord emphasizes that this is true even among pretribulational scholars who would gain by the alternative interpretation.[15] Two reasons reinforce the standard interpretation as defection from the faith. First is the fact that all other occurrences of the noun *apostasia* in the New Testament and in the Greek Old Testament refer to religious or political rebellion. Second, one must take into account the close association of the man of lawlessness mentioned in 2:3. Since he is described in terms of wickedness and rebellion (2:3–4), it may be more likely that the thought of wicked rebellion is also the intended meaning of *apostasia*. Consequently, it is much more likely that the word refers to religious defection of some kind rather than the departure of the church.

With that in mind, one immediately recalls that religious defection was something that existed in the beginnings of the early church (2 Pet. 2:1–22; Jude). But "apostasy" has the definite article (*hē apostasia*) in 2 Thessalonians 2:3 indicating a particular apostasy that will occur in the future. "Paul's use of the definite article reveals that he had in mind not a general flow or trend, but a specific, identifiable act of apostasy."[16]

However, the apostle does not explain himself further in this passage. Later, near the end of his life, he begins to flesh out the details of an end-time defection of the faith in his letters to Timothy (1 Tim. 4:1–3; 2 Tim. 3:1–9; 4:3–4). Paul speaks of false doctrine coming from deceitful spirits or demons. People will fall away chasing after these teachings that abandon basic Christian teaching (1 Tim. 4:1–3). It is a falling away that leads to a complete departure from genuine Christian behavior in all of life while at the same time trying to claim a form of Christian godliness (2 Tim. 3:1–9). It will also be a time when the truth of the Bible will be cast aside as people pursue myths that feed their desires (2 Tim. 4:1–4). Some Christians say we are already in such a time in the modern Western world. The rise of liberal Christianity in the nineteenth century and the advance of ecumenical movements in the twentieth century are seen as evidence of this perspective. While these developments are definitely a form of apostasy, the defection from the faith predicted by Paul in 1 Thessalonians 2:3 should probably be taken as a specific end-time event or development associated with the time immediately prior to the Day of the Lord and in connection with the rise of the man of lawlessness. It remains to be seen what connection there would be between that event and current times.

The Issue of the Antichrist

The Identification of Antichrist. Next Paul tells the saints in Thessalonica that the Day of the Lord will not come until the revelation of "the man of lawlessness," who is also called "the son of destruction" (2:3). This is not a reference to an impersonal force of evil in the world. Paul clearly describes him as a man (2:3) and as an individual who seeks worship (2:4). Furthermore, he is someone who performs false miracles (2:9–10) and who dies an individual death (2:8).

The man described here is described by the term "lawlessness" (*anomias*). The concept is repeated in 2:8 when he is portrayed as the "lawless one." The idea is fleshed out further when Paul notes that his coming is in agreement with the activity of Satan (2:9) and with all the deception of wickedness (2:10). Such a description shows this man to be not only against God's laws, but against God Himself. The pinnacle of this man's heinous lawlessness is when he sets himself up to be worshiped as God (2:4).

While the term "man of lawlessness" describes this man's character and actions, the second term, "son of destruction," speaks of his destiny. The phrase "son of destruction" is used elsewhere in the New Testament only one time in referring to Judas Iscariot who betrayed Christ (John 17:12; cf. Acts 1:25). Some popular presentations have suggested that the man of lawlessness (Antichrist) will be a resurrected or resuscitated Judas in light of the same use of terms. However, this should be treated no more seriously than the myth from the early church that the Antichrist would be the Roman emperor Nero raised from the dead. Just as Judas in his rebellion was destroyed, so also will be this future anti-God figure of the end-times. In 2:8 Paul reminds the Thessalonians that this person will be killed directly by the Lord Jesus when He returns, a turn of events that correlates well with Revelation 19:20.

The depiction of this lawless one given in 2:4 allows the drawing of a more precise portrait of him. He opposes all other objects that could be worshiped, including the one true and living God—"who opposes and exalts himself above every so-called god or object of worship." The word "opposes" (*antikeimenos*) carries the idea of showing open hostility, the very essence of an adversary. The term "exalts" (*huperairomenos*) refers to a placing of someone over someone else in the most extreme terms. In this case the exaltation is a self-exaltation by an arrogant and prideful man. In harmony with this action, he considers himself to be exalted above all others who would claim worship ("every so-called god"). The height of this rebellion is demonstrated by his wicked action of taking his seat in the Jewish temple of the tribulation (see below). Since the temple is the place that symbolizes God's presence, the man of lawlessness truly claims to be God. D. Michael Martin notes, "The image is one of extreme arrogance, the ultimate in megalomania, installing oneself not just as a god but as the greatest of the gods, the self-proclaimed ruler of all."[17]

This monstrously wicked man of lawlessness is not a new portrayal that Paul has created. The image follows the book of Daniel and also anticipates the book of Revelation. In Daniel it is the *little horn* (king) out of the fourth world empire (Rome), which emerges "speaking boastful words." However, he is destroyed as the Son of Man comes to establish the kingdom of God on earth (Dan. 7:7–14). This same personage appears to be the "prince who is to come" who will make a treaty with Israel for seven years but then break that treaty, stop the sacrifices in the Jewish temple, and set up the abomination of desolation (Dan. 9:27; cf. 12:11). He is also the *willful king* of Daniel 11:36–45 who will exalt himself above all gods and speak blasphemously against the God of the Jews as he abuses the nation of Israel. The book of Revelation designates him and his kingdom by the term "beast" coming up out of the sea (Rev. 13). He is a mighty political and military power speaking arrogant words and blasphemies against God. All of these descriptions match in the details. Paul calls this same person the *man of lawlessness* and the *son of destruction* (2 Thess. 2:3). The general term that is used most often for this evil man is *Antichrist,* a designation taken from 1 John 2:18–22 (see below).

The revelation of the Antichrist (2:3). The word "revealed" (*apokalupthē*) leaves the impression that this man of lawlessness was hidden from view but at the appropriate time would be made known. Paul's statement is simple enough on the face of it. The man of lawlessness must be made known in some way before the Day of the Lord arrives. However, as we saw earlier, the Day of the Lord in 1 and 2 Thessalonians refers to the entire seven-year tribulation, which is the Day of the Lord's wrath of God. That means that in some way the man of lawlessness appears on the scene before these seven years or at the beginning point of the seven years. There is no reason to see this teaching as referring to the birth of this person. Rather, it is a specific event in history where the man of lawlessness steps into God's timeline for end-time events. The most logical time to see this revelation occurring is the signing of the seven-year treaty between this Antichrist and the nation of Israel (Dan. 9:27). Thus the man of lawlessness is revealed at the beginning of the tribulation period and is, in fact, the one who humanly precipitates the start of the seven-year period.[18]

The Antichrist—1 John 2:18–22

Designation and Passage	Exalts Himself as God	Jewish Temple and Law	Deception	His Destruction
Little Horn *Dan. 7:7–12*	*Uttering great boasts (v. 8); boastful words (vv. 11, 20)*	*Intends alterations in times and law (v. 25)*	—	*The beast was slain and given to the burning fire (vv. 11, 26)*
Prince to Come *Dan. 9:24–27*	—	*Puts a stop to sacrifice and grain offering (v. 27)*	*Breaks his treaty with Israel (v. 27)*	*Complete destruction . . . poured out on the one who makes desolate*
Willful King *Dan. 11:36–45*	*Will exalt and magnify himself above every god, and will speak monstrous things against the God of gods (v. 36)*	*Will pitch the tents of his royal pavilion between the seas and the beautiful Holy Mountain (v. 45)*	—	*Comes to his end and no one helps him (v. 45)*
Beast *Rev. 13*	*Given a mouth speaking arrogant words and blasphemies (v. 5)*	*Compare Rev. 11 and 12*	*Through the False Prophet he will deceive those on the earth because of the signs (v. 14; cf. Rev. 20:20)*	*Beast and False Prophet will be thrown alive into the lake of fire (Rev.19:20)*
Man of Lawlessness, Son of Destruction *2 Thess. 2:3–8*	*Opposes and exalts himself above every so-called god or object of worship; displays himself to be God (v. 4)*	*He takes his seat in the temple of God (v. 4)*	*With all power and signs and false wonders, and with all deception (vv. 9–10)*	*The Lord will slay . . . and bring to an end by the appearance of His coming (v. 8)*

The significance of the Jewish temple (2:4). The arrogance and self-exaltation on the part of Antichrist reaches its pinnacle when he "takes his seat in the temple of God, displaying himself as being God." The idea of taking a seat (*kathisai*) in the temple is in this case to assume a high position. The reference to the temple is highly significant, although its meaning is debated. Beale rejects the idea that this is a reference to an end-time rebuilt Jewish temple in Jerusalem. His reasons can be summarized as (1) the apostasy or falling away mentioned in 2:3 does not involve Israel, since the majority of Jews have never believed in Christ and so cannot fall away, and (2) the worldwide apostasy really refers to the church and not national Israel, since all of Paul's other uses of the word *temple* refer to Christian believers (e.g., 1 Cor. 3:16–17; 2 Cor. 6:16). G. K. Beale's conclusion is that the temple referred to is the church. Antichrist would then be seen by Paul as taking his seat in the church, leading it into false worship and idolatry.[19]

In response to the first claim, it must be noted that the argument assumes what it is attempting to prove. Why not a worldwide apostasy associated with a defection from the Christian faith that is also coupled with the Antichrist setting himself up in an actual Jewish temple to lead false worldwide worship? There is no contradiction here if that is the case. The attempted proof otherwise almost begins from the assumption that national Israel has no real role in the end-times and then argues from that vantage point.

In response to the second claim regarding Paul's other uses of the word "temple," one must point out that none of those uses occurs in a context discussing the particulars of end-time events. At stake is the interpretation of a host of other passages. Is not Daniel 9:27 partly about the Antichrist and his relationship to a real Jewish temple during Daniel's Seventieth Week? Do not the discussions of the actions of the Antichrist in Daniel 11:36–45 include mention of the Beautiful Land (Israel (v. 41) and geographical markers that can refer only to Jerusalem in the land of Israel (v. 45.)? Is not the mention of the temple in the Olivet Discourse (Matt. 24:1–3) also associated with the real city of Jerusalem (Matt. 23:37–39) and the region of Judea (Matt. 24:16)? Does not the book of Revelation also show that there is an end-time temple (Rev. 11:1–2) and a persecution of national Israel (Rev. 12)? All of these end-time examples are impossible to harmonize with a view that *temple* means *church* unless some spiritualizing or allegorizing method of interpretation is used. Consequently, taking Paul's words at face value, the word "temple" in 2 Thessalonians 2:4 should be taken as a rebuilt Jewish temple that is prominent throughout passages regarding the tribulation and Antichrist.[20]

The wording for this arrogant action of the man of lawlessness that is most worthy of condemnation is "displaying himself as being God" (2:4). The word *"displaying"* (*apodeiknunta*) entails an attempt on the part of the Antichrist to demonstrate in a public fashion the claim that he is the deity with whom the world must reckon. Paul uses the same term in portraying God's desire to make the apostles an exhibit (put on display) in the world as condemned men who are a spectacle to the whole world (1 Cor. 4:9). The display of the Antichrist is, of course, a self-generated display (no doubt with Satan's help). Martin makes the keen observation that in Paul's day such pretension to deity was more readily understandable as a cultural phenomena than it is today in our modern world.[21]

Paul's prior instructions (2:5). Almost interrupting himself, the apostle Paul inserts a question into the flow of his argument—"Do you not remember that while I was still with you, I was telling you these things?" The question demands a yes answer. It could be taken as a rhetorical question and may suggest that the apostle is somewhat bothered by the fact that he has to go over old lesson plans again. However, he has throughout his epistles reminded them of things he said while he was with them. Therefore, it is probably not best to see Paul as flustered or impatient in his argumentation. He uses the question to remind the Thessalonians that he had already taught them about these end-time events. Interestingly, the tense of the verb "was telling" (*elegon*) can be taken to imply that his teaching had been ongoing about these matters when he was with them.[22] That is, he frequently touched upon these end-time subjects concerning the man of lawlessness on his visit to Thessalonica.[23] It is no wonder then that Paul moves from the usual "we" to the more personal "I" in this verse as he reminds them of past teaching done personally and forcefully.

This question reveals two things that are helpful. First, it shows that the information the Thessalonians possessed on end-time events is not restricted merely to I Thessalonians but also includes the oral presentations of Paul when he came through Thessalonica. Second, it reveals that the study of last things was a major priority in first-century apostolic preaching and teaching. A significant application of Paul's words for today is that end-time studies should not be relegated to a secondary place in theology.

The Issue of the Restrainer

The identity of the restrainer. The apostle indicates that the Antichrist would already be on the scene if there had not been a *restrainer*. Paul first gives this teaching in the form found in 2:6: "And you know what restrains him now, so that in his time he may be revealed." The verb "know" (*oidate*), in keeping with the apostle's question of 2:5, implies that the Thessalonians already possess an understanding of the idea of restraining, which Paul mentions. The word "*now*" (*nun*) shows that the restraining is going on at the time he writes. It is part of the experience of the first-century world. The one being restrained and the one who will eventually be revealed are the same person, namely, the man of lawlessness whose revelation is mentioned in the previous context (2:3). These points of interpretation are relatively easy to establish.

However, the meaning of the word "restrains" (2:6) has not admitted to any ease of understanding. The term (*katechōn*) in a negative use means "to hold down, confine, restrain." But such a negative sense is not the only way to take the word. In 1 Corinthians 15:2 it is translated "hold fast" in a context where Paul expects the Corinthians to hold fast or grasp tightly the gospel of Jesus Christ. However, the former sense of restrain is the only one that correlates well with the context of the chapter. Something or someone prevents the revealing or making known of the ultimate Antichrist. The expression "in his time" leads to the conclusion that in God's timetable there is a set moment in history when the man of lawlessness comes on the scene and is made known. In addition, the restraining here based on the word Paul uses is somewhat vague, coming across as an impersonal thing—*what* restrains. That is, some *thing* perhaps is holding back the coming forward of the man of lawlessness. At this point in Paul's argument, the impersonal or personal nature of the restraining influence cannot be determined.

The next verse, however, makes it clear that this restrainer must be a person (rather than an impersonal force), for it is "*he* who now restrains" (2:7). Various views have been put forth concerning who or what this restrainer will be—human government, angelic beings, certain Roman emperors, the Antichrist himself, or the church. The most likely candidate is that the restrainer should be identified as the Holy Spirit of God, for He alone could do the work required to restrain Satan's work of the Antichrist:

> Our identification of the Restrainer must ultimately be determined by the question, What person is able to hold back the efforts of Satan? To effectively counteract and restrain the personal activities of Satan demands a person, and one that is more than human. Only a supernatural person can truly frustrate the supernatural workings of Satan. This would at once rule out human agencies as well as all evil supernatural agents. Only a superhuman Restrainer can do the work.[24]

The interpretive decision to see the Holy Spirit as the restrainer is aided partly by the fact that He is personal and possesses force. However, it is the process of elimination that narrows down the choices to the work of the Spirit, who fits the details better than any other suggestion.

The restraining work of the Holy Spirit will continue until such time as He is "taken out of the way" (2:7). The Holy Spirit's restraining ministry will apparently be removed from earth during the future tribulation period. This does not mean that the Spirit of God will no longer work in the world at all. It simply means that His work of restraining the arrival of the Antichrist and holding him back will be stopped. Then God will allow the Antichrist to do Satan's final work at the end of the age. More information on the identity of the restrainer is provided in appendix B.

The mystery of lawlessness (2:7). Paul makes the claim in 2:7 that the "mystery of lawlessness is already at work." The word "mystery" refers to a truth that can now be known although it was once hidden. This particular mystery involves lawlessness, which in turn harks back to the man of lawlessness predicted in 2:3. The question naturally arises as to how a future reality is somehow tied to Paul's present time. The meaning is that the spirit of rebellion that characterizes the work of the future Antichrist is also present in the world now, although not in its ultimate and worst form. This is exactly parallel to 1 John 2:18–22. There the apostle John teaches that there is a personal Antichrist who is coming but that there are many antichrists already in the world. An antichrist in that particular passage is one who rejects Christ. So those opposing Christ in Paul's day, already at work in their lawlessness, will one day find their ultimate negative hero in the personal Antichrist, the man of lawlessness.

The Destiny of the Antichrist and His Followers

The destiny of the Antichrist. At this point Paul has answered the question that was disturbing the Thessalonians. They wondered whether the Day of the Lord had started. Paul tells them that it has not started, because the man of lawlessness, the Antichrist who dominates the tribulation period or Day of the Lord, has not arrived on the scene. If they were in the tribulation period, the Antichrist would be a well-known figure as Paul has characterized him. Even though the apostle has given the outline of an answer to the Thessalonians, he wants to take his sketch of the Antichrist to its logical conclusion.

Thus Paul notes that the removal of the restrainer leads to the truth that "the lawless one will be revealed" (2:8). The designation "lawless one" or "the one without law" (*ho anomos*) is a shorthand form of "man of lawlessness" and refers in context to the Antichrist. The mentioning of his revelation follows the same assertion given twice already in the chapter (2:3, 6). However, as F. F. Bruce notes, "He is revealed only to be destroyed."[25] From the vantage point of a pretribulational approach to the Rapture, the revelation of the Antichrist happens at the start of the seven-year tribulation, but his rise to power is short-lived. Paul describes the Antichrist and his end this way: "whom the Lord will slay with the breath of His mouth" (2:8). After Antichrist's rise to power and acclaim, Christ Jesus will kill him. The term "slay" (*anelei*) means "to do away with" or "kill." It carries the weight of a just execution. There is nothing wrong with this kind of killing. It is genuine righteous indignation meting out what is due to the man of lawlessness. The means of the killing is said to be "with the breath of His mouth." This picture is found in Isaiah 11:4: "But with righteousness He will judge the poor, and decide with fairness for the afflicted of the earth; and He will strike the earth with the rod of his mouth, and with the breath of His lips He will slay the wicked." The chief difference between Isaiah's use of the metaphor and Paul's is that Isaiah envisions the putting down of evil as an ongoing activity within the time of the kingdom (millennial phase). That is, it is part of the reign of Christ during the millennium. Paul, on the other hand, uses the imagery to describe the judgment at the Second Coming itself, which ends the tribulation and precedes the kingdom. Later on in history the book of Revelation will portray Christ at the Second Coming with a sword in his mouth as he slays His enemies, including the Antichrist (Rev. 19:11–21).[26]

The destiny of the man of lawlessness is also described by Paul's thought that the Antichrist is the one whom the Lord "will . . . bring to an end by the appearance of His coming" (2:8). In this context, the expression "bring to an end" (*katargēsei*) means to put a stop to something in the sense of absolute destruction. The word is used by Paul when he teaches that the "last enemy that will be *abolished* is death" (1 Cor. 15:26). The appearance of His coming can only refer to the second coming of Jesus, which according to the first chapter of 2 Thessalonians is a great hope for believers but is horrible affliction for those who do not know God. Antichrist is in the company of the latter.

The use of the term "coming" (*parousia*) in 2:8 to refer to the event of Christ's coming to earth is thought to be a problem for the pretribulational view because that position sees the word referring to the event of the Rapture (which is at least seven years earlier in that scheme) in virtually all other passages in 1 and 2 Thessalonians that apply to Jesus. However, the term is not a technical term that carries with it some encoded event. It is the *presence* of Christ that is in view no matter what the event or its timing. The context and the argument derived from each passage must carry the day. The term is even used with reference to the man of lawlessness in the very next verse where no specific event is in view. Therefore, caution should be urged before drawing conclusions too tightly on the basis of a single word.

The source of Antichrist's power. Paul adds a brief description of the enormous power behind the man of lawlessness. The Antichrist, the one destroyed by Jesus, is "the one whose coming is in accord with the activity of Satan" (2:9). The word "activity" (*energeian*) means "working, function, or practice." Paul usually uses the term relative to the working of God (e.g., Eph. 1:19) or the activity of the church (Eph. 4:16). Only here does he use the term to speak of Satan's activity, although he shows in his other epistles that he is quite aware of the devil's working (Eph. 6:11–16). Satan is none other than the adversary who hindered him from going to see the Thessalonians (1 Thess. 2:18), the chief among the fallen angels who deceives and tempts people.

Paul goes on to describe the manner or means of Satan's activity through the Antichrist: "with all power and signs and false wonders" (2:9). It is not clear if the adjective "false" should be taken only as describing the word "wonders" or should be applied also to the other terms.[27] Regardless, the overall meaning is clear. All of these same terms—"power" or "miracles," "signs," and "wonders"—are applied to Jesus in Peter's sermon in Acts 2:22—"Jesus the Nazarene, a man attested to you by God with miracles and wonders and signs." Thus Paul teaches that Satan is a counterfeiter who uses certain actions and methods to deceive people to believe a lie and come against God. Thomas Constable notes that Satan will "perform such powerful miracles that it will be evident to all that he has supernatural power, and people will stand in awe of him."[28] The idea of false wonders reminds one of Pharaoh's magicians who mimicked God's power through Moses during the time of the plagues (Exod. 7:11ff.). However, such duplicitous duplication can only go so far as the entire episode shows. How fitting that Paul would here discuss Satan's counterfeiting power through the Antichrist in the context of a description of the utter and final destruction of the man of lawlessness.

But Paul is not yet finished with his depiction of Satan's miracle-working through the Antichrist. He goes on to add the description "with all the deception of wickedness" (2:10). The apostle had reminded the Thessalonians that the apostolic missionary team had not come to them in any deceitful way (1 Thess. 2:3). It is also highly appropriate that in a section of his epistle designed specifically to help the Thessalonians avoid the deceit that comes with a false message (2 Thess. 2:3), Paul shows that Satan, who is alive and well in the present experience, will peak in terms of deceit during the coming Day of the Lord's wrath. The word "wickedness" (*adikias*) speaks of any action or work that is not right, an unjust deed. The phrase coupled with the term "all" may signify that Satan, during the Day of the Lord, will use every unrighteous means available to him to lead people astray.

The destiny of Antichrist's followers. Unfortunately, there will be individuals alive during the tribulation, who will follow the deceitful miracles of the Antichrist done by the power of Satan. Paul explains to the Thessalonian saints that the "deception of wickedness" of the Antichrist is "for those who perish" (2:10). The ones who are perishing are the ones on their way to perdition.[29] These are those who can be characterized as lost. The further descriptive language brings this home: "because they did not receive the love of the truth so as to be saved." These people are lost (i.e., not saved) because they have rejected the truth about Christ and the gospel. When the text refers to the "love" of the truth, it means to push our minds to thoughts of the great love of God that brought about the wonderful gospel of salvation. To reject the gospel is for Paul a denial of the astounding love of God (cf. John 3:16).

The apostle informs the Thessalonians of the tragic nature of this situation for those who perish. God does not sleep and ignore their embrace of Satan and his man of lawlessness, for the text says, "for this reason," or on account of this, God "will send upon them a deluding influence" (2:11). The time when God does this is during the Day of the Lord's wrath, a time future to the current state of the Thessalonians as the passage says through and through. He is not giving this information in case they find themselves in the midst of the tribulation one day. The term "sends upon" (*pempei*) conveys the truth that God will cause an experience of sorts, in this case a "deluding influence." The word for deluding or deception comes from a term meaning "the state of wandering," applied here to a wandering from the truth. It is a missing of the mark in what to hold as true and factual. The word "influence" (*energeian*) is actually the idea of working. It is the same term that is used of the working or activity of Satan in 2:9. The parallel is important. It is as if God, in light of their following after Satan's deception, uses their very deception and reinforces it—"so that they might believe what is false" (2:11). The reader must not be too casual here. "That which is false" is stated rather formally. It is *the* lie, not just any lie. In this context it refers to the rejection of the one true God and the acceptance in His place of the Antichrist, the one who has set himself up as God in the Jewish temple.

The teaching here bears some resemblance to the hardening of Pharaoh's heart in the Exodus story (cf. Rom. 9:17). Martin cautiously frames the meaning: "God does not cause their unbelief, but he does set the stage for them to demonstrate it and thus openly earn their own condemnation."[30] The summary of it all is given as the result of God sending them strong delusion—"in order that they all may be judged who did not believe the truth, but took pleasure in wickedness" (2:12). Concerning this section, and particularly verse 11, Morris astutely observes:

> The principle underlying this verse is of great importance for an understanding of the moral government of the universe. From the foregoing verses it might perhaps be thought that there is a contest in which Satan on one hand and God on the other hand makes their moves, but with God somewhat the stronger. But Paul has a much grander conception. God is using the very evil that people (and even Satan) do for the working out of his purpose. They think they are acting in defiance of him, but in the end they find that those very acts in which they expressed their defiance were the vehicle of their punishment.[31]

At this point it is necessary to review a couple of interpretations involving the identity of the particular unbelievers upon whom God sends the delusion so that they are condemned. The first interpretation, sometimes heard in popular pretribulational presentations, is that those who consciously reject Christ *before* the rapture of the church (2:10) will be sent a strong delusion by God after the rapture of the church (v. 11) so that they will not be saved. In other words, those who had heard the truth about Jesus but spurned it will have their hearts hardened after the Rapture with no opportunity for them to be saved. The context, however, knows nothing about those who have heard the gospel before the Rapture versus events after the Rapture. That is a theological reading into the text without scriptural warrant.

Therefore, a second interpretation is to be preferred. The deception of Satan that occurs in the passage involves the lying and wonders of the Antichrist's work during the tribulation. This is what the unbelievers being discussed embrace. People in the tribulation period, who follow Satan's and Antichrist's lying wonders, will have their minds deluded by God so that they will not believe in Christ. This fits nicely with the teaching in Revelation that those who receive the mark of the Beast (flowing from worship of Antichrist) will be doomed (Rev. 13:16–18; 19:20). The rejection of Christ that is envisioned occurs during the tribulation itself, not before the rapture of the church. This makes perfect sense in light of the fact that Paul's topic of discussion is the Day of the Lord. The unbelievers who are hardened in their thoughts are those who, during the tribulation, have accepted the Antichrist as their savior.

Study Questions

1. What caused the believers at Thessalonica to have their faith shaken?

2. What is the major concern of the Thessalonians in this passage? In light of this concern, is it better to see the Day of the Lord as a single event or a period of time?
3. To what does the word "apostasy" in verse 3 refer?
4. How is the Antichrist described by Paul? Can we know his identity? How does this compare to other descriptions of him throughout the Bible?
5. Will the temple be rebuilt in the tribulation? What does the Antichrist do in the temple?
6. What is the identity of the restrainer? Is the restrainer a force or a person? What does he restrain?
7. How will the Antichrist work miracles?
8. If people miss the Rapture, will they have a chance to get saved in the tribulation period? Why or why not?

CHAPTER 15

The Call of God
2 Thessalonians 2:13–17

Preview:

Paul encourages the believers at Thessalonica to remember God's choice of them and to stand firm on proper teaching. He adds a prayer that the everyday experience of the saints will be one of comforting and strengthening based on the love, comfort, and hope that God has already granted by His grace.

Paul follows up the doctrinal section of 2 Thessalonians with statements of encouragement just as he did in the first chapter. In particular Paul had already dealt with the call of God in 1:11, but now he gives the broad scope of salvation. He looks back to the past and ahead to the future to encourage the believers at Thessalonica to be faithful to God in the midst of their persecution. This section contrasts with the earlier concern that they would be shaken by a false message (2:2). Paul reminds the Thessalonians that they have no need to worry in light of God's great work in their behalf, a work that will lead ultimately to glory (2:14).

The Choice of God (2:13–14)

Paul begins this last section of chapter 2 with a familiar apostolic theme: "we should always give thanks" (2:13; see also 1 Thess. 1:2; 3:9; 2 Thess. 1:3). Gratitude is a debt that Paul owes to God and the Thessalonian believers, and he intends to fulfill it as a matter of obligation. The apostle combines the familial expressions "brethren" and "beloved by the Lord" to emphasize the personal nature of what is being said. To be a brother with Paul and to be the focus of God's love would certainly be in contrast to those persecutors who hated them in Thessalonica. It would also contrast with those he just described in the future tribulation period who would not receive the love of the truth.

The apostle reminds the Thessalonians that his thanksgiving stems from the knowledge that "God has chosen you from the beginning for salvation" (2:13). The word "chosen" (*eilato* from *haireō*) is not Paul's usual word to explain election. The word is used only two other times in the New Testament, neither of which speaks of God's choosing. Paul uses the word in Philippians 1:22 when talking about personal choice. It is also used in Hebrews 11:25 of Moses choosing to suffer affliction with the people of God rather than enjoy the blessings of Egypt. Here in 2 Thessalonians 2:13, the word shows God's active choice of the persecuted saints in that place, something intended to comfort. However, there is no real difference in its meaning from other words that speak of God's election of believers.

The time of being chosen, the apostle writes, is "from the beginning."[1] This could be interpreted to be from the beginning of Paul's ministry in Thessalonica and the time they became believers under his ministry. More likely, as evidenced by Paul's focus on election in other letters, the expression points to the call of God in eternity past: "The view that 'from the beginning' means 'from eternity past' is in full accord with Paul's teaching concerning the pretemporal beginning of the program of redemption (1 Cor. 2:7; Eph. 1:4; 2 Tim. 1:9; Titus 1:2). The readers are assured that their election was no recent innovation; they were included in God's plan from the dateless past."[2]

This choosing is "for salvation," which refers to a positive relationship with God and what we usually understand comes with eternal life, both in its present and future aspects (2:13). According to the passage, this salvation comes first through "sanctification by the Spirit." Sanctification (*hagiasmō*), as seen earlier in 1 Thessalonians 4:3–7, is the normal word for holiness and means set apart from something evil and for something good. The word "*Spirit*" (*pneumatos*) can refer only to the Holy Spirit of God in this context (cf. 1 Thess. 4:8). Paul's mention of the Spirit's work is in contrast to the work of the unholy spirit (Satan) in the preceding verses. The different results, which each one works in individuals, provide a stark contrast. The Spirit of God takes the sinner and sets him apart positionally at the moment of initial salvation. But He also sets apart the believer moment by moment practically, making him holy or sanctified. This is a process that continues throughout the believer's life, but it is still reckoned as part of the salvation package a believer receives through God's choice. The entire package is probably viewed holistically by the apostle as he thinks about the status of the Thessalonians.

The second means of salvation is through "faith in the truth" (2:13). In contrast to those Paul previously mentioned who would be deceived and thereby not believe the truth (2:10–11), the Thessalonian church was composed of those who had exercised genuine faith in the truth. Faith here is not mere intellectual acceptance of facts, but a real trust in and reliance upon God. So the divine element in election (sanctification by the Spirit) and the human element in personal salvation (faith in the truth) come together to bring about the salvation of the believers at Thessalonica in time under Paul's ministry, which was "through our gospel" (2:14). This truth of the gospel was what he preached everywhere he went (1 Cor. 15:1–4). He wanted all people to trust in the work of Christ on the cross and His resurrection in order to be forgiven of sin and to obtain the setting apart unto God that is part of the passage. The ultimate purpose of God's calling was "that you may obtain the glory of our Lord Jesus Christ" (2 Thess. 2:14), a point that the apostle had already made abundantly clear in the first chapter (1 Thess. 1:10–12). They would obtain this glory at the second coming of Christ Jesus.

Standing Firm on Proper Teaching (2:15)

Paul again appeals personally by addressing the Thessalonians as brothers. He connects their present and ultimate status as ones called by God to an obligation ("so then") that requires action on their part (2:15). The apostle instructs them to do two things, the first of which is to "stand firm." This term (*stēkete*) means to "be steadfast." Paul had used the word in 1 Thessalonians 3:8 when he told the saints that he would really live if they were standing firm in their faith. He is pleased with where they are in their stand but wants them to continue. The present tense here reinforces the notion already inherent in the word itself to go on maintaining their position. One is reminded of Paul's earlier warning that the Thessalonian believers should not be quickly shaken from correct thinking (2:2).

The second instruction that Paul gives is really a subset of the first—"hold to the traditions which you were taught" (2:15). Doing this is "one way of standing firm in the Lord."[3] The word "hold" (*krateite*) can have the nuance of seize or grasp, but in this context it conveys the notion of retaining something or holding on to it, that is, continuing to grasp. Specifically, what are believers supposed to hold to with such tenacity? "The traditions which you were taught." "Traditions" (*paradoseis*) refers to teachings, stories, and beliefs that have been passed down from one person to another. Tradition can be a bad thing as people follow after man-made regulations that are not rooted and grounded in divine revelation (Matt. 23:1–36; Mark 7:8; Col. 2:8). However, pure traditions that are built upon the truths of Scripture should be followed and imitated (1 Cor. 11:2; 2 Thess. 3:6). As shown here Paul used the word both ways. In this verse, it is the positive and good force of the term that is meant as Paul refers to apostolic tradition that represents the true Christ.

The action of both exhortations ("stand firm" and "hold to the traditions") should be ongoing. Paul is asking the believers never to stand down or cease to hold on to the truth. In short, the Thessalonians' reaction to the truth of God's calling should be one of never giving up in the pursuit of the truth and its implications for life. This required resolve would be necessary in the present climate of persecution, for the temptation might be to give in to the forces pressuring them as Thomas Constable describes:

> Christians are in constant danger of being swept downstream by the currents of an ungodly culture. They are also prone to let the truths they know and the relationship they enjoy with God grow cold. They need to vigorously **hold to** what they have been taught by God's servants. The Thessalonians were in danger of loosening their grip on the apostles' teachings which they had received (cf. 2 Thess. 3:6) in person from the missionaries and from their letters. They were in danger of slipping backward in their Christian experience because of the pressures of their trials and the daily negative influences of the world, the flesh, and the devil.[4]

Thus there is an urgency to Paul's tone here that betrays a deep concern of a spiritual father for his children.

Where were the Thessalonians to go to receive the teaching of the traditions that Paul speaks of in this verse? One source was "by word of mouth"—literally "through word" (2:15). It is unclear whether the phrase "from us" applies also to the word of mouth or just the letter that is mentioned next. If it applies to both the word of mouth and letter, the source of the oral message cannot be disputed. Even if not, certainly the verbal instruction that Paul mentions can be no other than apostolic teaching—Paul or his missionary team teaching the Thessalonians when they were with them initially. The second source of sound tradition is "by letter from us" (2:15). Since Paul treats this written tradition in a positive way, the letter is a reference to the first epistle to the Thessalonians that they had already received from the apostle. This stands in stark contrast to the complaint that Paul made earlier about a false spirit, message, or letter pretending to be of apostolic origin (2:2). Paul lets them know that they have access to enough information from truthful sources to make an enduring stand for God and the truth.

A Prayer of Comfort (2:16–17)

A prayerful benediction of comfort closes out the second chapter of 2 Thessalonians as it had the first chapter. The apostle begins 2:16 by calling on "our Lord Jesus Christ Himself and God our Father." Interestingly, Christ is mentioned before God. This, along with the pronoun "Himself," emphasizes the full equality of the Son with the Father (John 1:1, 14, 18) as other statements in the letters had done. Paul further describes the members of the Godhead (Son and Father) as one when he uses the singular "who" (2:16). In light of this and other grammatical considerations in the passage, Robert Thomas notes that "Paul conceived of Jesus Christ as God in the same full sense as he conceived of God the Father. No other explanation of this unusual combination of grammatical features is satisfying."[5]

Christ and God are said to have done three things for believers: loved, given eternal comfort, and given good hope by grace (2:16). All of these are viewed as already poured out by God but with continuing validity and ramifications as verse 17 will show. However, each has its own unique contribution to the possibility of ongoing and future strengthening of the Thessalonians.

The first element of *love* is an important theme in the Thessalonian letters. All eight occurrences in noun or verb form come from the usual Greek words *agapē* or *agapaō*, respectively. However, there is a contrast between its use in the two books. In the five references to love in 1 Thessalonians, it is always mentioned in the context of the need for believers to love each other, that is, the horizontal dimension. In 2 Thessalonians the vertical dimension is emphasized as God is viewed as loving (2 Thess. 2:10, 16; 3:5). The only possible exception is 2 Thessalonians 2:10, which mentions that those who will reject Christ during the tribulation will "not receive the love of the truth." The reference in this passage could be to the lack of love on the part of unbelievers who fail to exercise it in the pursuit of truth. In other words, their lack of pursuit of Christ is a failure to love the truth, namely, the gospel of Christ. It could also be, however, a reference to the love expressed by the truth which they did not receive. In that light God has loved them in providing Christ for them, but they reject that love in the rejection of the truth about Him. In light of the argument of the context, the latter view is to be accepted since the focus is on what God has done and is doing (see earlier comments).[6] This is in contrast to the fact that the unbelievers took pleasure in wickedness (2:12) rather than the love of the truth. Consequently, 2 Thessalonians focuses on the love that God expresses toward the saints.

We find the same arrangement regarding the word "comfort" or its verb form. In the first epistle, its six uses (2:11, 3:2, 7, 4:18, 5:11, 14) always refer to the horizontal dimension of Paul, Timothy, or the Thessalonians comforting other believers although the truth of God's plan and work is sometimes the basis for the comfort (e.g., 1 Thess. 4:18).[7] The idea of comfort occurs only in the second epistle here in 2:16–17. In verse 16 Paul has acknowledged that God has already provided an eternal comfort, while in verse 17 he calls upon God to continually supply comfort to the Thessalonians. The usual Greek words Paul uses are *parakaleō* ("to comfort") or *paraklēsis* ("comfort"). These words are related to *paraklētos* ("comforter"), which is used of the Holy Spirit elsewhere in the Bible (John 14:16). Even though the Spirit is not mentioned in this passage (only Christ and God), Paul is most certainly aware of the connection to the Spirit's ministry, for he mentions the role of the Spirit's work in sanctification a few verses earlier (2:13).

Concerning the element of *hope*, a similar difference exists between the two epistles as existed for love and comfort. In 1 Thessalonians the concept of hope is viewed from the human perspective. All four occurrences (1:3; 2:19; 4:13; 5:8) speak of hope as a present or potential possession of the believers or of its absence in unbelievers. On the other hand, Paul in 2 Thessalonians 2:16 treats hope as something that has already been given by God. It is described as "good," which heightens the positive side of the expectation that God has granted.

The three concepts of love, comfort, and hope all go together. Love and hope are certainly brought together in other lists given by Paul (1 Cor. 13:13). In addition, the term "by grace" (1 Thess. 2:16) modifies the entire phrase "eternal comfort and good hope." This highlights the fact that God's enablement is necessary before believers can experience these significant aspects of the Christian walk. While love, comfort, and hope are all human actions and expectations, they are possible only because God has already provided the basis for them through Jesus, is working diligently in believers through the Spirit, and is the faithful God who will keep His promises for the future. Only in light of this overwhelming sense of divine provision can Paul ask God that the ongoing actions and words of the Thessalonians would be enhanced by comfort and strength (2:17).

Study Questions

1. What comfort can a believer gain from understanding God's choice of him or her from the beginning?
2. Define *sanctification*. What areas of the Christian life does this word cover?
3. What leads a person to believe the gospel?

4. How can someone tell the difference between good and bad human traditions?
5. How can someone prove the deity of Christ from this passage?
6. How is God's work for believers the basis of hope for tomorrow?

CHAPTER 16

Dealing with Unruly Believers 2 Thessalonians 3:1–18

Preview:

Paul asks the Thessalonian saints to withdraw from association with unruly believers who are not working but are spending their time bothering others in the assembly. These disorderly believers should be admonished to work hard for their own upkeep and follow the example of the apostle in the matter.

Recall that Paul deals with three separate issues in the three chapters of 2 Thessalonians. In chapter 1 he gives comfort to the Thessalonians in light of severe persecution by reminding them that Jesus would come to vindicate them and destroy their enemies. In chapter 2 he responds to a false message pretending to be from him concerning the Day of the Lord. He explains that they are not in the Day of the Lord's wrath, or tribulation period, because the great apostasy and revelation of the Antichrist have not yet taken place. In chapter 3 he deals with unruly believers at Thessalonica, especially those who appear to be lazy.

On the face of things, one does not readily see the connection of chapter 3 to the other two chapters. The previous chapters deal with end-time issues of prophecy, issues of some importance and prominence. D. Michael Martin argues that most of the early verses of chapter 3 are too general to be tied with any specificity to any of the concerns in earlier chapters.[1] However, it is possible that some believers became unruly and lazy due to erroneous thinking concerning the Day of the Lord.[2] Some believers were perhaps thinking that if they were in the Day of the Lord, what use would working be? If this is the case, then Paul's move to the practical exhortation section of the second epistle is much more closely tied to the overall focus on end-time events in the letter. Christians should respond to prophetic teaching in the proper way, which Paul outlines in chapter 3.

Request for Prayer (3:1–5)

"Finally" does not mean that what remains is unimportant compared to other sections of the epistle. The correction to come in this chapter may have been a major concern and reason for writing the epistle. But in 3:1 Paul begins by asking the Thessalonian believers to be praying for the apostle and his associates (cf. Rom. 15:30–31; Eph. 6:18–19). This is the flip side of chapter 2, where he prays for them. The requests are simply that (1) the word of the Lord may spread rapidly, (2) the word of the Lord may be glorified, and (3) the missionary and his helpers would be delivered from wicked people (3:2).

A rapid spreading of the gospel is what took place when Paul ministered as a missionary in Thessalonica, for he says "just as it did also with you" (3:1). Paul wants to see the same results in Corinth, from where he wrote this epistle.

"Spread rapidly" (*trechō*) brings to mind the image of a runner in a race. It is Paul's prayer that the word of the Lord would run freely and rapidly and be victorious as in a race. The prayers of believers assist the preaching and teaching of the Word of God. This was not just true for Paul in his day. Today's preachers and missionaries need prayer support for the Word to spread rapidly in their ministries. "Be glorified" is naturally the result of the gospel running unfettered with power. Paul's desire reflects a long-term goal and an understanding of God's work: "Why does Paul desire to see the Word of the Lord glorified? Because he is aware of its great eternal value and worth, and, because its glory reflects back upon the God of mercy who wishes to save and bless all humanity. The Word is glorified when it is heard with respect and honor and when it is reverenced and highly esteemed. It is lifted up when it is accepted with love and greatly prized."[3]

The third part of Paul's request concerns deliverance from "perverse" and "evil" men (3:2). "Perverse" literally means "out of place" and refers to inappropriate behavior (Acts 25:5; 28:6). "Evil" literally means "aggressively evil or wicked."[4] It does not refer to a mere passive kind of opposition consisting of words only, but to active persecution. Paul and the Thessalonians would well remember, not only the current troubles of the saints in that city, but the experience of Paul and Silas culminating in their abrupt exit from the town (Acts 17:5–10).[5]

The apostle bases his request on the truth, "for not all have faith" (3:2). Not all people respond to the gospel in the way the church at Thessalonica had. The believers there needed to be reminded to pray for Paul and for themselves concerning those whom Satan would stir up to oppose the gospel. Paul had experienced this throughout his ministry even before coming to Thessalonica (Acts 13:50; 14:19; 16:19).

Paul's Confidence in the Lord (3:3–5)

Paul begins this section by pointing to the Lord as one who is "faithful" (3:3)—a divine characteristic revealed throughout the Scriptures (Deut. 7:8–9; Isa. 49:7; 1 Cor. 1:9; 10:13; 2 Cor. 1:18). The word (*pistos*) carries the thought of being trustworthy, reliable, sure, and unfailing. The God of Abraham, Isaac, and Jacob had revealed Himself to be unfailing throughout the history of the world as recorded in the Bible. Paul had reminded them of this pertinent aspect of God's character at the end of his first epistle: "Faithful is He who calls you, and He also will bring it to pass" (1 Thess. 5:24). The reminder here would also bring to mind his earlier words in chapter 1 of the second epistle when Paul speaks of their future vindication. Only God could help them to endure the perverse persecution they faced.

Because the Lord was faithful, He would "strengthen" the believers (3:3). Paul had *prayed* for God to strengthen them in 2:16–17. Here he *promises* or *predicts* that He will do so. No doubt Paul's certainty is tied to the fact that God had done the same for all the saints down through the centuries. However, the promise is a double-edged sword for the believers at Thessalonica. It virtually guarantees that the persecution will not end anytime soon. In fact, "by using the future tense, the apostle may be saying that 'the worst is yet to come,' that more hardship is certain."[6]

Paul adds the promise that the Lord would "protect" the believers "from the evil one." The word "protect" (*phulazei*) variously means "to guard, watch over, or preserve." It is used elsewhere by Paul only in his letters to Timothy, where it is usually translated "guard" and mostly speaks of human responsibility to guard or protect something. An example would be the instructions for Timothy to be "on guard" against Alexander the coppersmith who did harm to Paul (2 Tim. 4:14–15). Here in 2 Thessalonians 3:3, it is God who does the guarding, watching, or protecting relative to evil people. While believers must protect the truth and themselves against evil people, they can do so understanding that God is spiritually fighting the real battle for them.

The protection is said to be from "the evil one." This is most likely a reference to Satan, the enemy of Christ and His saints.[7] The New Testament gives several references to the devil as the evil one (Matt. 13:19, 38–39; Eph. 6:16; John 17:15; 1 John 2:13; 5:19). Behind "evil men" (3:2) is the "evil one" known as Satan. He is the one who stirs up unbelievers to cause opposition to the work of the gospel. Paul indicates forcefully that he is the source of the afflictions that the Thessalonian church must endure. In the previous chapter Paul had talked about Satan's activity as essentially the driving force for the man of lawlessness during the future Day of the Lord. Although the current situation of the Thessalonians did not rise to that level, the pattern is the same.

What does protection from Satan look like? Is God promising through Paul's letter that Christians will not die from Satan's attacks? Is the apostle saying that believers will never waiver in their faith? It is clear that Paul is not saying that God promises deliverance from every circumstance, trial, trouble, affliction, or persecution. If that were the case, the Thessalonians would have viewed Paul as a mocker, for they were experiencing such trials. Many martyrs down through the centuries stand as a stark reminder of the fact that God allows His saints to suffer. In fact, the Scripture speaks of both great deliverances for believers and serious hardships (Heb. 11). We are not able to sort out all of life's twists and turns on our own, but we can rest assured that God will be involved in our lives at all points. Paul probably says it best when he knows he is going to die a martyr's death: "The Lord will deliver me from every evil deed, and will bring me safely to His heavenly kingdom" (2 Tim. 4:18).

Paul's ultimate confidence did not rest in the ability of the Thessalonians themselves, but in the Lord (3:4). The apostle qualifies the word "confidence" with the phrase "concerning you." Paul was confident that the Lord would empower the Thessalonian believers to do right now (as they were doing) and continue to do in the future what the apostle had commanded. As Satan enables the opposition, God even more so enables the saints of God. Paul's shows his confidence in the Lord by asking that He would "direct your hearts into the love of God and into the steadfastness of Christ" (3:5). This is the same sentiment Paul expressed in 1 Thessalonians 5:23 and 2 Thessalonians 2:17.

The Command to the Unruly (3:6–15)

Second Thessalonians 3:6–15 forms a major part of the reason for this epistle as the apostle deals with a thorny issue within the church. He has commended them greatly for their Christian virtues (1 Thess. 1:3, 6; 2:13; 3:5, 2 Thess. 1:3–5) and has already dealt with wrong views received into the church about the Day of the Lord (2 Thess. 2:1–3). Now he addresses the problem of those in the church whom he describes as "unruly" (3:6).

He writes authoritatively: "Now we command you, brethren, in the name of the Lord Jesus Christ" (3:6). Paul is not giving a helpful suggestion but an apostolic directive. This is a command given in the full name of Christ, indicating that Paul believes the full force of Heaven is behind his command and therefore the Thessalonian believers must heed his admonition. By addressing them as "brethren," he maintains a loving relationship but still demands adherence to his directive. The command is as follows: "that you keep aloof from every brother who leads an unruly life and not according to the tradition which you received from us" (2 Thess. 3:6).

"You" is plural and refers to the whole church, which is to obey the command of the apostle. To "keep aloof" means to "withdraw from." Every brother walking in an "unruly" manner is to be avoided. The whole matter turns on the meaning of "unruly" life: "The offense was idleness, deliberate loafing which led some to interfere in the work of others (2 Thess. 3:11) and to expect others to provide for their needs (v. 12). This behavior was in direct disobedience to the apostles' teaching."[8] Paul puts forward the apostolic team as the example for the Thessalonians to follow. He points out that he and his coworkers did not act in an undisciplined manner; therefore no one in the church at Thessalonica should act that way either (3:7). The apostle makes it clear that the missionaries paid for their food (3:8) and worked jobs night and day in order not to burden the believers (3:8).

Paul did, however, explain that the missionaries had a right to be cared for by the church: "not because we do not have the right to this" (3:9). Paul gave the same teaching to other churches (1 Cor. 9:11–18). Nonetheless, he was sensitive to the churches he was starting and concerned about his testimony before them. He might not be able to correct this problem in the church at Thessalonica if he had not had the testimony of working hard while he was with them (1 Thess. 2:9).

Furthermore, the issue was not new. Paul, during his time with the Thessalonians, had instructed them that "if anyone will not work, neither let him eat" (2 Thess. 3:10). This strong and uncompromising language may come across as callous to a modern Western world steeped in government welfare. However, nothing more loving could be done for loafers than to force them to work. In light of this truth, it is hard to imagine a Christian view of wanting something for nothing. While work was required of Adam in the Garden of Eden before sin came (Gen. 2:15), the curse of sin made work miserable (Gen. 3:17–19). It would thereafter be hard to labor, and people would have to strive for a living.

Still, the lack of hard work by the unruly believers does not go to the heart of the problem. Paul primarily describes what he is hearing about them in reports from Thessalonica with the phrase "leading an undisciplined life" (3:11). The word "undisciplined" (*ataktōs*) refers to idleness or laziness. There is an attitude that lies beneath the inaction on the part of these people. Paul further describes what this attitude leads to. First, expected from the previous verses, is the description "doing no work at all." It is striking for its absolutism in the words "at all." Apparently they are making no attempt whatsoever to support themselves. Second is the flip side of doing no work: "but acting like busybodies." If one does not work, what is left but to interfere in the lives of others. "Busybodies" is mentioned here for the first time by Paul, and the word itself means "to go around performing."[9] That is, with nothing to do, they go around getting involved in other people's business, eating of their bread, and giving nothing in return (see 1 Tim. 5:13).

There is a possible connection between the problem of unruly believers in chapter 3 and the previous issue of the Day of the Lord from chapter 2. R. C. H. Lenski comments:

> Being busybodies" does not say with what they busied themselves; but we are right in connecting this with 2:2: agitating the claim that the Lord's day is already here, that in some indirect way they have received this information from Paul, Silvanus, and Timothy themselves. We may picture them sitting around for hours in the bazaars and little shops of the other members, making a nuisance of themselves, and trying to unsettle the stable members with their fanatical notions.[10]

Perhaps the lazy loafers in the church were partly justifying their lack of work on the claim that they were already in the tribulation period. Thus they would be spending their extra time in the homes of other working believers spreading their false understanding while they ate their food. While this scenario is possible, Paul does not clearly spell it out, so the interpretation must be held cautiously.[11]

Moreover, the apostle seems to be agitated because such unruly behavior is being tolerated "among you," or in the midst of the church. This expression "seems to suggest that their public conduct raised some question as to their true relationship to the church. The disorderly conduct was setting up a barrier between them and the other members. The present tense points to their persistence in conduct that is disorderly, underlining their guilt."[12]

In light of this discussion, Paul gives another command. The one in 3:6 was aimed at others in the church to avoid and withdraw from the unruly ones. Now in 3:12 he aims his command directly at those who are refusing to work. He instructs them strongly "to work in quiet fashion and eat their own bread." "Quiet" meant to be "settled down." They were to do work and do it in a quiet manner, not causing a stir for any reason. They were also to eat their own food so as not to be a burden to everybody else. This would maintain a spirit of harmony in the church.

Special Instructions (3:13–15)

When Paul says "But as for you, brethren" (3:13), he shifts gears and speaks to the whole church instead of to the unruly loafers. Another command is given: "Do not grow weary of doing good." Paul wrote the same words to the churches of Galatia: "And let us not lose heart in doing good, for in due time we shall reap if we do not grow weary" (Gal. 6:9). It takes perseverance to stay on a spiritual track, and Paul wanted them to know it was required that they not give up in the matter of doing good. The apostolic authority is still in force: "And if anyone does not obey our instruction in this letter, take special note of that man and do not associate with him, so that he may be put to shame" (2 Thess. 3:14).

The word "obey" (*hypakouei*) means "to be subject to or accept." It was used of the action of a doorkeeper who hears the knock on the door and responds. The phrase "take special note" means not simply to notice the person in question, but also to mark that person in a unique way. The passage does not immediately specify the details of how this is to be done. However, the next phrase, "do not associate with him," fills in some of the details. It is easy to draw an analogy between Paul's desire here and his instructions to the Corinthians who were commanded not to associate with the man who had committed incest.[13]

The purpose of the disassociation is so that the unruly person "may be put to shame" (*entrepō*). The disapproval of the church was, in Paul's mind, the way to accomplish this. But as the church was to withdraw from such a person, they were required to do so in a brotherly fashion and with godly intent. Paul warns the Thessalonians, "Do not regard him as an enemy, but admonish him as a brother" (3:15). There should be no feeling of hostility toward the unruly loafers. Such an attitude and any associated positive action would most likely backfire in its intentions of restoration (cf. 1 Cor. 5; Gal. 6:1). D. Edmond Hiebert notes that "aroused feelings must not lead to a wrong evaluation of the man's true character."[14]

Closing Remarks (3:16–18)

As the epistle comes to a close, the apostle prays to the "Lord of peace" to grant the church at Thessalonica "peace in every circumstance." They had been through much persecution and affliction. It is also an appropriate prayer in light of the division just discussed between unruly members and the rest. Paul knows that the Lord will be with them through it all and voices the sentiment directly (3:16).

Paul himself, who often dictated his letters, points out to the Thessalonians that he is writing this ending in his own handwriting. Four different expressions in 3:17 demonstrate what he is doing. First, he directly asserts, "I, Paul, write." If a secretary had been writing for him, at this point Paul took over and wrote these words himself. Second, he claims that he is writing the closing "with my own hand." He also notes that he is making a "distinguishing mark" that is "in every letter" (cf. 1 Cor. 16:21; Col. 4:18). Apparently Paul expected his handwriting to be recognized by those who read it. Finally, he comments that "this is the way I write." The need for this firm and strong claim that this epistle represents Paul's words and thoughts is the earlier false letter that had apparently been sent to the Thessalonians pretending to be from Paul (2:2).

The closing verse focuses on grace. As is his practice, Paul's letters usually begin with grace (1:1) and end with grace (3:18). Certainly, God's grace would be what the church of Thessalonica would need to heed the admonitions of the apostle given in his letters.

Study Questions

1. Why should believers pray for preachers and the preaching of the Word of God?
2. How is the word of the Lord glorified?
3. How do evil people oppose the gospel and the messengers of the gospel? What is the source of their opposition?
4. Who were the unruly ones at the church of Thessalonica? Do you have any people like that in your own church today?
5. How are believers to react to other believers who act unruly?
6. What response should an unruly person give to Paul's instructions?
7. How is work considered a noble act for a Christian?

8. How does the church acting together to deal with an unruly believer bring that person to repentance? How should that person be treated—as an enemy or as a brother or sister?

Appendix A

The Day of the Lord

Day of the Lord is one of the more controversial expressions in prophetic studies primarily because of the varying definitions that are assigned to it. Sometimes views seem to depend on one's overall preconceived eschatological viewpoint. Commentators will teach that it is the second coming of Christ, the seven-year tribulation period (Daniel's Seventy Weeks), or some other combination of end-time events without demonstrating why their interpretation is the correct one. With that in mind, the following discussion is offered to assist the interpreter of 1 and 2 Thessalonians (or any prophetic part of Scripture) in meditating on the concept as it appears in the biblical text.

The Term *Day of the Lord* in the Old Testament

Interestingly, the greater number of explicit Old Testament references to the expression *Day of the Lord* come from the preexilic prophets during the ninth and eighth centuries BC. The prophets Joel, Obadiah, Amos, Isaiah, and Zephaniah use the term, thereby forming the foundation of its usage, especially as it relates to questions about the end-times. In general they view the Day of the Lord as a time when the transcendent God will break through in history to judge and deliver in some respect.

The book of Joel (late ninth century BC) mentions the Day of the Lord five times (1:15, 2:1, 11, 31; 3:14), which is more than any other biblical writer, even taking into account the apostle Paul's letters combined. In 1:15 the Day of the Lord is viewed as a time when crops are destroyed (1:16–20). It is described as being near and as a time of destruction. Using the well-known picture of a locust plague sweeping the land, Joel portrays an invading army as judgment from God upon Judah and Jerusalem (1:4–7).

However, Joel quickly merges his discussion of a possible near fulfillment of the Day of the Lord with an apparent reference to end-time events. In Joel 2:1–11 the Day of the Lord is a time period described as darkness and gloom (2:2). It is a time that stands out with nothing like it before or after (2:2). It is a time of consuming fire (2:3), war (2:4–9), and cosmic signs (2:10) in the heavens that produce fear. Yet the goal of the time is the return of God's people Israel to Him (2:12–13). This time will precede the kingdom restoration and protection of Israel in its land (2:18ff.), the pouring out of the Spirit upon the people in fulfillment of the new covenant (2:28–32; cf. Jer. 31:31ff.), and the return of the fortunes of Judah and Jerusalem (3:1–2).

On the other hand, Joel also speaks of the Day of the Lord as coming *after* some of these things (e.g., cosmic signs precede it in 2:30–31; cf. 3:14). How can a period of destruction called the "Day of the Lord" precede a restoration of Israel in its kingdom, while at the same time apparent elements within that time period of destruction actually precede the Day of the Lord? In other words, the text can be understood to say that the Day of the Lord precedes the Day of the Lord! How can this be? Is this not a contradiction? The only solution is to see the expression *Day of the Lord* as being broad enough to encompass more than one breaking-through of God in history. In other words, as Joel uses the term, he does not treat it like a technical term related to a particular time, but as a concept for God's work in history. Within the sweep of end-time events, he actually speaks of God's work in a broad sense (a period of time emphasizing judgment) and a narrower sense (a beginning point for restoration for the nation of Israel).[1] It is probably accurate to suggest that any lone point of time within this end-time matrix of events could be singled out as the Day of the Lord. This is only possible when one realizes that the term *Day of the Lord,* as Joel uses it, is more a concept than a time designation.

The ninth-century prophet Obadiah emphasizes the fact that the Day of the Lord is a judgment time drawing near upon all the nations (v. 15). He especially focuses on Edom, an enemy in Israel's history, which through associated bloodline should have favored God's chosen nation instead of opposing it (vv. 10–12). While some interpreters do not see any future, end-time fulfillment in view, it is likely that Obadiah is thinking in far prophetic terms due to the fact that all nations are mentioned and that Israel is apparently blessed in ultimate kingdom restoration (vv. 17–21). There are also some similarities in language between Obadiah's statements and Christ's in the Olivet Discourse (cf. Matt. 25:31–46). But it is not clear if Obadiah has a singular event or a period of time in mind. Teaching elsewhere in Scripture points to judgment upon the nations both during the tribulation period (Rev. 6–19) and at the second coming of Christ (Matt. 25).

The eighth-century prophet Amos mentions the Day of the Lord twice in the span of three verses (5:18–20). With a focus on temporal judgment upon Israel, he chastises people in the nation for wanting the Day of the Lord. Apparently they were viewing it in terms of ultimate blessing and national bliss. But Amos tells them that is not what they are going to get. Instead, the nation will experience darkness and gloom instead of light. Although Amos anticipates an ultimate restoration of Israel's kingdom (9:11–15), the Day of the Lord that he identifies in 5:18–20 must be a time of judgment that precedes that time. It would be impossible to harmonize this negative understanding of the Day of the Lord with the second coming of Christ, since that will be a positive event of deliverance for the nation. Thus it is best to see the emphasis of Amos the same as the broad view of the Day of the Lord in Joel.

The eighth-century prophet Isaiah gives two references to the Day of the Lord in a context that is harder to interpret (see 13:6–16). These verses occur as part of the oracle concerning Babylon. A localized reference to the Medes in 13:17, who conquered Babylon near the end of the seventy years of captivity in the sixth century, opens the possibility that a near fulfillment is in view throughout the section rather than an end-time focus. However, the language is similar to that in Joel. It is a time of destruction (13:6), terror (13:8), God's wrath (13:9), cosmic signs (13:10, 13), and judgment upon the entire world (13:11). It is this reference to the entire world and not just Babylon that forces the likelihood that an end-time scenario is in view. Israel is really not in view in this particular passage. The image of ongoing war (13:14–16) makes it probable that a time period is in view and not a singular event like the Second Coming.

The seventh-century prophet Zephaniah speaks of the Day of the Lord in negative terms, but the target of God's activity initially is Judah and Jerusalem (1:4). The Day of the Lord is near and is a time of punishment (1:7–9). Almost gathering the terms used elsewhere in the Old Testament, Zephaniah calls the Day of the Lord a time of trouble, distress, destruction, desolation, darkness, and gloom (1:15). It is a terrifying time of the Lord's wrath (1:18). In chapters 2 and 3, Zephaniah expands the judgments to include the nations as well as Judah. But he envisions a remnant of Israel that will be delivered when the Lord restores the fortunes of His chosen people (3:12–20). Thus there is a clear use of the expression *Day of the Lord* relative to end-time events. Furthermore, it appears to be a time period that precedes the ultimate restoration of Israel, which, according to other Scriptures, takes place at the second coming of Christ.

The exilic prophet Ezekiel (sixth century BC) uses the phrase *Day of the Lord* in 13:5 and 30:3. In 13:5 it is doubtful that any end-time event is the prophet's meaning. A word is declared against false prophets who did not see the coming Day of the Lord as judgment from God when the Babylonian armies came to destroy the nation. The second use of the term (30:3) is found in a section where God through Ezekiel speaks against Egypt. The language in the context is similar to the negative imagery of Joel 2:15 and Amos 5:16–20. The reference to Nebuchadnezzar king of Babylon as a tool of God to destroy Egypt shows the near fulfillment of this particular Day of the Lord. Although no end-time event is in view, these occurrences in Ezekiel help to establish the fact that the term is not a technical term and should be understood carefully in context wherever it is used.

The only clear reference to the exact term *Day of the Lord* in the postexilic prophets is Malachi's prediction that God was going to send Elijah before "the great and terrible day of the LORD" (Mal. 4:5). This description of the Day of the Lord is consistent with the negative images given in earlier passages and points to a time of judgment especially related to Israel (see 4:6). This again cannot be harmonized precisely with the events associated with the Second Coming, because that time has positive ramifications for national Israel as its point of national and spiritual restoration. As one reviews the precise use of the phrase *Day of the Lord* throughout the Old Testament, it is clear that the expression was used early on, and its use declined after the exile of Israel into Babylon.

Other Terminology in the Old Testament

The survey of uses of *Day of the Lord* would be insufficient by itself to establish a doctrine of the Day of the Lord. Although it is beyond the scope here to cover all possible references to the same concept where the term does not precisely occur, a few examples will help to reinforce its proper interpretation.[2] For example, it is certain that Zechariah uses the terms "in that day" (12:3, 4, 6, 8, 9, 11; 13:1, 2; 14:4, 6, 8, 9), "a unique day" (14:7), and "a day is coming for the LORD" (14:1) to refer to the same general concept as Day of the Lord. God is breaking through in history in this case to deliver Israel while destroying her enemies. In this case, the language in Zechariah fits with teaching elsewhere about the second coming of Christ to earth to deliver Israel from her enemies.

Another example can be found by comparing the Old Testament passages Joel 2:1–2 and Daniel 12:1 with New Testament verses Matthew 24:21; Mark 13:19; and Revelation 16:18. Only Joel 2:2 uses the term *Day of the Lord*. What is important in this comparison is the similar language concerning the uniqueness of what is meant:

The Tribulation	
Joel 2:1–2	*For the day of the Lord is coming; surely it is near. . . . As the dawn is spread over the mountains, so there is a great and mighty people; there has never been anything like it, nor will there be again after it.*
Daniel 12:1	*There will be a time of distress such as never occurred since there was a nation until that time.*
Matthew 24:21	*For then there will be a great tribulation, such as has not occurred since the beginning of the world until now, nor ever shall.*
Mark 13:19	*For those days will be a time of tribulation such as has not occurred since the beginning . . . until now, and never shall.*
Revelation 16:18	*There was a great earthquake, such as there had not been since man came to be upon the earth.*

The similarity of the terminology is unmistakable. In Joel the Day of the Lord is described as a time of foreboding like an army coming in a way that has never been seen before or after. The same sentiment is given in Daniel 12:1. Later in Daniel 12:7 this time of distress appears to be at least three and a half years long and not a singular event. In a similar way, Jesus in the Gospel accounts listed above describes it as an unequaled time of great distress. In Matthew's context, Jesus has just mentioned the abomination of desolation which occurs half way through the Seventieth Week of Daniel (Dan. 9:27; cf. 12:11). Thus this time of distress is associated with the events of that time—a time often called the tribulation. The Revelation passage is in the sequence of the seventh bowl judgment and speaks of a particular event that is within the tribulation period, an event that precedes the Second Coming. Taking all of these things together, one can see how easily it is to associate the concepts of the Day of the Lord, the tribulation, and the Seventy Weeks of Daniel in some passages.

The Day of the Lord in the New Testament

There are six occurrences of the exact phrase *Day of the Lord* in the New Testament: Acts 2:20; 2 Peter 3:10; 1 Corinthians 5:5; 2 Corinthians 1:14; 1 Thessalonians 5:2; and 2 Thessalonians 2:2. The Acts 2:20 passage is Peter's quote of Joel 2:31 in his sermon on the Day of Pentecost. While this entire passage has engendered a great deal of debate, one thing the passage does not do is advance beyond Joel's understanding anything about the precise nature of the Day of the Lord.

On the other hand, Peter's use of the term *Day of the Lord* in 2 Peter 3:10 provides some alternatives for additional understanding. Various interpreters see this mention of the term as pointing to the second coming of Christ to earth at the end of the tribulation period.[3] This view fits nicely with the prior context of 2 Peter 3:3–9, which is a discussion about the delay of the Second Coming in light of current mockers who question the teaching. The destruction with intense heat and the burning of the earth in verse 10 would then be the work of God that introduces the Millennium. Thus it also fits the narrow use of the term *Day of the Lord* as it is sometimes found in the Old Testament.

A second approach is to see the reference as pertaining to the end of the Millennium so that the destruction of the earth by fire would precipitate the transition from the end of the Millennium to the start of the eternal state with its new earth. This view fits the later context of 2 Peter 3:11–13 with its mention of the new heavens and the new earth. The passage is then correlated to Revelation 21:1, where the new heavens and the new earth clearly follow the Millennium of the previous chapter. If the Day of the Lord in this passage is God's intervention in history at the end of the Millennium, then Peter has applied the term to a particular time not envisioned in any of the Old Testament texts that use the term. However, since the term *Day of the Lord* is not a technical term that refers to the same exact event every time it is mentioned, there is no problem with this use by Peter. This approach to the passage is probably the correct one.

In light of Peter's use of the phrase *Day of the Lord* to refer to an event at the end of the Millennium, a commonly held interpretation of the entire scope of the Day of the Lord is to view it as the time period beginning with the tribulation and ending with the start of the eternal state. In other words, it would consist of the tribulation plus the Millennium.[4] However, this approach to stretching the term as an umbrella term to cover the time period during which the term is applied in individual instances suffers from a wrong focus on the time element instead of the concept of the Day of the Lord. It is best to simply assert that at points along the timeline of end-time events, God breaks through in history to judge and restore, and such points can be called the "Day of the Lord." While the tribulation as a period can safely be called one of those points as it is viewed in its entirety, it is not clear that the Millennium can be viewed the same way.

The apostle Paul refers to the Day of the Lord four times, two in the Corinthian letters and two in 1 and 2 Thessalonians. In 1 Corinthians 5:5, Paul speaks of the man who had committed incest with the words "I have decided to deliver such a one to Satan for the destruction of his flesh, that his spirit may be saved in the day of the Lord Jesus." In some manuscripts the name Jesus is omitted, giving the phrase as precisely *Day of the Lord*. What day is meant here? At the pretribulation Rapture, it would certainly be true that such a believer would be among the accepted by God. This would also be true at the second coming of Christ to earth when his accepted ones enter the kingdom and are declared to be the true sons of God. The passage does not give us enough information to know with precision which specific event Paul had in mind. It is possible that the Rapture would be preferred by Paul's later reference to it in 1 Corinthians 15:51–52. However, the pride in them that Paul mentions will be his on that day (2 Cor. 1:14) may fit the time of the vindication of the saints (2 Thess. 1:5–12) which is at the Second Coming. The two occurrences of the term *Day of the Lord* in the Thessalonian letters will be discussed below.

Is the *Day of the Lord* a Technical Term?

At this point we have surveyed all the occurrences of the "day of the Lord" in the Old and the New Testaments (excluding the Thessalonian references). We have also alluded to the breadth of other terminology that must be taken into account. The upshot of this review is that the phrase *Day of the Lord* is not a technical term. It does not refer to the same exact event(s) in every single case in Scripture. At times it appears to be a period when God judges severely. In other instances, it is a single event, such as the Second Coming with its associated judgments. In one case it may even refer to the end of the Millennium. The significance of all of this is that the term is more a concept than a specific time. Each passage must be examined in its own right to see if there are any contextual clues that help to pinpoint any time factors that might identify the time frame meant in the passage. Consequently, when we come to the two occurrences of the "day of the Lord" in the Thessalonian epistles, we cannot assume any prior time association with the term. We cannot, for example, assume that it refers to the event of the second coming of Christ at the end of the tribulation because that fits some Old Testament uses of the term. In the end it is the context of 1 and 2 Thessalonians that will be decisive in conjunction with some correlation to other passages.

The Day of the Lord in 1 and 2 Thessalonians: Singular Event or Time Period?

The references to the Day of the Lord in 1 Thessalonians 5:2 and 2 Thessalonians 2:2–3 indicate in context the idea that a period of time is meant and not the single event of the Second Coming. The primary reasons for this view are the following:

1. In 1 Thessalonians 5:2–3 Paul teaches that the Day of the Lord will come during a time when the world is crying, "Peace and safety!" The general thought is not that they want peace and safety, but that they are in a time of relative peace and safety so that the words describe the tenor of history at that moment. However, if the Day of the Lord (5:2) means the second coming of Christ to earth, we know from Revelation that this coming of Christ is preceded by Armageddon, hardly a time to be describing history with the words "peace and safety." It is also true that the midpoint of the tribulation period will not qualify as the start of the Day of the Lord. The period preceding the midpoint consists of the seal judgments with much war (Rev. 6:4, 8) and the intrigues of war involving the Antichrist (Dan. 11:36–45). Thus the only time that fits the time of peace is a time before the tribulation begins. This implies that Paul's meaning is that the Day of the Lord is the entire seven years of the tribulation. As a consequence the pretribulation rapture view is verified, because the church is exempt from that time (5:9).

2. In 2 Thessalonians 2:2–3 the Thessalonians are concerned that the Day of the Lord has already come. Which makes better sense? Were they concerned that Jesus had already returned in the Second Coming, or were they concerned that the tribulation period had already started? If they were concerned that Christ had already come, it is hard to understand how the concern makes sense, for they would be in the kingdom. Surely they understood the kingdom as a time of restoration and the presence of the Lord. It is much more likely that they are asking a different question. In light of the great persecution they were enduring (chapter 1), they were more likely wondering if such persecution constituted a sign that they were in the predicted end-time tribulation that Paul taught them preceded the kingdom.

It is safe to assume that Paul, in two letters written close in time to the same recipients, is using the term *Day of the Lord* the same way. The contextual evidence favors the notion that the "day of the Lord" in both books refers to a period of time called the seven-year tribulation period. Thus, in light of that, the exemption from the Day of the Lord's wrath taught in 1 Thessalonians 5:9 refers to an exemption from all seven years. One implication is that the rapture of the church must be pretribulational.

Appendix B

The Identification of the Restrainer

In 2 Thessalonians 2:2–3, Paul tells the believers at Thessalonica that the Day of the Lord has not yet occurred because two other events had to happen first—the apostasy and the revelation of the man of lawlessness (Antichrist). Related to the latter, Paul goes on to note that the Antichrist has not yet been revealed because of the restraining work of some entity or person (2:6–7). The verses give no particular identification of this restrainer. Therefore the interpreter must ultimately compare Scripture with Scripture to see if it is possible to discern with more precision the identity of Paul's restrainer.

Several views have been advanced. Various commentators have suggested the following identifications: Roman Empire, a particular Roman emperor, human government, law, Satan, church, Holy Spirit, the gospel, demons, Israel, Michael the archangel, binding of Satan by believers, James of Jerusalem, Paul, Elijah, and the providence of God. Such a varied list is only possible because of the scant information the apostle provides. In light of the context of Paul's oral teaching when he was in Thessalonica, we can be certain that the Thessalonians understood what he meant.

At the outset there are a couple of interpretive problems we must address. First, one is confronted by Paul's generalized statement in verse 6—"*what* restrains him now" (emphasis added). The words are not personal, and taken by themselves they make one think about an impersonal force. However, in the next verse, Paul uses the masculine when he says "only *he* who now restrains will do so until *he* is taken out of the way" (emphasis added). This shows that the restrainer must be personal. A person may exercise force (thus the wording of verse 6), but an impersonal force could not be described in the manner of Paul's words in verse 7. Thus any of the options that have been advanced that can only be construed in terms of an impersonal force must be eliminated from consideration.

Second, the translation of the word for "restrains" must be examined. The idea of the concept *restrains* can be understood as "holds back," which is the normal way one would take the English word. However, the Greek term can also be translated as "holds sway" which gives it an altogether different sense.[1] In this light verse 6 would mean "that which holds sway," and verse 7 would mean "he who now controls." This raises the question in the context of whether the restrainer is someone good or evil. If taken in the sense of "holds sway," then the most probable meaning is that the person meant in the passage is either the Antichrist himself or Satan. For example, if it is Satan, he would be the one who would be controlling the man of lawlessness until some point when he allows the unleashing of the full evil fury that is in the Antichrist.

However, it is unlikely that Satan would be involved in holding back or controlling lawlessness in the sense of diminishing it. A better approach is to see the restrainer and his restraining influence as a positive thing. The main interpretive options along these lines would be human government, the church, and the Holy Spirit. As to human government, one could point out that its establishment in Genesis 9 had a restraining character, as evidenced by the establishment of capital punishment for murder (Gen. 9:5–6). Similarly, Paul taught the Roman Christians that government was ordained by God to put down evildoers even with the sword if necessary (Rom. 13:1–7). It can also be said that the general character of law that comes with various governments as portrayed throughout Scripture demonstrate a controlling influence relative to evildoers.

However, the idea that the restrainer is human government in general conflicts with the personal description of him in 2 Thessalonians 2:7. One could suggest that often in Scripture a nation or empire is associated with the leader of that nation or empire. For example, Nebuchadnezzar and the empire of Babylon were both the head of gold in his dream (Dan. 2). The beast in Revelation appears to be both the revived Roman Empire as well as the head of that empire, the personal Antichrist (Rev. 13). In this way the impersonal nature of 2 Thessalonians 2:6 can be harmonized with the personal description of 2:7. Some who go this route make the specific choice of the Roman Empire and view one of the Caesars as the personal Antichrist. This approach usually mentions Nero and is part of the preterist understanding that the tribulation was fulfilled during his reign and that Jesus came back (in a second coming) to judge Israel in AD 70. This view is entirely untenable due to its rejection of any future for national Israel in contradiction to many prophecies that affirm Christ's final deliverance of that nation (e.g., Zech. 12–14; Rev. 12).

The church is sometimes mentioned as the restrainer that Paul had in mind. It is certainly true that the church, acting as salt and light in the world, functions with a kind of restraining influence over against evil. Such restraining would be removed when the church is taken out of the way in the Rapture. Under this scheme the removal of the church facilitates the true revelation of the Antichrist, which in the pretribulational understanding, takes place at the signing of the treaty with Israel at the beginning of the tribulation. However, as with human government, it is hard to see how the church would qualify as a person as required in 2 Thessalonians 2:7. While it is made up of persons, it can not easily be described in the language Paul uses.[2]

Perhaps the best option is to see the restrainer as the Holy Spirit of God. The Holy Spirit is characterized in other Scriptures as having a kind of restraining influence (Gen. 6:3; John 16:8–11). In this understanding God through His Spirit is preventing the Antichrist from coming on the end-time scene until the appointed time. While the lawlessness that characterizes the Antichrist is already in the world (2 Thess. 2:7), it will not reach its ultimate evil expression until God permits it. This view has several advantages. The Holy Spirit is a person (2:7) who has restraining power (2:6). He has the power to countermand Satan (2:8–10). It is doubtful that such could be said of human government or even the church.[3]

While Paul does not precisely identify the restrainer in his letter, the most likely choice is the Holy Spirit. Such identification is not necessary for the reader to get the main message that Paul is trying to convey: the lawless spirit that will characterize the coming Antichrist will be held in check by a superior power until the appointed time. In the context of the book, he informs the Thessalonians that this time had not yet occurred.

Bibliography

Baxter, J. Sidlow. *A New Call to Holiness*. Grand Rapids: Zondervan, 1967.

Beale, G. K. *1–2 Thessalonians*. IVP New Testament Commentary. Downers Grove, IL: InterVarsity, 2003.

Bruce, F. F. *1 and 2 Thessalonians*. Word Biblical Commentary. Waco: Word, 1982.

Couch, Mal. *The Hope of Christ's Return*. Chattanooga, TN: AMG, 2001.

Eadie, John. *A Commentary on the Greek Text of the Epistles of Paul to the Thessalonians*. Reprint ed., Minneapolis, MN: James and Klock, 1977.

Ellicott, Charles John. *Commentary on the Epistles of St. Paul to the Thessalonians*. Reprint ed., Grand Rapids: Zondervan, 1957.

Frame, James Everett. *A Critical and Exegetical Commentary on the Epistles of St. Paul to the Thessalonians*. The International Critical Commentary. Reprint ed., Edinburgh: T. & T. Clark, 1960.

Hiebert, D. Edmond. *1 and 2 Thessalonians*. Rev. ed. Chicago: Moody, 1992.

Larson, Knute. *I and II Thessalonians, I and II Timothy, Titus, Philemon*. Holman New Testament Commentary. Nashville: Broadman & Holman, 2000.

Lenski, R. C. H. *The Interpretation of St. Paul's Epistles to the Colossians, to the Thessalonians, to Timothy, and to Philemon*. Minneapolis: Augsburg, 1937.

MacArthur, John. *1 and 2 Thessalonians*. MacArthur New Testament Commentary. Chicago: Moody, 2002.

Mayhue, Richard. *First and Second Thessalonians*. Berkshire, UK: Christian Focus, 1999.

Neil, William. *The Epistle of Paul to the Thessalonians*. Moffatt New Testament Commentary. London: Hodder and Stoughton, 1965.

Showers, Renald E. The *Pre-wrath Rapture View: An Examination and Critique*. Grand Rapids: Kregel, 2001.

Walvoord, John F. *The Thessalonian Epistles*. Findlay, OH: Dunham, 1955.

Wanamaker, Charles A. *The Epistles to the Thessalonians*. New International Greek Testament Commentary. Grand Rapids: Eerdmans, 1990.

NOTES

BOOK OF FIRST THESSALONIANS
Introduction–Background of 1 Thessalonians

1. F. F. Bruce, *1 and 2 Thessalonians* (Waco: Word, 1982), xxxiii–xxxiv. Here Bruce gives a general and brief summary of the nineteenth-century F. C. Baur school of thought relative to 1 and 2 Thessalonians.
2. Ibid., xxxii.
3. Karl Paul Donfried, *Paul, Thessalonica, and Early Christianity* (Grand Rapids: Eerdmans, 2002), 75–76.
4. F. F. Bruce, *The Book of Acts* (Grand Rapids: Eerdmans, 1977), 368.
5. Donfried, *Paul, Thessalonica, and Early Christianity*, 74.
6. For some examples, see John Eadie, *A Commentary on the Greek Text of the Epistle of Paul to the Thessalonians* (London: Macmillan, 1877; repr., Minneapolis: James and Klock, 1977), 22.
7. F. F. Bruce, *1 and 2 Thessalonians* (Waco: Word, 1982), xxxiv–xxxv.
8. For analysis of information concerning the date of 1 Thessalonians, see Mal Couch, *The Hope of Christ's Return* (Chattanooga, TN: AMG, 2001), 28–29; D. Michael Martin, *1, 2 Thessalonians*, New American Commentary (Nashville: Broadman & Holman, 2001), 33–34; Leon Morris, *The First and Second Epistles to the Thessalonians*, New International Commentary on the New Testament (Grand Rapids: Eerdmans, 1991), 12–15; and G. K. Beale, *1–2 Thessalonians*, IVP New Testament Commentary (Downers Grove, IL: InterVarsity, 2003), 14. There is little controversy over the general time frame for 1 Thessalonians, but 2 Thessalonians is another matter.
9. Bruce, *1 and 2 Thessalonians*, xxxiv.
10. The best summary of this structure to Paul's argument in 1 Thessalonians can be found in Zane Hodges, "The Rapture in 1 Thessalonians 5:1–11," in *Walvoord: A Tribute*, ed. Donald K. Campbell (Chicago: Moody, 1982), 68–70. I am generally following this approach. While Paul in 1 Thessalonians comes back to the same topic at times (e.g., thanksgiving, coming of Christ), it is best

to see the general outline he provides early in the book rather than forcing a different outline upon it. Although the chapters of this commentary must by necessity be structured with a different outline for presentation purposes, that outline should not be confused with the Pauline outline given in the book itself.

Chapter 1—Opening Remarks

1. D. Edmond Hiebert, *1 and 2 Thessalonians*, rev. ed., Chicago: Moody, 1992), 39.
2. G. K. Beale, *1–2 Thessalonians*, IVP New Testament Commentary (Downers Grove, IL: InterVarsity, 2003), 14–15.
3. Ibid., 43.
4. Leon Morris, *The First and Second Epistles to the Thessalonians*, New International Commentary on the New Testament (Grand Rapids: Eerdmans, 1991), 36.
5. D. Michael Martin, *1, 2 Thessalonians*, New American Commentary (Nashville: Broadman & Holman, 2001), 52.

Chapter 2—A Testimony of Thanksgiving

1. G. K. Beale, *1–2 Thessalonians*, IVP New Testament Commentary (Downers Grove, IL: InterVarsity, 2003), 45.
2. Ibid.
3. The word *constantly* is actually the last word of verse 2 in the Greek text. There is some question as to whether the meaning in verse 2 is the *constant* mentioning in prayer or if Paul is attaching the word *constantly* to "bearing in mind" or "remembering" in verse 3. In the end, the overall meaning is unaffected by the placement.
4. D. Edmond Hiebert, *1 and 2 Thessalonians*, rev. ed. (Chicago: Moody, 1992), 51.
5. Harold J. Ockenga, *The Church in God: Expository Values in Thessalonians* (Westwood, NJ: Revell, 1956), 36.
6. Beale voices this idea (*1–2 Thessalonians*, 47–48). However, Beale sees immediate application to the first-century experience because the end-times had already started with the First Advent. The application is better seen based on a look forward, although some of the Thessalonians perhaps had mistaken notions about end-time events relative to their own time.
7. Leon Morris, *The First and Second Epistles to the Thessalonians*, New International Commentary on the New Testament (Grand Rapids: Eerdmans, 1991), 42–43.
8. William MacDonald, *Believer's Bible Commentary: New Testament* (Nashville: Thomas Nelson, 1995), 840.
9. F. F. Bruce, *1 and 2 Thessalonians* (Waco: Word, 1982), 13.
10. Ibid., 14.

11. Frame holds that the certainty or full assurance belongs to the entire missionary team (James E. Frame, *Epistles of Saint Paul to the Thessalonians* [Edinburgh: T. & T. Clark, 1912], 81).
12. Leon Morris notes that the absence of the preposition *en* ("in") in front of the terms for "full conviction" in the Greek text ties the phrase more closely to what goes before (the Holy Spirit) rather than to what follows. However, Morris appears to interpret the phrase "with full conviction" to refer simultaneously to the work of the Holy Spirit, the product it produces in the Thessalonians, and the assurance the Spirit gave to the preachers. It could be, however, that he sees the work of the Spirit more on the speakers than on the hearers (*The First and Second Epistles to the Thessalonians*, rev. ed. [Grand Rapids: Eerdmans, 1991], 46–47).
13. Bruce, *1 and 2 Thessalonians*, 17.
14. Hiebert, *1 and 2 Thessalonians*, 66.
15. This statement should not be taken to mean that there were no Jews in the church at Thessalonica. According to Acts 17:4, there were some Jews in the synagogue who were persuaded by Paul along with some God-fearing Greeks.
16. MacDonald, *Believer's Bible Commentary*, 841.
17. I am reminded of Francis Schaeffer's classic work *The God Who Is There* (Chicago: InterVarsity Press, 1968).
18. For a discussion of the various pagan cults in Thessalonica in the first century, see Karl P. Donfried, *Paul, Thessalonica, and Early Christianity* (Grand Rapids: Eerdmans, 2002), 21–48.
19. Bruce, *1 and 2 Thessalonians*, 18–19.
20. Hiebert, *1 and 2 Thessalonians*, 72–73.

Chapter 3—The Testimony of Paul's Ministry

1. F. F. Bruce, *1 and 2 Thessalonians* (Waco: Word, 1982), 24.
2. It is true that the character of the missionary team is invoked by Paul later in chapter 2 in harmony with 1:5. However, that is simply not the chief point in 2:1.
3. Bruce, *1 and 2 Thessalonians*, 24.
4. G. K. Beale, *1–2 Thessalonians*, IVP New Testament Commentary (Downers Grove, IL: InterVarsity, 2003), 64.
5. Mal Couch, *The Hope of Christ's Return* (Chattanooga, TN: AMG, 2001), 64.
6. Beale, *1–2 Thessalonians*, 64–65. Beale's point is not entirely clear in this matter.
7. Bruce, *1 and 2 Thessalonians*, 26.

8. R. C. H. Lenski, *The Interpretation of St. Paul's Epistles to the Colossians, to the Thessalonians, to Timothy, to Titus and to Philemon* (Minneapolis: Augsburg, 1937), 243.

9. In many Greek texts, this expression is actually the beginning of verse 7 rather than the end of verse 6.

10. Beale, *1–2 Thessalonians*, 70–71n.

11. Some Greek manuscripts have the term *infants* or *babes* instead of the word *gentle*. Thus some English translations follow this reading. If this is Paul's wording, the thought is something akin to the sweetness of children. However, this reading does not seem to fit well, since the next analogy he makes is of himself and a nursing mother. It is a bit incongruous to say "as infants among you, as a nursing mother."

12. Leon Morris, *The First and Second Epistles to the Thessalonians*, New International Commentary on the New Testament, rev. ed. (Grand Rapids: Eerdmans, 1991), 71.

13. Bruce, *1 and 2 Thessalonians*, 32.

14. Ibid.

15. It is somewhat surprising how often Paul in the New Testament thinks in terms of *threes*. Sometimes this is at the detailed level here in our discussions of descriptions of various human actions. Other times it appears at the level of God's dealings with humans, such as God's deliverance of people past, present, and future (e.g., note the past, present, and future work of Christ in behalf of the elect cited in Rom. 8:32–34). This often-used threefold focus should make one pause before overdosing on the typical already–not yet scheme so many New Testament scholars hold today.

16. In many Greek texts, the expression involving the three descriptive verbs is actually the beginning of verse 12 rather than in verse 11.

17. The Greek text of 1 Thessalonians 2:11 is troublesome due to the absence of a main verb that must be supplied by the context. Consequently the concepts of exhorting, encouraging, and imploring are supplied to give the reader the full import of the meaning. See Morris, *First and Second Epistles to the Thessalonians*, 75–76.

18. D. Michael Martin, *1, 2 Thessalonians*, New American Commentary (Nashville: Broadman & Holman, 2001), 85.

19. See Couch's brief discussion of some interpreters who see the kingdom here as present and not future (*Hope of Christ's Return*, 74).

20. D. Edmond Hiebert, *1 and 2 Thessalonians*, rev. ed. (Chicago: Moody, 1992), 113.

21. Mal Couch, *Hope of Christ's Return*, 76–77.

22. For an interpreter who sees Paul emphasizing both Jews and Gentiles among the persecutors, see Beale, *1–2 Thessalonians*, 81, and Morris, *First and Second Epistles to the Thessalonians*, 82.
23. In the order of the Hebrew Bible, Genesis is naturally the first book, but 2 Chronicles is the last book. So, Jesus is asserting a truth covering the entire Old Testament canon.
24. Morris, *First and Second Epistles to the Thessalonians*, 84.
25. Hiebert, *1 and 2 Thessalonians*, 122.
26. For an excellent summary of the use of *parousia*, see Couch, *Hope of Christ's Return*, 83–86. For an apparent posttribulational view of the meaning of *parousia* in 1 Thessalonians, see Martin, *1, 2 Thessalonians*, 154–55.

Chapter 4—The Testimony of Timothy's Ministry

1. F. F. Bruce, *1 and 2 Thessalonians* (Waco: Word, 1982), 60.
2. Knute Larson, *I and II Thessalonians, I and II Timothy, Titus, Philemon*, Holman New Testament Commentary (Nashville: Broadman & Holman, 2000), 39.
3. Mal Couch, *The Hope of Christ's Return* (Chattanooga, TN: AMG, 2001), 89.
4. D. Edmond Hiebert, *1 and 2 Thessalonians*, rev. ed. (Chicago: Moody, 1992), 148–49.
5. Leon Morris, *The First and Second Epistles to the Thessalonians*, New International Commentary on the New Testament, rev. ed. (Grand Rapids: Eerdmans, 1991), 100.
6. This implies that the term should not be taken as a technical term meaning the same thing in every context.
7. Bruce, *1 and 2 Thessalonians*, 66.
8. Morris, *First and Second Epistles to the Thessalonians*, 101.
9. Ibid., 102.
10. R. C. H. Lenski, *The Interpretation of St. Paul's Epistles to the Colossians, to the Thessalonians, to Timothy, to Titus and to Philemon* (Minneapolis: Augsburg, 1937), 290.

Chapter 5—Praying for the Church

1. F. F. Bruce, *1 and 2 Thessalonians* (Waco: Word, 1982), 68.
2. D. Michael Martin, *1, 2 Thessalonians*, New American Commentary (Nashville: Broadman & Holman, 2001), 109.
3. Leon Morris, *The First and Second Epistles to the Thessalonians*, New International Commentary on the New Testament, rev. ed. (Grand Rapids: Eerdmans, 1991), 105.

4. Mal Couch, *The Hope of Christ's Return* (Chattanooga, TN: AMG, 2001), 96.
5. Morris, *First and Second Epistles to the Thessalonians*, 107–8.
6. The only other occurrence of the word in the entire New Testament is when Luke records the final words of the praise of Zacharias, father of John the Baptist: "to *guide* our feet into the way of peace" (Luke 1:79).
7. Charles A. Wanamaker, *The Epistles to the Thessalonians*, New International Greek Testament Commentary (Grand Rapids: Eerdmans, 1990), 138–39.
8. Couch, *Hope of Christ's Return*, 85; John F. Walvoord, *The Thessalonian Epistles* (Findlay, OH: Dunham, 1955), 50.

Chapter 6—Morality and Genuine Love

1. John MacArthur, *1 and 2 Thessalonians*, MacArthur New Testament Commentary (Chicago: Moody, 2002), 102.
2. William Neil, *The Epistle of Paul to the Thessalonians*, Moffatt New Testament Commentary (London: Hodder and Stoughton, 1965), 75.
3. John Stott, *The Gospel and the End of Time: The Message of 1 and 2 Thessalonians* (Downers Grove, IL: InterVarsity, 1991), 82; I. Howard Marshall, *1 and 2 Thessalonians*, New Century Bible Commentary (Grand Rapids: Eerdmans, 1983), 107.
4. Mal Couch, *The Hope of Christ's Return* (Chattanooga, TN: AMG, 2001), 106. We must be careful not to read the breadth of possible meanings for *porneia* into every occurrence of the word. However, in 1 Thessalonians 4:3, the apostle Paul seems to be speaking broadly of all kinds of sexual impurity.
5. D. Edmond Hiebert, *1 and 2 Thessalonians*, rev. ed. (Chicago: Moody, 1992), 180.
6. Leon Morris, *The First and Second Epistles to the Thessalonians*, New International Commentary on the New Testament, rev. ed. (Grand Rapids: Eerdmans, 1991), 120.
7. Ibid., 120–21.
8. The term may have been used as a euphemism for sexual intercourse (Morris, *First and Second Epistles to the Thessalonians*, 121).
9. Couch, *Hope of Christ's Return*, 108.
10. F. F. Bruce, *1 and 2 Thessalonians* (Waco: Word, 1982), 84. Bruce does a good job of refuting the notion that defrauding in this text is financial. Those who argue for this idea emphasize the connection to covetousness as greed in the word. However, a person can be desirous of more than he or she should have in different areas of life than money matters.
11. Couch, *Hope of Christ's Return*, 110.
12. Morris, *First and Second Epistles to the Thessalonians*, 126–27.

13. Ibid., 131.
14. Ibid., 132.
15. Bruce, *1 and 2 Thessalonians*, 91.

Chapter 7—The Comfort of the Rapture

1. I have not listed the *partial rapture view* since its following is quite small. Its primary weakness is that it splits the church into one group of believers who go to be with Christ in a pretribulational rapture because they are spiritual, watching Christians and another group of believers who are not spiritual and must wait until some later time to be raptured. Such a position is untenable because of Paul's statement in 1 Corinthians 15:51, which insists that all believers shall be changed at the point they are resurrected. Paul does not envision a divided church relative to the doctrine of the rapture of the church. The two major views within evangelicalism today are the pretribulational and posttribulational rapture positions.
2. Paul does not deal with the issue here, but the Bible does teach a resurrection of sorts for those who are unbelievers (Dan. 12:2; Rev. 20:11–15). The timing of the raising of their bodies (although presumably not to a glorified state) appears to be at the end of the millennium with respect to what has been called the Great White Throne Judgment.
3. The NIV translates the verse as "we believe that Jesus died and rose again" without any introductory "if" attached. See D. Michael Martin, *1, 2 Thessalonians*, New American Commentary (Nashville: Broadman & Holman, 2001), 145.
4. The first two options would also fit the midtribulational and prewrath rapture views as well. In other words, they fit any two-phase view of the Second Coming since the return to heaven would entail a later coming down to earth of Christ and the saints. I have here discussed the issue only in terms of the primary two views on the timing of the Rapture.
5. F. F. Bruce, *1 and 2 Thessalonians* (Waco: Word, 1982), 98–99.
6. Concerning Paul's description of the Parousia, Martin comments, "Its brevity is evident. Detail is lacking. Also the sequence of events is truncated" (*1, 2 Thessalonians*, 150).
7. Mal Couch, *The Hope of Christ's Return* (Chattanooga, TN: AMG, 2001), 125.
8. Bruce, *1 and 2 Thessalonians*, 100.
9. D. Edmond Hiebert, *1 and 2 Thessalonians*, rev. ed. (Chicago: Moody, 1992), 213.
10. Thomas L. Constable, "1 Thessalonians," in *Bible Knowledge Commentary*, New Testament Edition, ed. John F. Walvoord and Roy B. Zuck (Wheaton: Victor, 1983), 704.
11. Hiebert, *1 and 2 Thessalonians*, 214.
12. See Bruce, *1 and 2 Thessalonians*, 102.

13. Under the posttribulational rapture view, the catching up into the clouds is followed immediately by the coming to earth. However, even if this were so, one cannot say that 1 Thessalonians 4:13–18 actually gives us any information about that coming to earth.

14. See Bruce, *1 and 2 Thessalonians*, 102–3.

Chapter 8—The Day of the Lord

1. John MacArthur, *1 and 2 Thessalonians*, MacArthur New Testament Commentary (Chicago: Moody, 2002), 142.

2. D. Michael Martin, *1, 2 Thessalonians*, New American Commentary (Nashville: Broadman & Holman, 2001), 156.

3. Mal Couch, *The Hope of Christ's Return* (Chattanooga, TN: AMG, 2001), 135. We must be careful not to overstate the implications of watchful language, such as "thief in the night" or "be alert." Some pretribulational proponents view such language as implying imminency in the sense that the event can happen at any moment. Then they move from there to prove a pretribulational rapture of the church. Although I am strongly pretribulational in interpretation, I admit that such an approach does not follow the Bible carefully. Watchful language is clearly used in Scripture of events that cannot happen at any moment. Two clear examples are Armageddon (Rev. 16:15–16) and the second coming of Christ to earth (Matt. 24:29–50; cf. Luke 17:22–37). What must be understood in 1 Thessalonians 5:1–2 is that the Day of the Lord, which is the tribulation period, will come upon the world unexpectedly. So it is imminent from the point of view of unbelievers. This actually says nothing about the imminence of the rapture of the church one way or the other. The fact that the Day of the Lord will not overtake believers suddenly at all shows that their posture relative to the timing of the Day of the Lord is not in view. The passage is simply asserting an exemption from that time for the church.

4. The idea that Revelation 6–19 covers the full seven years of the tribulation period or Daniel's Seventieth Week is based partly on a correlation of the seal judgments in Revelation 6 with the early portions of the Olivet Discourse (Matt. 24:4–14). The happenings discussed appear to take place before the abomination of desolation (Matt. 24:15), which is halfway through the tribulation period. This points to the likelihood that the seal judgments of Revelation 6 start in the first half of the tribulation. It is relatively easy to show that these seal judgments are indeed the wrath of God, since Jesus, who is God, is the one who unleashes the seal judgments upon the earth. In addition, the four living creatures at the throne of God announce the first four seals and the fourth seal quotes from Ezekiel where the wrath of God is in view. Consequently, the midtribulational and prewrath views, which depend upon the notion that the seals are not the wrath of God, cannot be maintained.

5. Zane Hodges, "The Rapture in 1 Thessalonians" in *Walvoord: A Tribute*, ed. Donald K. Campbell (Chicago: Moody, 1982), 70.

6. A. T. Robertson, *Word Pictures in the New Testament,* (Nashville: Broadman, 1931), 4:34.
7. G. K. Beale, *1–2 Thessalonians,* IVP New Testament Commentary (Downers Grove, IL: InterVarsity, 2003), 144.
8. Hodges, "Rapture in 1 Thessalonians," 73–74.
9. Leon Morris, *The First and Second Epistles to the Thessalonians,* New International Commentary on the New Testament, rev. ed. (Grand Rapids: Eerdmans, 1991), 155.
10. In the Qumran literature, the term *sons of light* refers to the elect, while the term *sons of darkness* refers to the nonelect. See F. F. Bruce, *1 and 2 Thessalonians* (Waco: Word, 1982), 111.
11. MacArthur, *1 and 2 Thessalonians,* 160.
12. Couch, *Hope of Christ's Return,* 138.
13. Bruce, *1 and 2 Thessalonians,* 112.
14. MacArthur, *1 and 2 Thessalonians,* 162.
15. Martin, *1, 2 Thessalonians,* 154–67. This is similar to Leon Morris who, following Ladd, argues in an irenic way for a posttribulational rapture of the church (*The First and Second Epistles to the Thessalonians,* New International Commentary on the New Testament, rev. ed. [Grand Rapids: Eerdmans, 1991], 150–52). However, Morris sometimes speaks of the events (plural) of the Day of the Lord, while at other times he describes it as a singular event.
16. Many pretribulationalists note that the term *Day of the Lord* is not a technical term that is used the same way in every passage. Ryrie summarizes the futurist use of the term as related to three ideas: the tribulation years, the second coming of Christ, and the millennium, while noting that the expression can be found "sometimes focusing on one or another of these future events" (Charles C. Ryrie, *First and Second Thessalonians* [Chicago: Moody, 1959], 67). Renald Showers also views the passages about the Day of the Lord as emphasizing both a narrow use of the term associated with the event of the Second Coming and a broad use of the phrase coinciding with the Seventieth Week of Daniel and the Millennium (*The Pre-wrath Rapture View* [Grand Rapids: Kregel, 2001], 152–71).
17. Hodges, "Rapture in 1 Thessalonians 5:1–11," 77. It is the context of Paul's statement more than the tense of the Greek verb that leads to the transparent conclusion of which Hodges speaks.

Chapter 9—A Church in Harmony

1. Leon Morris, *The First and Second Epistles to the Thessalonians,* New International Commentary on the New Testament, rev. ed. (Grand Rapids: Eerdmans, 1991), 165.

2. William MacDonald, *Believer's Bible Commentary: New Testament* (Nashville: Thomas Nelson, 1995), 858.
3. Mal Couch, *The Hope of Christ's Return* (Chattanooga, TN: AMG, 2001), 145.
4. A. T. Robertson, *Word Pictures in the New Testament,* (Nashville: Broadman, 1931), 4:36.
5. Morris, *First and Second Epistles to the Thessalonians,* 166–67.
6. Couch, *Hope of Christ's Return,* 147.
7. John MacArthur, *1 and 2 Thessalonians,* MacArthur New Testament Commentary (Chicago: Moody, 2002), 177.
8. Michael W. Holmes, *1 and 2 Thessalonians,* NIV Application Commentary (Grand Rapids: Zondervan, 1998), 180.
9. F. F. Bruce, *1 and 2 Thessalonians* (Waco: Word, 1982), 124.
10. Ibid.
11. Couch, *Hope of Christ's Return,* 150.
12. Morris, *First and Second Epistles to the Thessalonians,* 172.
13. Thomas L. Constable, "1 Thessalonians," in *Bible Knowledge Commentary,* New Testament Edition, ed. John F. Walvoord and Roy B. Zuck (Wheaton: Victor, 1983), 708.
14. G. K. Beale, *1–2 Thessalonians,* IVP New Testament Commentary (Downers Grove, IL: InterVarsity, 2003), 170.
15. D. Michael Martin, *1, 2 Thessalonians,* New American Commentary (Nashville: Broadman & Holman, 2001), 182.
16. Beale, *1–2 Thessalonians,* 171.
17. Morris, while not holding this view, gives it a good review (*First and Second Epistles to the Thessalonians,* 175–76).
18. Lewis Sperry Chafer, *He That Is Spiritual,* rev. ed. (Grand Rapids: Zondervan, 1967), 23.
19. D. Edmond Hiebert, *1 and 2 Thessalonians,* rev. ed. (Chicago: Moody, 1992), 263.
20. Beale, *1–2 Thessalonians,* 173.
21. Constable, "1 Thessalonians," 709.
22. Couch, *Hope of Christ's Return,* 155.
23. Hiebert, *1 and 2 Thessalonians,* 266.

Chapter 10—The Faithfulness of God

1. F. F. Bruce, *1 and 2 Thessalonians* (Waco: Word, 1982), 129.

2. Ibid.
3. D. Edmond Hiebert, *1 and 2 Thessalonians*, rev. ed. (Chicago: Moody, 1992), 250–51.
4. I am thinking here of Wesley and his particular struggle with the notion of entire sanctification.
5. J. Sidlow Baxter, *A New Call to Holiness* (Grand Rapids: Zondervan, 1967), 148. I am actually using the revised edition of three volumes in one entitled *Christian Holiness Restudied and Restated* (1977).
6. Mal Couch, *The Hope of Christ's Return* (Chattanooga, TN: AMG, 2001), 157.
7. Henry C. Thiessen, *Lectures in Systematic Theology* (Grand Rapids: Eerdmans, 1949), 226. See also the complete discussion of the issues in Millard Erickson, *Christian Theology*, 2nd ed. (Grand Rapids: Baker, 1998), 537–57.
8. John MacArthur, *1 and 2 Thessalonians*, MacArthur New Testament Commentary (Chicago: Moody, 2002), 207.
9. G. K. Beale, *1–2 Thessalonians*, IVP New Testament Commentary (Downers Grove, IL: InterVarsity, 2003), 176. Beale argues that both progressive and ultimate sanctification are in view in the passage.
10. Leon Morris, *The First and Second Epistles to the Thessalonians*, New International Commentary on the New Testament, rev. ed. (Grand Rapids: Eerdmans, 1991), 184.
11. Couch, *Hope of Christ's Return*, 160.
12. Hiebert, *1 and 2 Thessalonians*, 277.
13. Bruce, *1 and 2 Thessalonians*, 135.
14. D. Michael Martin, *1, 2 Thessalonians*, New American Commentary (Nashville: Broadman & Holman, 2001), 193.

BOOK OF SECOND THESSALONIANS
Introduction—Background of 2 Thessalonians

1. Leon Morris, *The First and Second Epistles to the Thessalonians*, New International Commentary on the New Testament, rev. ed. (Grand Rapids: Eerdmans, 1991), 27.
2. Morris summarizes this objection; see ibid., 18.
3. D. Michael Martin, *1, 2 Thessalonians*, New American Commentary (Nashville: Broadman & Holman, 2001), 28.
4. Morris, *First and Second Epistles to the Thessalonians*, 18–19.
5. For further discussion of this argument, see Morris, *First and Second Epistles to the Thessalonians*, 21–22.
6. Ibid., 14.

7. Martin, *1, 2 Thessalonians*, 32.
8. Michael W. Holmes, *1 and 2 Thessalonians*, NIV Application Commentary (Grand Rapids: Zondervan, 1998), 28.
9. D. Edmond Hiebert, *1 and 2 Thessalonians*, rev. ed. (Chicago: Moody, 1992), 290.
10. Ibid.
11. Ibid., 290–91.
12. Ibid., 291.
13. D. Michael Martin, *1, 2 Thessalonians*, 32.
14. Morris, *First and Second Epistles to the Thessalonians*, 28.
15. Ibid., 29. See also G. K. Beale, *1–2 Thessalonians*, IVP New Testament Commentary (Downers Grove, IL: InterVarsity, 2003), 17.
16. Holmes, *1 and 2 Thessalonians*, 28.
17. Beale, *1–2 Thessalonians*, 18.
18. Hiebert, *1 and 2 Thessalonians*, 292.

Chapter 11—Encouraging the Church

1. Leon Morris, *The First and Second Epistles to the Thessalonians*, New International Commentary on the New Testament, rev. ed. (Grand Rapids: Eerdmans, 1991), 37.
2. Robert L. Thomas, "2 Thessalonians," in *Expositor's Bible Commentary*, vol. 11, ed. Frank E. Gaebelein (Grand Rapids: Zondervan, 1978), 307.
3. Mal Couch, *The Hope of Christ's Return* (Chattanooga, TN: AMG, 2001), 181.
4. Ibid., 183.
5. R. C. H. Lenski, *The Interpretation of St. Paul's Epistles to the Colossians, to the Thessalonians, to Timothy, to Titus and to Philemon* (Minneapolis: Augsburg, 1937), 380.
6. Couch, *Hope of Christ's Return*, 183; D. Michael Martin, *1, 2 Thessalonians*, New American Commentary (Nashville: Broadman & Holman, 2001), 203.
7. Some have imagined a contradiction in Paul's words here, which stress ongoing persecution, and the apostle's statement in 1 Thessalonians 2:14, which view the believers at Thessalonica as having endured suffering as a past event. However, a statement about past suffering does not contradict a statement about ongoing suffering unless it is qualified in such a way as to imply that such past suffering is the *only* suffering involved. See Martin, *1, 2 Thessalonians*, 203–4.
8. D. Edmond Hiebert, *1 and 2 Thessalonians*, rev. ed. (Chicago: Moody, 1992), 306.

9.Morris, *First and Second Epistles to the Thessalonians,* 196.

10. Hiebert, *1 and 2 Thessalonians,* 307.

11. Morris, *First and Second Epistles to the Thessalonians,* 196–97.

12. Charles C. Ryrie, *First and Second Thessalonians* (Chicago: Moody, 2001), 97. Also holding the same view is Richard L. Mayhue, *First and Second Thessalonians* (Berkshire, UK: Christian Focus, 1999), 157–58. Couch comes close to the same position in *Hope of Christ's Return,* 184–85.

Chapter 12—The Judgment of God

1. Mal Couch, *The Hope of Christ's Return* (Chattanooga, TN: AMG, 2001), 186
2. D. Edmond Hiebert, *1 and 2 Thessalonians,* rev. ed. (Chicago: Moody, 1992), 310.
3. Leon Morris, *The First and Second Epistles to the Thessalonians,* New International Commentary on the New Testament (Grand Rapids: Eerdmans, 1991), 200.
4. Harry Buis, "Retribution," in *Zondervan Pictorial Encyclopedia of the Bible,* ed. Merrill Tenney (Grand Rapids: Zondervan, 1975), 5:85.
5. In some Greek texts, the words "in flaming fire" are the first words of verse 8 rather than the last words of verse 7.
6. Hiebert, *1 and 2 Thessalonians,* 312.
7. Ibid.
8. F. F. Bruce, *1 and 2 Thessalonians* (Waco: Word, 1982), 151. Bruce interacts with Lightfoot's argument that the Greek construction requires two separate groups in Paul's statement.
9. Morris, *First and Second Epistles to the Thessalonians,* 203.
10. Ibid.
11. Couch, *Hope of Christ's Return,* 190.
12. Morris, *First and Second Epistles to the Thessalonians,* 204.
13. John MacArthur, *1 and 2 Thessalonians,* MacArthur New Testament Commentary (Chicago: Moody, 2002), 245.
14. G. K. Beale, *1–2 Thessalonians,* IVP New Testament Commentary (Downers Grove, IL: InterVarsity, 2003), 189.
15. For more discussion on the culture of postmodern "softness," see Mike Stallard, "The Tendency to Softness in Postmodern Attitudes about God, War, and Man," *Journal of Ministry and Theology* (Spring 2006): 92–114.
16. For one of the best discussions of the biblical doctrine of hell, see Robert Peterson, *Hell on Trial: The Case for Eternal Punishment* (Phillipsburg, NJ: P & R, 1995).
17. Morris, *First and Second Epistles to the Thessalonians,* 206.

18. Couch, *Hope of Christ's Return,* 192.
19. Thomas L. Constable, "1 Thessalonians," in *Bible Knowledge Commentary,* New Testament Edition, ed. John F. Walvoord and Roy B. Zuck (Wheaton: Victor, 1983), 716.
20. Robert H. Gundry, *The Church and the Tribulation* (Grand Rapids: Zondervan, 1973), 113. See also Douglas Moo, "The Case for the Posttribulational Rapture Position," in *The Rapture: Pre-, Mid-, or Post-Tribulational?* (Grand Rapids: Zondervan, 1984), 169–211.
21. Vern S. Poythress, "2 Thessalonians 1 Supports Amillennialism," *Journal of the Evangelical Theological Society* (December 1994): 529–38.
22. Paul D. Feinberg, "Response," in *The Rapture: Pre-, Mid-, or Post-Tribulational?* (Grand Rapids: Zondervan, 1984), 227. This is Feinberg's response to Douglas Moo. Feinberg gives a helpful summary of a few pretribulational approaches to 2 Thessalonians 1:5–7.
23. Ibid.
24. Charles Ryrie, *Come Quickly Lord Jesus: What You Need to Know about the Rapture* (Eugene, OR: Harvest House, 1996), 55–62. I have provided an article defending Ryrie's overall position titled "The Post-Trib and Amillennial Use of 2 Thessalonians 1," in *Journal of Ministry and Theology* 6 (Fall 2002): 60–80.

Chapter 13—The Focus of Paul's Prayer

1. D. Edmond Hiebert, *1 and 2 Thessalonians,* rev. ed. (Chicago: Moody, 1992), 317.
2. Mal Couch, *The Hope of Christ's Return* (Chattanooga, TN: AMG, 2001), 193.
3. D. Michael Martin argues for inclusion of a transformative view in Paul's statement based largely on the later context of the verse (*1, 2 Thessalonians,* New American Commentary [Nashville: Broadman & Holman, 1995], 217–18). G. K. Beale argues for the likelihood of the judicial understanding (count worthy) in light of the earlier context of the chapter and the fact that the Greek word being used is always used elsewhere in the New Testament in a forensic way (*1–2 Thessalonians,* IVP New Testament Commentary [Downers Grove, IL: InterVarsity, 2003], 193–94).
4. Hiebert, *1 and 2 Thessalonians,* 318.
5. John MacArthur, *1 and 2 Thessalonians,* MacArthur New Testament Commentary (Chicago: Moody, 2002), 257–58.
6. This adjective *every* probably applies to the second expression "the word of faith" as well as to the first one. So it is "every desire for goodness" and "every work of faith."
7. Hiebert, *1 and 2 Thessalonians,* 319–20.
8. Leon Morris, *The First and Second Epistles to the Thessalonians,* New International Commentary on the New Testament (Grand Rapids: Eerdmans, 1991), 210.

9. MacArthur, *1 and 2 Thessalonians,* 259–60.
10. Beale, *1–2 Thessalonians,* 195; See also Morris, *First and Second Epistles to the Thessalonians,* 210n51.
11. Charles Ryrie, *First and Second Thessalonians* (Chicago: Moody, 2001), 102.
12. Martin, *1, 2 Thessalonians,* 219.
13. The fact that the believers in the church age have been and will be used to glorify Christ in similar ways and using similar language for saints in national Israel should not be used to downplay or eliminate a distinction between Israel and the church. Angels are also used to glorify God, but that does not make them part of either Israel or the church. Although angels do not share the redemptive position in God as saints from all ages, they frequently share in the experience of the open expression of God's greatness and glory (Matt. 16:27; 25:31; Mark 8:38; Luke 9:26).
14. The two occurrences of the word *glorified* in 2 Thessalonians 1:10–12 are from the Greek word *endoxazomai*. The word carries the idea of receiving glory or of being honored. Its only two occurrences in the New Testament are here in 2 Thessalonians. In other passages, the same concept is described in other ways using terms related to "glory" (*doxa*) without the prefix of the preposition *en* (in) added to the verb.

Chapter 14–Prophetic Issues about the Day of the Lord

1. John MacArthur, *1 and 2 Thessalonians,* MacArthur New Testament Commentary (Chicago: Moody, 2002), 268.
2.D. Edmond Hiebert, *1 and 2 Thessalonians,* rev. ed. (Chicago: Moody, 1992), 326.
3. Bob Gundry, *First the Antichrist* (Grand Rapids: Baker, 1997), 109; see also G. K. Beale, *1–2 Thessalonians,* IVP New Testament Commentary (Downers Grove, IL: InterVarsity, 2003), 199–201.
4. The gathering outside of a city to meet a dignitary and escort him back into the city is found in the experience of the apostle Paul when he was taken prisoner to Rome. Many Christians from Rome went out to meet him and return to the city with him (Acts 28:15–16). However, a different word is used for the idea of meeting together and does not contain within it the idea of the return to the city, which is expressed by context.
5. Beale, who apparently holds to a posttribulational rapture, comments, "Scholars generally do not see any specific relationship between chapters 1 and 2" (*1–2 Thessalonians,* 199).
6. Ibid., 198. Beale argues that the burden of proof is on the pretribulationalist to show that there can be a change from 2:1 to 2:8 to allow two different comings of Christ.

7. Leon Morris, *The First and Second Epistles to the Thessalonians*, New International Commentary on the New Testament (Grand Rapids: Eerdmans, 1991), 214.

8. R. C. H. Lenski, *The Interpretation of St. Paul's Epistles to the Colossians, to the Thessalonians, to Timothy, to Titus and to Philemon* (Minneapolis: Augsburg, 1937), 402.

9. Mal Couch, *The Hope of Christ's Return* (Chattanooga, TN: AMG, 2001), 203.

10. Beale, *1–2 Thessalonians*, 201. Some might argue from the posttrib vantage point that the Day of the Lord had come in some nebulous manner apart from the end-time events of the resurrection and the return of Christ. However, Beale, who does not hold to a pretrib rapture, correctly suggests that 2:8, with its reference to the actual coming of Christ, makes a nebulous or spiritual coming impossible.

11. I have couched the arguments in terms of two positions: pretribulational and posttribulational views of the rapture of the church. These are the overwhelming favorites among evangelicals. However, to be more precise, one would have to say that the argument presented here actually only proves a two-phase Second Coming and does not necessarily rule out the midtribulational or prewrath rapture views. Further analysis from other passages concerning the nature of the Day of the Lord's wrath of God throughout the entire tribulation would have to be incorporated into the discussion (e.g., Revelation 6) to show that the pretribulational position is the correct view. In addition, a full understanding of Old Testament understanding of the Day of the Lord would be essential. See J. Randall Price, "Old Testament Tribulation Terms," in *When the Trumpet Sounds*, ed. Thomas Ice and Timothy Demy (Eugene, OR: Harvest House, 1995), 57–83.

12. Hiebert, *1 and 2 Thessalonians*, 331.

13. H. Wayne House, "Apostasia in 2 Thessalonians 2:3: Apostasy or Rapture?" in *When the Trumpet Sounds*, ed. Thomas Ice and Timothy Demy (Eugene, OR: Harvest House, 1995), 286.

14. Couch, *Hope of Christ's Return*, 206.

15. John F. Walvoord, *The Rapture Question* (Grand Rapids: Zondervan, 1979), 239–40.

16. MacArthur, *1 and 2 Thessalonians*, 272.

17. D. Michael Martin, *1, 2 Thessalonians*, New American Commentary (Nashville: Broadman & Holman, 2001), 235.

18. One's view of the timing of the revelation of Antichrist (1 Thess. 2:3) is intertwined with one's view of the timing of the Rapture and the associated definition of the Day of the Lord. A posttrib rapturist would suggest that the Day of the Lord is the second coming of Christ to earth at the end of the tribulation and that Antichrist obviously shows up on the scene before that (Beale, *1–2 Thessalonians*, 205). A midtrib rapturist would likely hold that the revelation of the Antichrist comes with the establishment of the abomination of desolation, which proves his identity and occurs halfway through the tribulation

just prior to the rapture of the church (J. Oliver Buswell, *A Systematic Theology of the Christian Religion* [Grand Rapids: Zondervan, 1962], 2:431). A prewrath rapturist would also likely see the midpoint of the tribulation as the time of the revelation of Antichrist, although the Rapture is later in that particular scheme (Marv Rosenthal, *The Pre-wrath Rapture of the Church* [Nashville: Nelson, 1990], 197ff.). As stated in the commentary, the pretrib rapturist generally holds to the signing of the treaty with Israel at the beginning of the tribulation as the revelation of the Antichrist (Charles Ryrie, *First and Second Thessalonians* [Chicago: Moody, 2001], 110). This has the distinct advantage of being the first major historical event associated with the Antichrist in relation to the end-time tribulation. I have also argued earlier that a two-phase Second Coming better fits the concerns that the Thessalonians were having, that is, believing that they were in the tribulation rather than that they had missed the Second Coming (posttrib explanation). When trying to decide between a prewrath, midtrib, or pretrib rapture, the first two are ruled out because of their inability to handle teachings elsewhere, particularly concerning the nature of the seal judgments in Revelation as the wrath of God.

19. Beale, *1–2 Thessalonians*, 205–8.

20. Hiebert also points out the significance of the particular word used for temple by Paul: "As contrasted to the Greek term *hieron*, also translated 'temple' and denoting the entire complex with its courts, the word here, *naos*, when used of a pagan temple, indicated an inner shrine where the image of the god was placed. For a Jew 'the temple' (*ton naon*) could only denote the holy place of the Jerusalem temple, that portion into which the priests alone could lawfully go. The construction used (*eis* with the accusative) implies motion toward and indicates that by his impious act the man of sin puts himself 'into' God's seat in the inner sanctuary" (*1 and 2 Thessalonians*, 333–34). It is, however, true that Paul uses the Greek word *naos* to refer to the church (1 Cor. 3:16–17) or to the physical body of a Christian (1 Cor. 6:19). However, Hiebert's argument is that the word with the article (*the* temple) must be taken into account in 2 Thessalonians 2:4 as a designation that Jewish ears would hear in a certain way.

21. Martin, *1, 2 Thessalonians*, 238.

22. Ibid.

23. Morris, *First and Second Epistles to the Thessalonians*, 224.

24. Hiebert, *1 and 2 Thessalonians*, 339.

25. F. F. Bruce, *1 and 2 Thessalonians* (Waco: Word, 1982), 172.

26. The sword in Christ's mouth is for more than the destruction of the Antichrist and his armies at the Second Coming. The passage also envisions a ruling of the nations with a rod of iron, which presumably entails the reign of Christ in the following kingdom. This understanding is similar to the Isaiah 11 passage.

27. Bruce, *1 and 2 Thessalonians*, 173.

28. Thomas L. Constable, "1 Thessalonians," in *Bible Knowledge Commentary,* New Testament Edition, ed. John F. Walvoord and Roy B. Zuck (Wheaton: Victor, 1983), 720.
29. Bruce, *1 and 2 Thessalonians,* 173.
30. Martin, *1, 2 Thessalonians,* 247.
31. Morris, *First and Second Epistles to the Thessalonians,* 235.

Chapter 15—The Call of God

1. There is a textual variant that affects one's interpretation of this particular verse even though it does not affect one's overall theology. The phrase translated "from the beginning" (*ap' archēs*) is not found in a large number of Greek manuscripts. Instead, the word "as a firstfruit" (*aparchēn*) is found. One can easily see the spelling similarity of the two options so that a scribal error in copying could be easily imagined. But which is the original? The English Standard Version chooses the second option and translates the verse as "God chose you to be the firstfruits to be saved." In a comparable vein, the New Living Translation reads, "God chose you to be among the first to experience salvation." Both of these translations provide footnotes with the alternate option. The KJV, NASB, and NIV all select "from the beginning" instead of any reference to firstfruits. The external evidence of the manuscripts favors "as a firstfruit" both by sheer number of manuscripts and by geographical distribution of text-types representing that particular reading. However, the use of "from the beginning" and the associated context of 1 Thessalonians 2:13 would be in harmony with Paul's teaching elsewhere (Eph. 1:4).
2. D. Edmond Hiebert, *1 and 2 Thessalonians* (Chicago: Moody, 1992), 350.
3. F. F. Bruce, *1 and 2 Thessalonians* (Waco: Word, 1982), 193.
4. Thomas L. Constable, "1 Thessalonians," in *Bible Knowledge Commentary,* New Testament Edition, ed. John F. Walvoord and Roy B. Zuck (Wheaton: Victor, 1983), 721.
5. Robert L. Thomas, "2 Thessalonians," in *Expositor's Bible Commentary* (Grand Rapids: Zondervan, 1978), 11:330.
6. Leon Morris, *The First and Second Epistles to the Thessalonians,* New International Commentary on the New Testament (Grand Rapids: Eerdmans, 1991), 233.
7. The idea of comfort is actually not stated but understood in the Greek text in 1 Thessalonians 2:11. See the earlier part of the commentary that deals with that passage.

Chapter 16—Dealing with Unruly Believers

1. D. Michael Martin, *1, 2 Thessalonians,* New American Commentary (Nashville: Broadman & Holman, 2001), 261.

2. D. Edmond Hiebert, *1 and 2 Thessalonians* (Chicago: Moody, 1992), 367. Hiebert suggests that the bad thinking about the Day of the Lord did not cause the unruly behavior, but it may have stimulated an existing situation into becoming worse.
3. Mal Couch, *The Hope of Christ's Return* (Chattanooga, TN: AMG, 2001), 242–43.
4. John MacArthur, *1 and 2 Thessalonians*, MacArthur New Testament Commentary (Chicago: Moody, 2002), 295.
5. R. C. H. Lenski, *The Interpretation of St. Paul's Epistles to the Colossians, to the Thessalonians, to Timothy, to Titus and to Philemon* (Minneapolis: Augsburg, 1937), 447.
6. Couch, *Hope of Christ's Return*, 244.
7. The term *evil one* could refer to evil in general, that is, the general opposition the Thessalonians were facing. This is how Martin interprets the designation (*1, 2 Thessalonians*, 266). However, Paul's earlier reference to Satan as energizing the future persecution led by the man of lawlessness during the formal tribulation period (2:3–10) makes this conclusion less likely. By way of analogy, Paul probably has Satan in mind here.
8. Thomas L. Constable, "1 Thessalonians," in *Bible Knowledge Commentary*, New Testament Edition, ed. John F. Walvoord and Roy B. Zuck (Wheaton: Victor, 1983), 723.
9. Couch, *Hope of Christ's Return*, 254.
10. Lenski, *Interpretation of St. Paul's Epistles*, 463.
11. I alluded to this possibility in my comments at the beginning of the discussion of 2 Thessalonians 3. G. K. Beale believes there is a strong connection between the unruly loafers of chapter 3 and the issue of the Day of the Lord in chapter 2 (*1–2 Thessalonians*, IVP New Testament Commentary [Downers Grove, IL: InterVarsity, 2003], 251). From his posttrib perspective and the belief that the Day of the Lord is the Second Coming, Beale argues that the loafers thought Christ had come so they were in paradise and had no need to work. It is highly unlikely that they thought they were in paradise in light of all the persecution they were enduring (chap. 1). Although Beale is wrong in his overall posttrib perspective and definition of the Day of the Lord, he may be right that the end-time questions drove the loafers' inactivity. They may have simply assumed that since the tribulation had begun, Christ's coming was near, so there was no need to exert themselves. This attitude has been repeated throughout history among groups who believed they knew specifically when Christ would return and sold all they owned and waited (e.g., the Millerites of the 1840s in the northeast United States).
12. Hiebert, *1 and 2 Thessalonians*, 375.
13. Couch, *The Hope of Christ's Return*, 258.
14. Hiebert, *1 and 2 Thessalonians*, 380.

Appendix A—The Day of the Lord

1. I am following here the same general approach as Renald E. Showers (*The Prewrath Rapture* [Grand Rapids: Kregel, 2001], 152–71). Showers demonstrates that the use of the term *Day of the Lord* by prewrath rapturists is too restricting to handle the full orb of information about the concept given in the prophets including Joel.
2. For a more complete discussion of terms related to the Day of the Lord, see J. Randall Price, "Old Testament Tribulation Terms," in *When the Trumpet Sounds*, ed. Thomas Ice and Timothy Demy (Eugene, OR: Harvest House, 1995), 57–83. This is one of the best surveys in print of the various terms and issues. See also the helpful survey in Arnold G. Fruchtenbaum, "Day of the Lord," in *Dictionary of Premillennial Theology*, ed. Mal Couch (Grand Rapids: Kregel, 1996), 87–88.
3. Tim LaHaye and Thomas Ice, *Charting the End Times* (Eugene, OR: Harvest House, 2001), 75. Some interpreters see the reference in 2 Peter 3:10 with its focus on the judgment by fire as not only speaking of the Second Coming itself, but of the entire tribulation period leading up to the Second Coming. See William Baker, *The Books of James and First and Second Peter* (Chattanooga, TN: AMG, 2004), 220.
4. J. Dwight Pentecost, *Things to Come* (Grand Rapids: Zondervan, 1964), 231; Kenneth O. Gangel, "2 Peter," in *Bible Knowledge Commentary*, New Testament Edition, ed. John F. Walvoord and Roy B. Zuck (Wheaton: Victor, 1983), 876–77.

Appendix B—The Identification of the Restrainer

1. D. Michael Martin, *1, 2 Thessalonians*, New American Commentary (Nashville: Broadman & Holman, 2001), 240–41. Martin does not necessarily hold this view. He simply offers it as an exegetical possibility as one sorts out the various interpretive options.
2. It is possible that the church is the impersonal restraining power in 2:6, while the Holy Spirit is the personal restrainer of 2:7. This would require some relationship between the two. Options for describing the relationship are plentiful in light of the many ministries the Spirit has relative to church age believers. The two could work together in the restraining ministry. However, it is doubtful that Paul is being this complicated.
3. John MacArthur, *1 and 2 Thessalonians*, MacArthur New Testament Commentary (Chicago: Moody, 2002), 277. In rejecting the many interpretive options for the restrainer that involve human beings in the identification in some way, MacArthur notes, "Human power, ingenuity, and institutions cannot restrain the supernatural power of Satan that seeks to release the Antichrist." In the final analysis, only God can restrain the evil that is being discussed by Paul.

About the Author

Dr. Mike Stallard is currently serving as Professor of Systematic Theology and Director of Ph.D. Studies at Baptist Bible Seminary in Clarks Summit, Pennsylvania, where he has been teaching since 1994. Dr. Stallard is the founder and director of Mission Scranton (a ministry of Heritage Baptist Church in Clarks Summit) established in 1994 to foster church planting and inner city outreach in the Scranton, Pennsylvania area. Dr. Stallard has authored articles for numerous periodicals and journals, as well as the *Dictionary of Premillennial Theology.* He is a frequent speaker at the Evangelical Theological Society, the Conservative Theological Society, and the Pre-Trib Study Group. Dr. Stallard was for eight years an aerospace engineer, with time served on-site in Israel as a technical advisor to the Israeli Air Force concerning F-16 jet fighters. He and his wife Cindy have three children: David, Philip, and Tiffany.

About the General Editors

Mal Couch is founder and former president of Tyndale Theological Seminary and Biblical Institute in Fort Worth, Texas. He previously taught at Philadelphia College of the Bible, Moody Bible Institute, and Dallas Theological Seminary. His other publications include *The Hope of Christ's Return: A Premillennial Commentary on 1 and 2 Thessalonians, A Bible Handbook to Revelation,* and *Dictionary of Premillennial Theology.*

Edward Hindson is professor of religion, dean of the Institute of Biblical Studies, and assistant to the chancellor at Liberty University in Lynchburg, Virginia. He has authored more than thirty books, served as coeditor of several Bible projects, and was one of the translators for the New King James Version of the Bible. Dr. Hindson has served as a visiting lecturer at Oxford University and Harvard Divinity School as well as numerous evangelical seminaries. He has taught more than fifty thousand students in the past twenty-five years.